Handwriting Without Tears®
by Learning Without Tears

Printing Power
Teacher's Guide

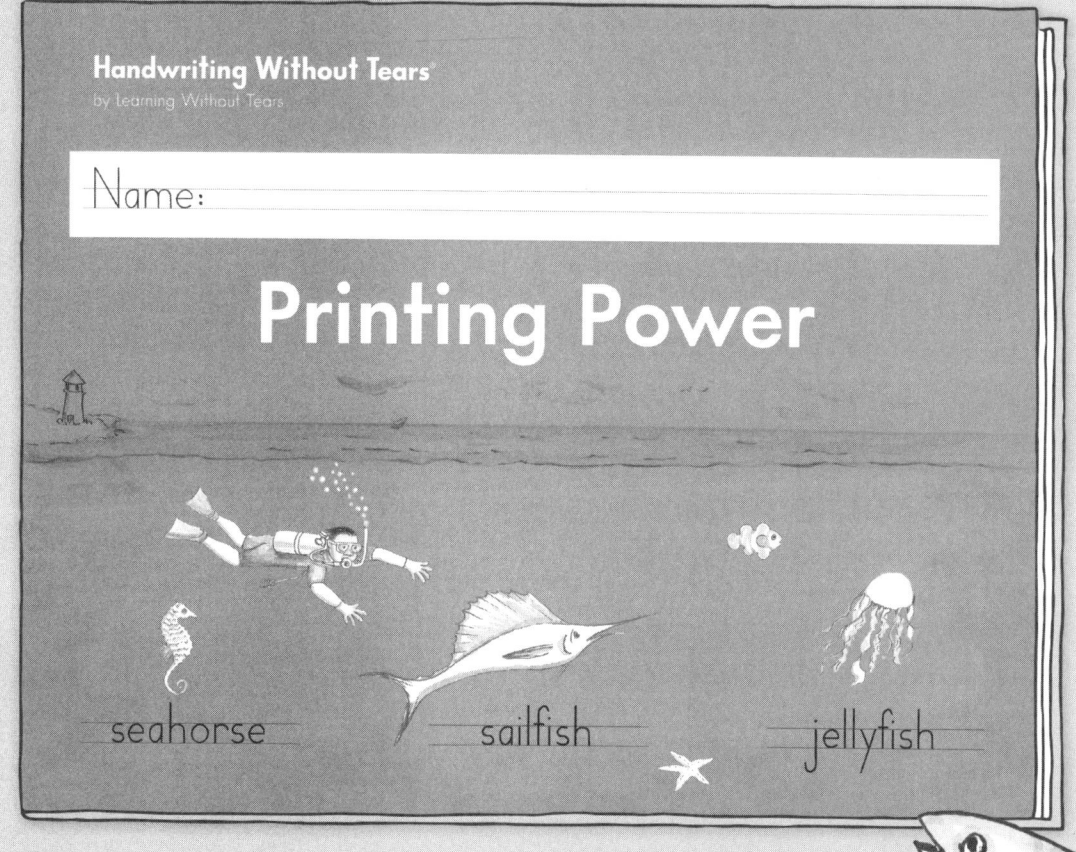

Guide to Workbook Lessons
and Multisensory Activities

by Jan Z. Olsen, OTR

LEARNING
Without Tears®

8001 MacArthur Blvd.
Cabin John, MD 20818
LWTears.com | 888.983.8409

Author: Jan Z. Olsen, OTR
Curriculum Designers: Christina Bretz, MS, OTR/L and Tania Ferrandino, OTR/L
Content Advisor: Elizabeth DeWitt, Ed. D.
Illustrators: Jan Z. Olsen, OTR and Julie Koborg
Graphic Designers: Sammie Simon and Julie Koborg
Editors: Annie Cassidy, Kathryn Fox, and Megan Parker

Copyright © 2022 Learning Without Tears
Fourth Edition
ISBN: 978-1-952970-85-6
123456789PAH232221
Printed in the USA

Welcome

Welcome to Handwriting Without Tears® by Learning Without Tears!

This is your teacher's guide, not only for the student edition, but for a way of teaching handwriting that is effective for children. Your children will be moving, singing, and playing with you as they build and write letters. That's how good handwriting starts—with hands-on materials and teaching that bring the curriculum to life.

We believe that good habits lead to good handwriting, which directly links to literacy and overall school success (Lust and Donica 2011). For this reason, explicit, multisensory handwriting instruction in is crucial, and we are committed to ensuring students can access it regardless of where they are learning. We are excited to offer an integrated print and digital approach, so students can learn handwriting actively and joyfully in any learning environment.

Handwriting Without Tears is part of the Learning Without Tears family. We started in the 1970s and have evolved based on our continued and direct experience with students, teachers, occupational therapists, and administrators around the country. Our 35 years of experience and ongoing collaboration solve the problems associated with early writing and do so in a way that is joyful, effective, and innovative.

Our materials and teaching strategies make learning a positive, successful experience for children in just 15 minutes a day. You will help your students build strong printing skills for writing letters, words, and sentences. Every lesson includes a multisensory element and has additional, optional connections to tie handwriting to other parts of the school day.

We support teacher directed learning. We believe you'll enjoy using our program and are excited to have you bring the program to life in your classroom.

Jan Z. Olsen

Table of Contents

1 – INTRODUCTION
- 4   This Is Handwriting Without Tears!
- 6   Simply Smart Student Materials
- 8   Features of the Student Edition
- 10   Get to Know the Teacher's Guide
- 12   Accessing Digital Products in +Live Insights
- 13   Using the Interactive Digital Teaching Tool
- 14   Teaching Handwriting in All Settings

17 – TEACHING HANDWRITING
- 18   Stages of Learning
- 19   Intent to Prevent
- 20   Handwriting in the Literacy Block
- 21   Connecting Handwriting and Fluent Writing
- 22   Scope & Sequence

25 – TEACHING GUIDELINES
- 26   UNIT 1: Capitals, Numbers 1–5
- 27   UNIT 2: c o s v w – t; a d g; u i e
  Numbers 6–10
- 28   UNIT 3: l k y j; p r n m h b
- 29   UNIT 4: f q x z
- 30   UNIT 5: Writing Activities
- 31   UNIT 6: Writing Activities

33 – GET READY! POSTURE, PAPER & GRIP
- 34   Preparing for Paper & Pencil
- 35   Stomp Your Feet
- 36   Paper Placement & Pencil Grip
- 37   The Correct Grip
- 38   Picking Up My Pencil
- 39   Grasping Grip

41 – CAPITALS
- 42   Developmental Teaching
- 43   Student Edition Design
- 44   Capital Teaching Order/Learn & Check
- 45   Pencil Pick-Ups
- 46   Frog Jump Capitals:
  F E D P B R N M
- 48   Starting Corner Capitals
  H K L U V W X Y Z
- 49   Center Starting Capitals
  C O Q G S A I T J
- 50   Capital Review
- 51   Number Review

53 – LOWERCASE LETTERS, WORDS & SENTENCES

TEACHING STRATEGIES
- 54   Student Edition Design
- 55   Double Line Success
- 56   Lowercase Teaching Order
- 57   Learn & Check

SAME AS CAPITALS AND t: c o s v w – t
- 58   Same as Capitals: c o s v w
- 59   t + words

MAGIC c LETTERS: a d g
- 60   a + words
- 61   d + words
- 62   g + words
- 63   Magic c Mystery Letters
- 64   Punctuation

MORE VOWELS: u i e
- 65   u + words
- 66   i + words
- 67   e + words
- 68   Letter Size & Place
- 69   Rhymes

TRANSITION GROUP: l k y j
- 70   l + words
- 71   k + words
- 72   y + words
- 73   j + words
- 74   Singular & Plural
- 75   Paragraph

DIVER LETTERS: p r n m h b
- 76   p + words
- 77   r + words
- 78   n + words
- 79   m + words
- 80   h + words
- 81   b + words
- 82   Turn h into b
- 83   Word Search

FINAL GROUP: f q x z
- 84   f + words
- 85   q + words
- 86   Greek and Latin
- 87   Paragraph
- 88   x + words
- 89   z + words
- 90   Lowercase Review
- 91   Capital & Lowercase

93 – WRITING ACTIVITIES

- 94 Sentences – Spacing
- 96 Paragraph – Paintings
- 97 Writing – Self-Portrait
- 98 Words – Homophones
- 99 Paragraph – Sign Language
- 100 Punctuation – Quotations
- 101 Paragraph – Training Boo
- 102 Words – Compound Words
- 103 Syllables – pre-cip-i-tate
- 104 Words – Land Words
- 105 Words – Sea Words
- 106 Labels – Continents & Oceans
- 107 Words – Geography
- 108 Poem – "Apostrophe"
- 109 Writing – Antonyms
- 110 Question & Answer – Strange Sleepers
- 111 Question & Answer – Picky Eaters
- 112 Words – Dates & Closings
- 113 Friendly Letter – Thank You
- 114 Vowels – a, e, i, o, u + y
- 115 Poem – "Four Wheel Drive"
- 116 Labels – Guitar & Violin
- 117 Paragraph – Violin
- 118 Paragraph – QWERTY Keyboard
- 119 Math – Calendar Surprise
- 120 Words – Irregular Nouns & Verbs
- 121 Sentences – Building Sentences
- 122 Paragraph – Elevators
- 124 Capitals – Usage
- 125 Sentences – Alliteration
- 126 Sentences – Languages

129 – NUMBERS

- 130 Teaching Numbers
- 131 Number Stories
- 132 About Reversals
- 133 1–10
- 143 Math Problems
- 144 1 & 2 Digit Numbers
- 145 2 & 3 Digit Numbers
- 146 Final Check

149 – MULTISENSORY ACTIVITIES

- 150 Multisensory Cues
- ♫ 151 Songs for Readiness
- 152 Shake Hands With Me
- 153 Top to Bottom
- ♫ 154 "Where Do You Start Your Letters?"
- 155 Capitals on the Door
- 156 Wet-Dry-Try for Capitals
- 157 Mystery Letters on the Slate Chalkboard
- ♫ 158 Songs for Capitals
- ♫ 159 Songs for Lowercase
- 160 Letter Stories
- 162 Air Writing
- 163 Laser Letters
- 164 Digital Formation Tools: Letter & Number
- 165 A+ Worksheet Maker
- 166 Wet-Dry-Try App
- 167 Hand Activity
- 168 Wet-Dry-Try for Lowercase Letters
- 169 Voices
- ♫ 170 "Sentence Song"
- 171 Syllables

173 – RESOURCES

- 174 School-to-Home Connections
- 175 Remediation Tips
- 182 Strategies for English Language Learners
- 185 Strategies for Children with Special Needs
- 188 Handwriting Standards for Written Production
- 190 References
- 191 Index

This Is Handwriting Without Tears®!

The award-winning Handwriting Without Tears curriculum draws from years of innovation and research to provide developmentally appropriate, multisensory strategies for early writing.

Whether you're using a physical, digital, or integrated approach to teach handwriting, our superior teacher and student materials provide an effective and engaging experience for all learners.

Explicit, thoughtful, and targeted handwriting instruction:

- Multisensory teaching strategies appeal to all learning modalities
- Child friendly, simple language to reach every student
- Large step-by-step models provide a clear example
- Innovative, developmentally appropriate letter order promotes easy learning
- Cross-curricular connections reinforce content being taught in other subjects
- Lefty-friendly design ensures all students can succeed in handwriting
- Easy-to-use assessments track students' progress and supports instruction

This Is Handwriting Without Tears®!

Teacher's Guides and Student Editions
The teacher's guides provide scaffolded instruction that allow educators to differentiate lessons for various learners and learning styles. Multisensory strategies to reach every learner are integrated in every lesson, as well as cross-curricular connections. The Student Editions feature child friendly language and a clean, simple, and intuitive approach that invites personalization and fosters handwriting success. Every page has large step-by-step models that show students how to sequence the letter. Double lines and line generalization activities promote legible writing that will transfer to success on all paper styles.

Manipulatves
A wide range of thoughtful and purposefully created manipulatives engage multiple modalities while bringing learning to life. The Handwriting Without Tears hands-on manipulatives are proven to stimulate and strengthen visual, tactile, kinesthetic, and auditory learning styles, while teaching children to build and sequence their letters prior to writing on paper.

Interactive Digital Teaching Tool (IDTT)
IDTT includes pre-loaded lesson plans aligned with the Handwriting Without Tears developmental order, and the ability to change the order of letter instruction to fit your core ELA curriculum. Digital teacher's guides and student editions make planning easy, and educators can also access, and assign, digital letter formations, teaching videos, and fun animations students will love. IDTT supports group or individual instruction. Educators can easily assign lessons remotely. Plus, the reporting feature easily identifies when students have completed assignments.

Digital Student App
Using the Digital Student App, students can complete lessons and received music, videos, and messages from their teacher. They'll also have access to a digital toolbox, including Letter and Number Formations, Wood Pieces, and Wet-Dry-Try, they can use anytime.

Simply Smart Student Materials

ABOUT THE SECOND GRADE CURRICULUM
Our intuitive and engaging student materials make learning handwriting joyful and fun. The materials below were created to fit into your daily routine. As you become familiar with the program, gradually incorporate new activities and choose those that suit your students' needs.

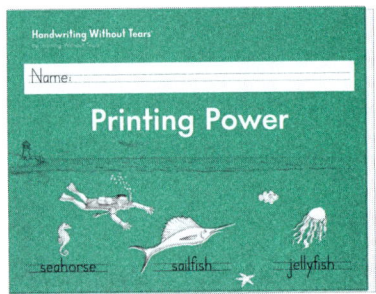

Printing Power Student Edition
The Student Edition is loaded with capital, lowercase, word, sentence, and number practice. Your students will love the fun activities, which develop their handwriting and sentence skills. We developed teaching guidelines in this teacher's guide to help you plan your lessons.

The Digital Student App
Our Digital Student App allows students to access the full Handwriting Without Tears curriculum virtually. In a student friendly digital environment, they complete lessons assigned by their teacher that include, music, animations, and digital formation tools. The physical Student Edition and Digital Student App work together to provide a perfectly integrated print and digital solution for handwriting.

Regular Double Line Notebook Paper & Writing Journal
Solve the problem of line confusion and help children place letters on the lines correctly. The bottom line keeps the writing straight, and the mid line controls the size of the letters. With regular double lines covering the pages, the Writing Journal and double line paper is a great supplement to encourage independent writing.

Simply Smart Student Materials

Color Print & Number Wall Cards and Print Alphabet Desk Strips
Students need correct models to form letters properly. When children aren't writing in the workbook, they need visual guides in the classroom to help them form letters. These eye-catching cards and helpful desk strips promote correct letter and number formation in the classroom.

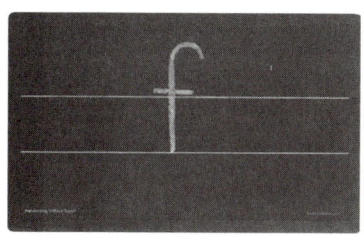

Blackboard with Double Lines
Use the Blackboard with Double Lines to teach lowercase letters. Incorporate our Wet-Dry-Try technique to add endless opportunities to trace, write, and learn to form letters and numbers.

Magic C Bunny
Make the puppet your teaching assistant. Access A Click Away 😊 for directions to make your own Magic C Bunny out of a paper napkin. Your students will form letters correctly when they learn the Magic C way.

Pencils for Little Hands
Our golf-size pencils are perfect for young students because they can write with pencils that fit their hand size.

Features of the Student Edition

We carefully plan every workbook page and everything that's on it. Our workbooks are accessible and friendly, yet also promote excellence. We want children to practice correctly, so our student edition pages promote efficient, effective practice for each letter.

Child Friendly, Simple Language
Our child-friendly language evolved in response to complicated letter formation terminology in other programs. When teaching letter formation, we eliminate language that assumes children understand left/right orientation, clockwise/counterclockwise, or forward/backward circles. We make it easy by using few, carefully selected words that all children know and understand.

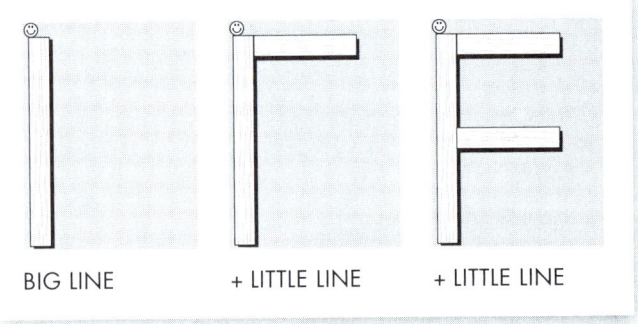

Large Step-by-Step Models
It is much easier for children to understand how to form letters if you show them step by step. Our workbooks contain large step-by-step images that show students how to make each part of every letter.

Lefty Friendly
Our workbooks are lefty friendly. Teaching pages provide models on the left and right so left-handed children can easily see the model they are copying. Lefties never have to lift their hands or place them in an awkward position to see a model.

Developmental Teaching Order
Teaching in a developmental order helps children master skills and boosts confidence. We teach the easiest skills first, then build on prior knowledge. We teach capitals first and follow with lowercase letters. We also teach in small groups of similar formation.

Features of the Student Edition

Black & White, Simple, Clean Design & Illustrations
The black and white pages in our workbooks are clean and clear. We deliberately avoid visually confusing backgrounds, colored graphics, crowded pages, and multicolored lines. Our simple workbook pages are appealing and invite children to color and draw once they have finished the lesson.

Our illustrations promote left-to-right directionality. This is a unique feature of our workbooks. The car, helicopter, horse, and other drawings move left to right across the page to encourage correct visual tracking and writing direction.

Continuous, Meaningful Review
Children retain skills better if they have continuous, meaningful review. That's why each new letter is used in words and sentences that emphasize practice of the new letter and help children review and practice previously learned letters.

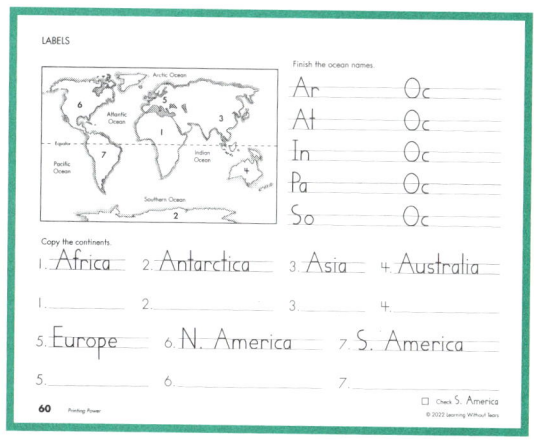

Cross-Curricular Connections
In addition to handwriting, we want the pages to have connections to other grade-appropriate curricula. We created activities that help you teach handwriting and review other grade-appropriate skills.

Simple Spatial Organization
We begin by teaching capital letters and numbers with Gray Blocks. The Gray Blocks prevent reversals and help children learn how to place letters and numbers.

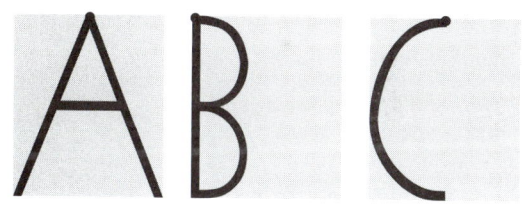

As children move to lowercase, our double lines foster handwriting success. The mid line is for size, and the base line is for placement. The middle space is for small letters, the top space is for tall letters, while the bottom space is for descending letters.

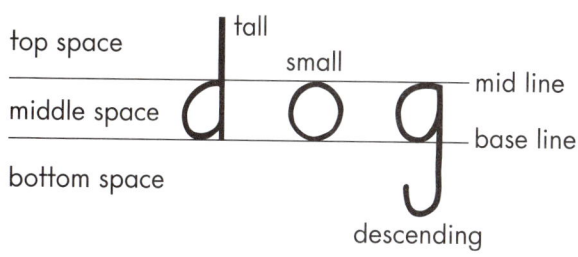

When children are learning to print, they need extra room to write. Our landscape style workbooks give them the space they need to write and develop good spacing habits.

Line Generalization: Success on All Paper Styles
Our workbooks provide activities for children to experience different types of lined paper. We start them with simple double lines, then teach them to master all lines.

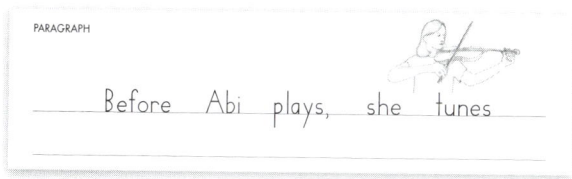

Get to Know the Teacher's Guide

Lesson Overview
There is a lesson plan for every student edition page. Below is a sample of how a letter formation lesson is organized.

STARTING THE LESSON
Letter, student edition page, and objectives are shown in the top corner. Start each lesson with the suggested multisensory activity.

TEACHING THE LESSON
Lesson Plan
The letter lesson follows these steps:

1. **Direct Instruction (Demo)** – Actively demonstrate the letter for children to finger trace and then copy.

2. **Guided Practice** – Children finger trace and copy the letter.

3. **Check Letter** – Children check their letter and evaluate formation.

Read, Color & Draw
You and your children read the sentence. Children color and draw.

A a
Printing Power – p. 16

OBJECTIVES
To use correct habits for writing capital **A** and lowercase **a**; to build fluency by practicing previously learned letters.

LESSON INTRODUCTION (Warm Up)
Introduce Magic C Bunny

Additional digital resources are available in the Interactive Digital Teaching Tool (IDTT).

LESSON PLAN

1. **Direction Instruction (Demo)**
   Demonstrate **A**, **a** on double lines.
   Say the words for each step.
   Demonstrate the words **act** and **was**.

Magic c — up like a helicopter — bump — back down, bump

2. **Guided Practice**
   Children copy: **A**, **a**, **act**, and **was**.
   Monitor as children write the other words on their own.

3. **Check Letter & Word**
   Help children ✓ their letter for correct start, steps, and bump.
   Help children ✓ their word for correct size, placement, and closeness.

READ & DISCUSS
Read the words together and discuss.

ENRICHMENT	SUPPORT/ELL	CROSS-CURRICULAR CONNECTIONS
Have children write **C c**, **O o**, and **A a** on double line paper. Discuss how **C c** and **O o** are Magic C Letters, but **A** is not even though **a** is a Magic c letter.	If children write lowercase **a** too skinny, encourage them to start on the dot and travel on the mid line before curving down.	Language Arts: Look around the room to find things that have the short /a/ sound in them. Make a class list of the things you find.

EXTENDING THE LESSON
Differentiated Instruction

Enrichment
Ways to extend learning by adding complexity or variety.

Support/ELL
Suggestions for adapting or simplifying the activity.

Cross-Curricular Connections
Connect the lesson to another subject.

Get to Know the Teacher's Guide

Multisensory Activities

Many multisensory activities for handwriting practice are implemented repeatedly throughout the curriculum. Below is an example of the step-by-step directions we provide for each activity. These multisensory activity pages can be found starting on p. 147.

ABOUT THE ACTIVITY
Introduction gives you background and guidance for the activity.

MATERIALS
Materials list helps you organize and plan for the activity.

ACTIVITY PLAN
Step-by-step directions along with illustrations to guide you through.

Wet-Dry-Try for Lowercase Letters

Wet-Dry-Try is an innovative teaching strategy. We use a slate chalkboard for capitals and numbers. For lowercase letters and words we use the Blackboard with Double Lines. This is the physical version. The digital version is available on the Interactive Digital Teaching Tool and Digital Student App. The latest research on brain development supports this activity. This research calls for fewer elements (just two lines), modeling, sensory engagement, and immediate feedback (Sousa 2011).

Materials
- Blackboard with Double Lines* (1 per child)
- Little Chalk Bits (1")
- Little Sponge Cubes (1/2")
- Little cups of water
- Paper towel pieces

Activity

1. **Prepare Blackboards**
   Write letter with chalk as a model to trace.

2. **Teacher's Part – Write f with Chalk**
   Use chalk to write a letter on double lines.
   Say the step-by-step directions.

3. **Child's Part – Wet-Dry-Try**
   As the child does each part, say the step-by-step directions to guide the child. The child is encouraged to join in, saying the words.
   Wet: The child uses a Little Sponge Cube to trace the letter.
   Dry: The child uses a little piece of paper towel to trace the letter.
   Try: The child uses a Little Chalk Bit to write the letter.

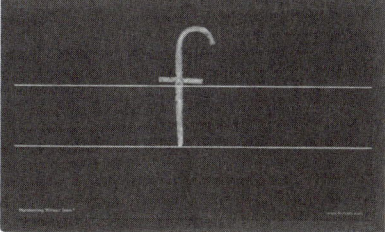 

*If you don't have a Blackboard with Double Lines, consider using our Double Line Writer on your whiteboard. This product is available at LWTears.com

Digital Version

 Interactive Digital Teaching Tool: Share via your interactive whiteboard or smartboard

 Digital Student App: Integrated in lessons and on "My Tools" for additional practice

168 Printing Power Teacher's Guide: *Multisensory Activities*   © 2022 Learning Without Tears

Accessing Digital Products in +Live Insights

Go to +Live Insights at **pli.LWTears.com** to manage and access all of your digital Learning Without Tears products. The Interactive Digital Teaching Tool and Digital Student App are located in +Live Insights.

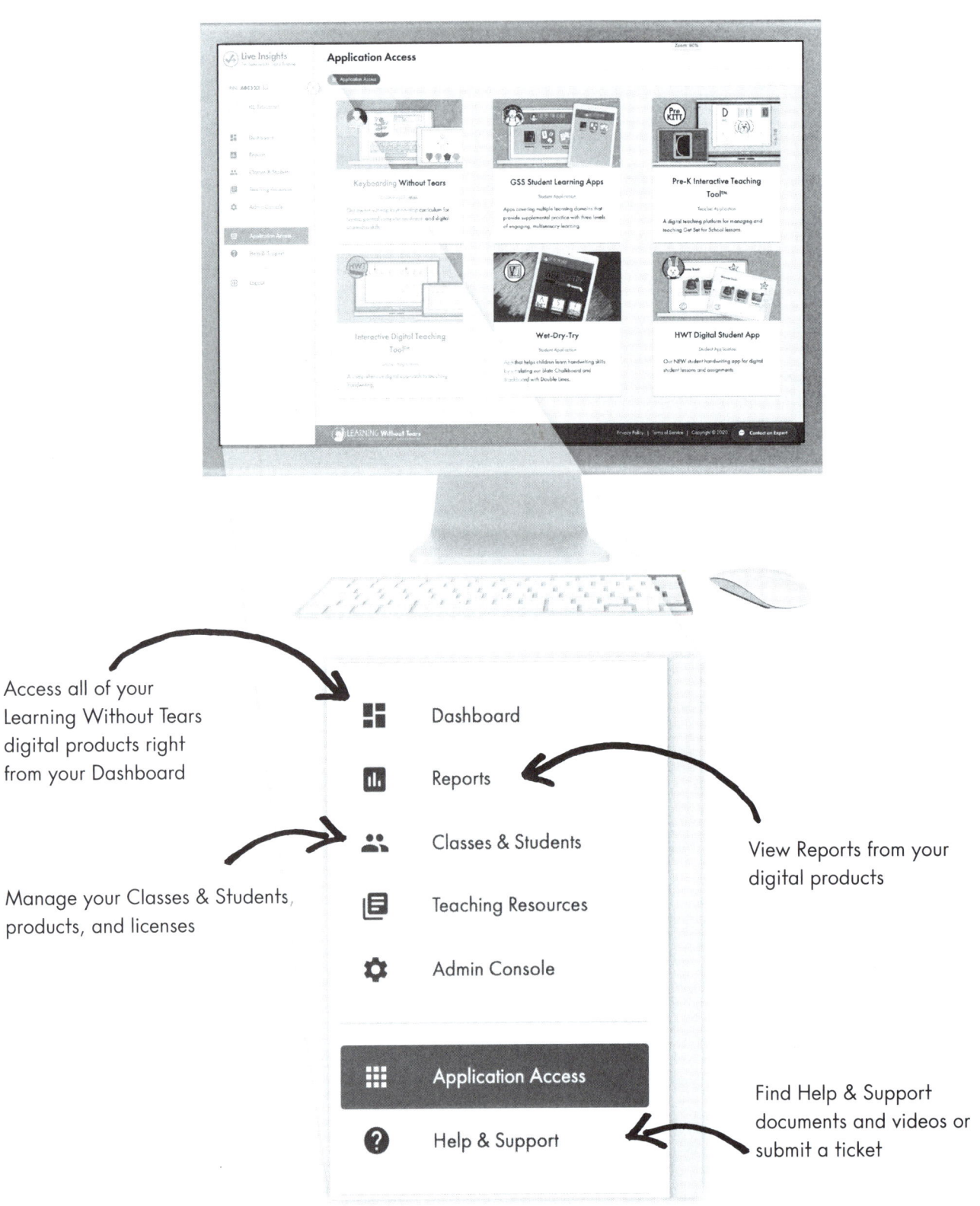

Access all of your Learning Without Tears digital products right from your Dashboard

Manage your Classes & Students, products, and licenses

View Reports from your digital products

Find Help & Support documents and videos or submit a ticket

Using the Interactive Digital Teaching Tool

The Interactive Digital Teaching Tool (IDTT) makes planning Handwriting Without Tears lessons effortless, and provides digital resources to engage students in any learning environment.

Teachers send lessons and activities to students.

Students access lessons in their Digital Student App.

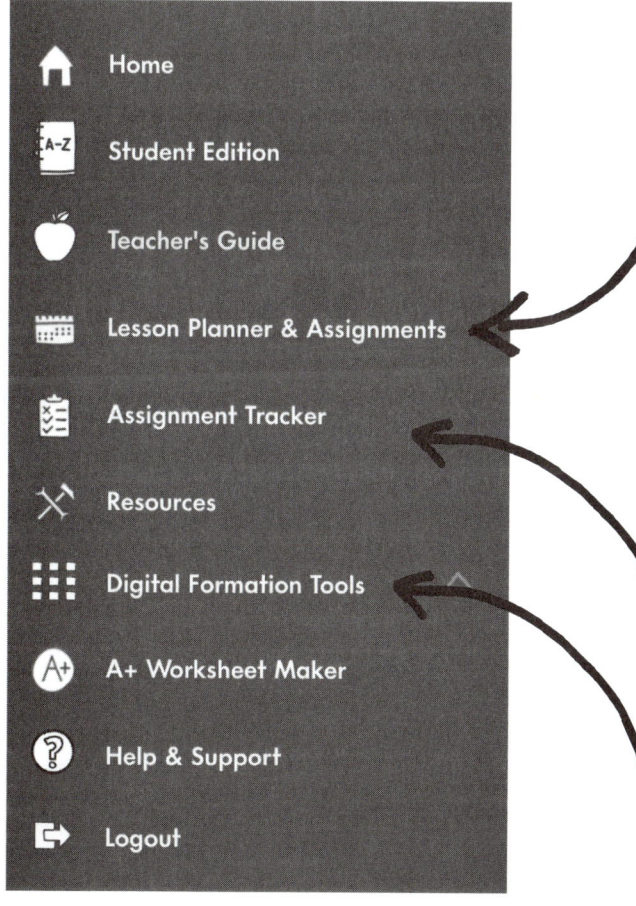

In IDTT, educators can:

1. Access digital student editions and teacher's guides

2. Plan and assign handwriting instruction
   - Choose from dozens of pre-loaded lesson plans aligned with the Handwriting Without Tears developental order, or choose your own order
   - Create lesson plans lessons that include animation, music and model lessons taught by master teachers
   - Assign Lessons directly to students they can easily access via the Digital Student App

3. Track whether student assignment has been completed

4. Access digital formation tools
   - Wet-Dry-Try
   - Letter & Number Formations
   - Wood Pieces

Teaching Handwriting in All Settings

The print and digital components in Handwriting Without Tears support a variety of different use cases. The Lesson Planner in the Interactive Digital Teaching Tool (IDTT) contains lessons pre-populated with recommended activities. However, you can easily customize a lesson to best fit your needs.

	In-Person: All learning is happening in the classroom—whether it's hands-on activities, a teacher projecting on a whiteboard, or students working on the Digital Student App on a computer during center time.
Lesson Time	10–15 mins
Lesson Introduction (Warm Up)	**Hands-on Learning** (in-person) Choose one or more of the following activities: Wood Piece Play, Music, Capitals on the Mat for Wood Pieces, Wet-Dry-Try on the Slate, Wet-Dry-Try on the Blackboard with Double Lines, Air Writing, or Hand Activity. **Digital: IDTT** Share one or more of the following activities via smartboard, or send to students via the Digital Student App: Animations, Letter & Number Stories, Wood Pieces, Hand Activity.
Direct Instruction (Demo)	**In-Class Demo** Demonstrate letter formation via the Interactive whiteboard, Slate or Blackboard with Double Lines, flip chart, or whiteboard or **Digital: IDTT** Share and demomonstrate letter formation via smartboard, or send to students via the Digital Student App: Letter & Number Formations, Wet-Dry-Dry, or Live Teaching videos.
Practice	Students complete appropriate lesson pages in their Student Edition in the classroom.

Teaching Handwriting in All Settings

Hybrid: Instruction and practice are split between school and at home.	**Virtual:** All instruction and practice is happening at home via the computer.
5–10 mins home/independent 5–10 mins in class	Lesson Time: 10–15 mins
Hands-on Learning (live in the classroom) Choose one or more of the following activities: Wood Piece Play, Music, Capitals on the Mat for Wood Pieces, Wet-Dry-Try on the Slate, Wet-Dry-Try on the Blackboard with Double Lines, Air Writing, or Hand Activity. **Digital: IDTT** Assign one or more of the following activities to the Digital Student App: Animations, Letter & Number Stories, Wood Pieces, or Hand Activity.	**Hands-On Learning** (Not recommended for virtual learning unless students have access to manipulatives at home.) **Digital: IDTT** Assign one or more of the following activities to the Digital Student App: Animations, Letter & Number Stories, Wood Pieces, or Hand Activity.
Digital: IDTT Demonstrate letter formation by assigning one or more of the following activities to the Digital Student App: Letter & Number Formations, Wet-Dry-Dry, or Live Teaching videos.	**Digital: IDTT** Demonstrate letter formation by assigning one or more of the following activities to the Digital Student App: Letter & Number Formations, Wet-Dry-Dry, or Live Teaching videos.
Students complete the appropriate lesson pages in their Student Edition in the classroom.	If students have access to their student edition at home, they can complete the assigned lesson pages. There is also the option to print the assigned pages from the Digital Student App.

TEACHING HANDWRITING

Children's handwriting matters. Handwriting skills affect school success (Feder and Majnemer 2007). When children master handwriting, they are free to focus on the content of their writing instead of the mechanics. With our easy-to-teach, easy-to-learn curriculum, you will be empowered to teach handwriting efficiently and well. With your guidance, children will learn correct letter formation and good handwriting habits that will serve them well in every subject.

The Handwriting Without Tears curriculum draws from years of innovation and research to provide developmentally appropriate, multisensory tools and strategies for your classroom.

"Writing fluency frees attention for content."

(Lichsteiner et al., 2018)

Stages of Learning

PRE-INSTRUCTIONAL STAGE – PRE-K, TRANSITIONAL KINDERGARTEN, AND KINDERGARTEN

The focus is on building readiness skills essential for learning. Pre-instructional readiness activities promote social-emotional learning, fine motor skills, drawing, coloring, alphabet knowledge, pre-writing, writing, number, and counting skills. Most handwriting lessons will begin with multisensory hands-on learning, which will boost these skills prior to writing letter and numbers.

INSTRUCTIONAL STAGES

Because research shows that children can imitate months before they can copy lines and shapes, the first stage of handwriting instruction is demonstration-imitation. When you demonstrate, children can see your physical motions. They imitate how you move to write a letter or number. For handwriting success in your classroom, use these three stages.

Stage 1 – Direct Instruction (Demo)

The child watches as the teacher writes and then imitates.
Ready for next stage?

- No: Do more multisensory activities.
- Yes: Let children finish a student edition page by copying models.

Stage 2 – Guided Practice

The child looks at the completed model of a letter, word, or sentence and copies it to match the model.
Ready for next stage?

- No: Go back to demonstrating the letter.
- Yes: Supervise copying.

Stage 3 – Independent Practice

The child writes unassisted, without a demonstration or a model.

You will know when your children are ready for independent writing when they can:

- Write their names correctly.
- Write letters and numbers from memory.
- Write dictated words (assist with spelling).
- Enjoy free writing.

The Intent to Prevent

THE HANDWRITING PROCESS

Good handwriting skills result from your thoughtful attention and instruction. Students need deliberate instruction to develop good habits and overcome bad ones.

With this guide and Handwriting Without Tears® materials, you will be prepared to help students make writing a natural and automatic skill. You'll find that their handwriting abilities and habits vary. Regardless of where they start, you can help them develop and improve their skills:

TEACH	TO FIX
How to hold the pencil correctly	Awkward pencil grip
Letters/numbers that face the right way — 3 cats	Reversals — Ɛ cɒtꙅ
Letters/numbers that start at the top — top	Starting at the bottom — bottom
Letters/numbers that are formed correctly and consistently — 10 right	Incorrect letters/numbers — 9 vvrong

Handwriting in the Literacy Block

Handwriting is an essential component of a complete literacy curriculum, and can be integrated within daily literacy activities. Our handwriting lessons take 10–15 minutes a day. It's easy to connect your handwriting lessons to other parts of your literacy block. Below are some possibilities:

Guided & Independent Reading

Instruct students on the formation of letters and words from the text after shared reading.

Guided & Independent Writing

Take turns practicing a specific letter's formation during interactive activites.

Word Work & Phonics

Provide direct instruction on features of the letters in target words. Utilize Handwriting Without Tears mulitisensory activities to practice correct letter formation while writing words.

Integrating Handwriting & Reading

The three options below work best because they adhere to the fundamental principles of each discipline and incorporate lesson work from each in a way that fully supports skill development. Find one that works best for you. In the Lesson Planner in the Interactive Digital Teaching Tool (IDTT), you can modify the lesson order to align to any one of the following sequences.

1. **Separate the handwriting and reading teaching order**

Teach both programs in the recommended orders. Keep instruction separate until familiar letters appear. Then remind children of letters they know from handwriting or reading instruction.
- During handwriting, remind students of letter sounds they know.
- During reading, remind students how to write letters previously taught.

2. **Integrate the handwriting and reading teaching orders**

Teach both programs in the recommended order, but make connections between them to facilitate learning.
- During handwriting, integrate reading instruction for that letter by saying, "We are learning to write letter a. Letter a makes the /a/ sound."
- During reading, integrate handwriting instruction for that letter by having students finger trace the letter in their handwriting books while you say the letter's formation. Or, print additional practice pages using A+ Worksheet Maker.

3. **Follow the reading teaching order**

Teach both reading and handwriting in the reading teaching order. During handwriting, simply go to the letter teaching page you are covering in reading. Complete the word and sentence pages after you have taught all the letters.

Connecting Handwriting and Fluent Writing

Handwriting Without Tears helps children become fluent at forming letters correctly. Students then need additional practice to transfer that skill into fluent composition. Building Writers and our Writing Journal serve as the perfect bridges to support your students as they become independent writers.

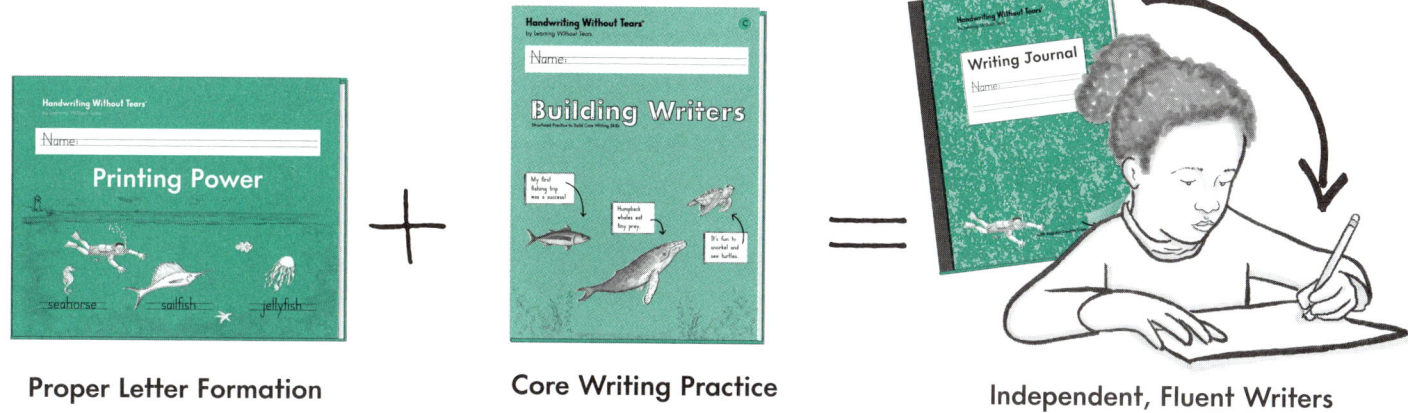

Proper Letter Formation + Core Writing Practice = Independent, Fluent Writers

What is Building Writers?

Building Writers is an interactive student work text that offers extra practice for writing skills development. It can be easily integrated into an existing writing program, and incorporated as independent writing or as whole group practice.

How does Building Writers work?

- Addresses critical writing standards at each grade level in the three main writing genres: narrative, information, and opinion
- Releases responsibility to grow independent writing in carefully scaffolded, intuitive activities
- Engages students with cross-curricular and high interest topics
- Reinforces correct letter formation on familiar double lines
- Provides a bridge between the mechanics of handwriting and the fluency required for creative composition

What support does Building Writers provide?

- Strong examples to use as a model for their writing
- Vocabulary-rich resources on each page
- Genre-specific graphic organizers to organize ideas
- Writing checklists guide students to plan and organize their writing in each genre.

Scope & Sequence

The Scope & Sequence of Printing defines the content and order of printing instruction. The skills needed for printing develop as early as Pre-K. Although we do not teach printing formally at the Pre-K level, we can create an environment and encourage activities to develop good habits that students need in kindergarten. The secret is to teach skills in a way that makes learning natural, easy, and fun.

Type of Instruction
Informal/Structured: A variety of activities address the broad range of letter and school readiness skills.
Formal/Structured: Teacher-directed activities are presented in a more precise order with specific objectives.

Handwriting Sequence
Pre-Strokes: These are beginning marks that can be random or deliberate.
Shapes: These are often introduced before letters and are a foundation for letter formation skills.
Capitals/Numbers: These use simple shapes and strokes. They have the same size, start, and position.
Lowercase Letters: These are tall, small, and descending symbols with more complex strokes, sizes, starts, and positions.

Stages of Learning
Pre-Instruction Readiness: Attention, behavior, language, and fine motor skills for beginning writing.
Stage 1–Direct Instruction: Watch someone form a letter first, and then write it.
Stage 2–Guided Practice: Look at a letter and then write it.
Stage 3–Independent Practice: Write without watching someone or even seeing a letter.

Physical Approach
Crayon Use: Crayons prepare children to use pencils. Small crayon use encourages proper grip.
Pencil Use: Proper pencil grip facilitates good handwriting. In kindergarten, children transfer their crayon grip to pencils.
Posture: Good sitting posture promotes good handwriting. This is taught in kindergarten.
Paper Placement: Correct paper placement helps children move the writing hand across the page. Paper placement is different for left- and right-handed children.

Printing Skills
Primary Skills
– Memory: Remember and write dictated letters and numbers.
– Orientation: Face letters and numbers in the correct direction.
– Start: Begin each letter or number correctly.
– Sequence: Make the letter strokes in the correct order.

Secondary Skills
– Placement: Place letters and numbers on the base line.
– Size: Write in a consistent, grade-appropriate size.
– Spacing: Place letters in words close, put space between words.

Functional Writing
Letters/numbers, words, sentences, paragraphs, and writing in all subjects

Scope & Sequence

SCOPE & SEQUENCE OF PRINTING					
	Pre-K	Transitional K	Kindergarten	1st Grade	2nd Grade
Type of Instruction					
Informal/Structured	✓				
Formal/Structured		✓	✓	✓	✓
Handwriting Sequence					
Pre-Strokes	✓				
Shapes	✓	✓			
Capitals/Numbers	✓	✓	✓	✓	✓
Lowercase Letters	*See note below	✓	✓	✓	✓
Stages of Learning					
Pre-Instruction Readiness	✓	✓	✓		
Stage 1–Direct Instruction	✓	✓	✓	✓	✓
Stage 2–Guided Practice		✓ Emerging	✓	✓	✓
Stage 3–Independent Practice		✓ Emerging	✓	✓	✓
Physical Approach					
Crayon Use	✓		✓		
Pencil Use		✓ Emerging	✓	✓	✓
Posture		✓ Emerging	✓	✓	✓
Paper Placement			✓	✓	✓
Printing Skills					
Primary Skills					
– Memory	✓	✓	✓	✓	✓
– Orientation	✓	✓	✓	✓	✓
– Start	✓	✓	✓	✓	✓
– Sequence	✓	✓	✓	✓	✓
Secondary Skills					
– Placement		✓ Emerging	✓	✓	✓
– Size		✓ Emerging	✓	✓	✓
– Spacing			✓	✓	✓
Functional Writing					
Letters/Numbers		✓	✓	✓	
Words		✓ Emerging	✓ Short	✓ Short	✓ Long
Sentences			✓ Short	✓ Short	✓ Long
Paragraphs				✓ Short	✓ Long
Writing in All Subjects			✓	✓	✓

*Children in Pre-K are taught lowercase letter recognition and introduced to writing lowercase letters. They may be taught to write the lowercase letters in their names.

TEACHING GUIDELINES

To help you plan your instruction, we have provided teaching guidelines. Units include a set of letters, numbers, and/or writing skills to teach in a developmentally appropriate manner. You have flexibility to stay on a unit until students have success with those skills and are ready to move ahead. The units progress through the skills needed for printing.

UNIT 1: Get Ready!
Review Capitals and Review Numbers: 1–5

UNIT 2: Lowercase – Same as Capitals and t: c o s v w – t
Magic c Letters: a d g, Vowels: u i e, Numbers: 6–10

UNIT 3: Lowercase – Transition Group: l k y j, Diver Letters: p r n m h b

UNIT 4: Lowercase – Final Group: f q x z
Numbers in Math

UNIT 5: Writing Activities

UNIT 6: Writing Skills, Independent Writing

Each of the six units has daily lessons with multisensory activities.
On days that indicate Review/Multisensory, choose one of the activities from pp. 149–171.

When the student edition is complete, maintain good habits with Handwriting All Year Activities.
Visit ☺ A Click Away for free Handwriting All Year downloads.

UNIT 1: Get Ready! Capitals — Numbers 1–5

Unit Summary:
1. Teach **Name**
2. Review/Teach **Capitals**
   - Frog Jump Capitals   F E D P B R N M
   - Starting Corner Capitals   H K L U V W X Y Z
   - Center Starting Capitals   C O Q G S A I T J
   - Capital Review
3. Review **Numbers**   **1–10** with gray blocks
   Teach Numbers   **1–5** on a single line with math sentences

Week	Monday	Tuesday	Wednesday	Thursday	Friday
1*	**Foundation Skills: Paper, Posture, Pencil Grip** pp. 33–39 Help Me Write My Name. Use template on ☺ A Click Away	**Pencil Pick-Ups** p. 45	**Frog Jump Capitals** F E D P B R N M pp. 46–47	**Number Review** p. 51 For Educators: pp. 129–130 (teaching numbers)	**Frog Jump Capitals** F E D P B R N M pp. 46–47 For Educators: pp. 41–44 (writing capitals)
2	**Number 1** p. 133 Math Sentence	**Starting Corner Capitals** H K L U V W X Y Z p. 48	**Number 2** p. 134 Math Sentence	**Starting Corner Capitals** H K L U V W X Y Z p. 48	**Number 3** p. 135 Math Sentence
3	**Number 4** p. 136 Math Sentence	**Center Starting Capitals** C O Q G S A I T J p. 49	**Number 5** p. 137 Math Sentence	**Center Starting Capitals** C O Q G S A I T J p. 49	**Capital Review** p. 50

* Handwriting Without Tears assessment: The Screener of Handwriting Proficiency includes evaluation of children's posture and grip along with capital and lowercase letters. We recommend administering this assessment at the beginning of the year to help drive instruction. You will need 15–20 minutes to prepare for the assessment and 20–30 minutes to administer and score. Full directions can be found on **LWTears.com/screener**.

☺ Handwriting Record idtt.LWTears.com/ext/TGPP/2022 (resources section)

UNIT 2: Lowercase c o s v w – t, a d g, u i e   Numbers 6–10

Unit Summary:
1. Review/Teach **Numbers**   6 –10 on a single line with math sentences
   Teach **Lowercase**
   Same as Capitals and **t**   c o s v w – t
   Magic c Letters   a d g
   Vowels   u i e
   Review Capitals with Lowercase
2. Develop **Writing Skills**
   Week 1   Words
   Week 2   Onset/Rime, Magic c Spelling,
   Week 3   Punctuation, Onset/Rime, Words
   Week 4   Hand Activity, Review

Week	Monday	Tuesday	Wednesday	Thursday	Friday
1	c o s p. 58 (Begin Same as Capitals and t)	v w p. 58 (End Same as Capitals and t)	t p. 59 T t Twin Words	Review Letter Group with a multisensory activity (Select from pp. 149–171).	Number 6 p. 138 Math Sentence
2	a p. 60 A a Twin Words (Begin Magic c Letters)	d p. 61 D d Add Rimes: -ad, -od, -oad, -ood	g p. 62 G g Add Rimes: -ag, -og	Magic c Mystery Letters p. 63	Numer 7 p. 139 Math Sentence
3	Sentences – Punctuation p. 64	u p. 65 U u Add Rimes: -ut, -ust, -ug, -out (Begin Vowels)	i p. 66 I i Twin Words	e p. 67 E e Add Rimes: -eed, -et, -est, -ed	Number 8 p. 140 Math Sentence
4	Review Letter Groups with a multisensory activity (Select from pp. 149–171).	Hand Activity p. 167	Same as Capitals and t, Magic c Letters, and Vowels Review	Number 9 p. 141 Math Sentence	Number 10 p. 142 Math Sentence

UNIT 3: Lowercase l k y j p r n m h b

Unit Summary:
1. Teach **Lowercase**
   - Transition Group — l k y j
   - Diver Letters — p r n m h b
   - Review Capitals with Lowercase
2. Develop **Writing Skills**
   - Week 1 — Rhymes, Words, Onset/Rime
   - Week 2 — Onset/Rime, Syllables, Singular & Plural Nouns, Paragraph
   - Week 3 — Words, Onset/Rime, Comparative
   - Week 4 — Words, Onset/Rime, Syllables

Week	Monday	Tuesday	Wednesday	Thursday	Friday
1	Letter Size & Place p. 68	Rhymes p. 69	l p. 70 L l Twin Words (Begin Transition Letter Group)	k p. 71 K k Add Rimes: -ack, -ick, -ake, -ike	Free Choice Friday! Choose an activity from 😊 A Click Away or create one using the A+ Worksheet Maker.
2	y p. 72 Y y Add Rime: -y Add Syllable: -ty	j p. 73 J j Twin Words	Singular & Plural – Nouns p. 74	Paragraph – Lucky p. 75	Free Choice Friday! Choose an activity from 😊 A Click Away or create one using the A+ Worksheet Maker.
3	p p. 76 P p Twin Words (Begin Diver Letters)	r p. 77 R r Words Add comparative Add Rimes: -ere, -ear, -ar	n p. 78 N n Twin Words	m p. 79 M m, Add Rimes: -ame, -ime, -im, -oom	Free Choice Friday! Choose an activity from 😊 A Click Away or create one using the A+ Worksheet Maker.
4	h p. 80 H h Twin Words	b p. 81 B b, Add Rimes: -ab, -ub Add syllable: -ble	Turn h into b p. 82	Transition Group and Diver Letters Review	Word Search p. 83*

* Administer mid-year assessment of the Screener of Handwriting Proficiency (LWTears.com/screener). Update scoring online and review individual student reports.

😊 Handwriting Record idH.LWTears.com/ext/TGPP/2022 (resources section)

UNIT 4: Lowercase f q x z

Unit Summary:
1. Teach **Lowercase**
   Final Group   f q x z
   Review Capitals with Lowercase
2. Review **Numbers**
   Using the calendar
   Math Problems
   1 & 2 and 2 & 3 Digit Numbers
3. Develop **Writing Skills**
   Week 1   Onset/Rimes, Words, Greek & Latin
   Week 2   Paragraph, Words
   Week 3   Lowercase Review
   Week 4   Math

Week	Monday	Tuesday	Wednesday	Thursday	Friday
1	f p. 84 F f Add Rimes: -aft, -ift Add syllable: -fle	q p. 85 Q q Twin Words	Greek & Latin p. 86 Prefixes, Root Words	Hand Activity p. 167 Practice this week's spelling words using the Hand Activity as a multisensory review.	Free Choice Friday! Choose an activity from ☺ A Click Away or create one using the A+ Worksheet Maker.
2	Paragraph – Rome p. 87	X p. 88 X x Twin Words	Z p. 89 Z z Twin Words	Review Letter Group with a multisensory activity (Select from pp. 149–171).	Free Choice Friday! Choose an activity from ☺ A Click Away or create one using the A+ Worksheet Maker.
3	Final Group Review Available on ☺ A Click Away	Lowercase Review p. 90	Capitals & Lowercase p. 91	Final Check p. 146	Free Choice Friday! Choose an activity from ☺ A Click Away or create one using the A+ Worksheet Maker.
4	Number – Calendar Surprise p. 119	Math Problems p. 143	1 & 2 Digit Numbers p. 144	2 & 3 Digit Numbers p. 145	Free Choice Friday! Choose an activity from ☺ A Click Away or create one using the A+ Worksheet Maker.

UNIT 5: Writing Activities

Unit Summary:
1. Develop **Writing Skills**
   - Week 1 — Sentence Spacing, Paragraphs, Homophones
   - Week 2 — Paragraphs, Quotations, Compound Words, Syllables
   - Week 3 — Words, Capitalization, Poem
   - Week 4 — Antonyms, Question & Answer, Abbreviations, Thank you Letter

Week	Monday	Tuesday	Wednesday	Thursday	Friday
1	Sentence Spacing p. 94 For Educators: p. 93 (writing activities)	Sentence Spacing p. 95	Paragraph – Van Gogh p. 96	Writing – Self-Portrait p. 97	Homophones p. 98
2	Paragraph – Sign Language p. 99	Punctuation – Quotations p. 100	Paragraph – Julie Trains Boo p. 101	Compound Words p. 102	Syllables p. 103
3	Words – Sea & Land p. 104	Words – Sea & Land p. 105	Capitalization – Continents & Oceans p. 106	Capitalization – Geography p. 107	Poem – "Apostrophe" p. 108
4	Antonyms p. 109	Question & Answer – Strange Sleepers (Animals) p. 110	Question & Answer – Picky Eaters (Animals) p. 111	Dates & Closings p. 112	Thank You Letter p. 113

UNIT 6: Writing Activities

Unit Summary:
1. Develop **Writing Skills**
    - Week 1 — Vowels, Poem, Labels, Paragraphs
    - Week 2 — Irregular Nouns & Verbs, Sentence Building, Paragraph, Thank You Letter
    - Week 3 — Paragraph, Capitalization, Proper Nouns, Alliteration, Sentences

Week	Monday	Tuesday	Wednesday	Thursday	Friday
1	Vowels – Vehicle Vowels p. 114	Poem – "Four-Wheel Drive" p. 115	Labels – Guitar & Violin p. 116	Paragraph – Violin p. 117	Paragraph – QWERTY p. 118
2	Irregular Nouns & Verbs p. 120	Sentence Building – Subject, Verb, and a Phrase p. 121	Paragraph – Elevators & Buildings p. 122	Thank You Letter Thursday: Have students write a thank you letter to one person at the school who has made them feel special.	**Free Choice Friday!** Choose an activity from ☺ A Click Away or create one using the A+ Worksheet Maker.
3	Paragraph – Elevators & Buildings p. 123	Capitalization – Proper Nouns p. 124	Alliteration p. 125	Sentences – Numbers p. 126	**Free Choice Friday!*** Choose an activity from ☺ A Click Away or create one using the A+ Worksheet Maker.

* Administer end of year assessment using the Screener of Handwriting Proficiency. Update scoring online and review individual student reports.

☺ Handwriting Record **idtt.LWTears.com/ext/TGPP/2022** (resources section)

GET READY! POSTURE, PAPER & GRIP

Grip is one of the foundations of handwriting. Children need to hold and use a pencil correctly (Dennis and Swinth 2001). We've planned pre-writing and grip guidelines for you so your students will be ready to learn and engage through three-dimensional, musical, joyful learning that supports your teaching all year long.

To make sure children are ready to learn, begin the year with readiness activities that focus on prewriting and pencil grip. The proper grip will develop the hand muscles and build the fine motor skills that are needed for successful handwriting. We begin with simple kinesthetic activities and work toward seated writing practice.

In this section, we include activities to develop, promote, and solidify good habits for grip and posture.

- Paper Placement & Pencil Grip
- The Correct Grip
- Picking Up My Pencil
- Grasping Grip

Preparing for Paper & Pencil

THREE EASY STEPS

When it comes to handwriting, children must be taught everything! That includes how to sit, position the paper, and hold a pencil. This is the physical approach to handwriting. Sometimes it's the physical approach, not the letters and numbers, that causes a child to struggle with handwriting. Think of it like playing a musical instrument. If you don't know how to position yourself and hold the instrument correctly, how can you play beautiful music? The same is true with writing letters and numbers. The ability to position yourself and hold your pencil correctly has a lot to do with being able to write legibly.

Important questions:
- What affects children's posture?
- How should the paper be placed?
- What is the secret to a good pencil grip?

STEP 1 – POSTURE

Does the furniture fit? The right size and style of chair and desk affect school performance. Children don't come in a standard size. Check that every child can sit with feet flat on the floor and arms resting comfortably. Children who sit on their feet often will lose stability in their upper torso. On the following page, we show you how good posture can be fun. We have a secret for getting children to stop sitting on their feet.

STEP 2 – PAPER PLACEMENT

There's a misconception that people should slant their paper to make slanted writing. Not true. In fact, we slant paper so that it fits the natural arc of the forearm. Children who slant their papers properly can write faster because the arm moves naturally with the paper.

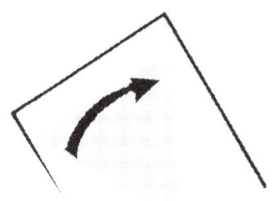

STEP 3 – GRASPING GRIP

The most important thing to understand about pencil grip is that it doesn't develop naturally—it is learned. Based on our years of experience helping children, we developed our own theories about how to develop good pencil grip habits effectively. Because children are born imitators, demonstration will lead to success.

On the next few pages, you will find fun strategies to help you teach posture, paper, and pencil skills.

Stomp Your Feet

Stomping is fun and really works because it keeps students' feet on the floor and parallel in front of them. The arm movements make their trunks straight. The noise lets them release energy, but it's under your control. When you have them stop stomping, they'll have good posture and be ready to pay attention. Use Stomp Your Feet a few times a day.

Materials
- "Stomp Your Feet" from *Rock, Rap, Tap & Learn* music album

Activity

1. Sit down and show the children how to stomp their feet and wave their arms.
2. Have them shout, "Na, na, naaaah, na, na naaah," with you as they wave and stomp.
3. Have children push and pull their hands. Have them hug themselves.
4. End by having children raise their shoulders up, pull shoulders back, and let them down.

Push palms

Pull hands

Hug yourself tightly

Raise shoulders

Pull shoulders back

Let them down

ENRICHMENT

 Video Lesson: View "Stomp Your Feet" at **idtt.LWTears.com/ext/TGPP/2022**

SUPPORT/ELL

While doing the motions, say the words out loud: "stomping," "pulling," "pushing."

Paper Placement & Pencil Grip

PLACE THE PAPER

How do you position paper correctly? Some children may lean over in an awkward position to write. Children who put their paper in front of them and slant it properly can write more efficiently because they position their arms naturally with the paper. You need to teach them how to place their papers appropriately. Have your students turn to p. 6 in *Printing Power*, and teach them how to slant their papers for their handedness.

Children who are able to print sentences across the page are ready to tilt the paper at a slight angle to follow the natural arc of the writing hand. The correct way to tilt the paper is easy to remember (see illustrations below). For right-handed children, put the right corner higher; for left-handed children, put the left corner higher. The writing hand is below the line of writing. This practice encourages a correct, neutral wrist position.

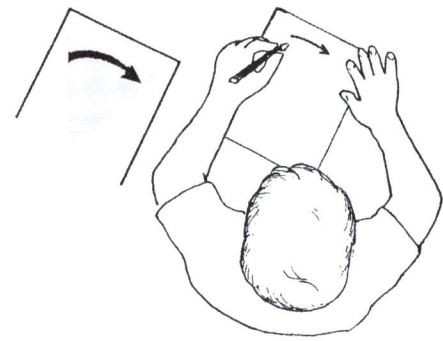
Left–Handed Students

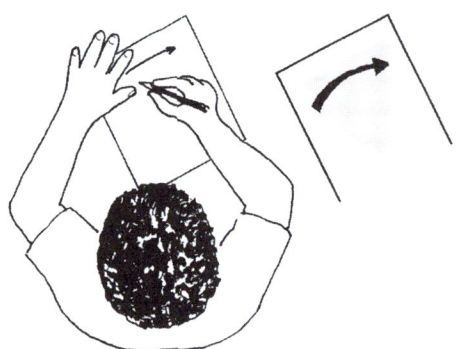
Right–Handed Students

LOOKING OUT FOR LEFTIES

 You might observe some left-handed children slanting their papers too much. They do this to prevent their wrists from hooking. Allow them to exaggerate the slant on their papers if it doesn't cause speed or neatness trouble. Visit **idtt.LWTears.com/ext/TGPP/2022** for more information about the left-handed writing position.

Cross Strokes

When writing, we typically travel from top to bottom and left to right. At times, left-handed children may choose to cross letters by pulling their writing hand from right to left. This is natural. Model it for them in their student editions for the letters below.

Mark arrows → for right-handed students. Mark arrows ← for left-handed students.

A E F G H I J T - f t

The Correct Grip

The standard way for children to hold their pencil is illustrated below. If you write using a grip that is different than tripod or quadropod, alter your grip for classroom demonstration.

Tripod Grip
Standard grip:
Hold pencil with
thumb + index finger.
Pencil rests on middle finger.

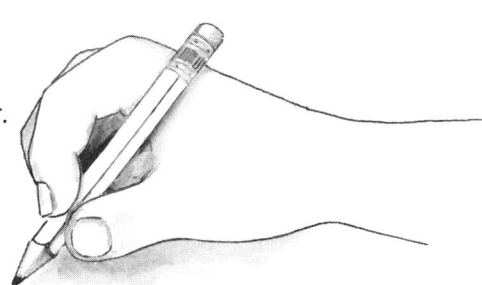

Quadropod Grip
Alternate grip: Hold pencil with
thumb + index and middle fingers.
Pencil rests on ring finger.

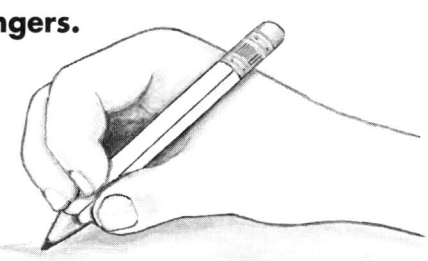

Flip the Pencil Trick
Here is another method that someone introduced to us at a workshop. It's such fun that we love to share it. Children like to do it and it puts the pencil in the correct position. (Illustrated for right-handed students.)

 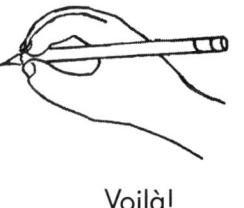

Place pencil on table pointing away from you. Pinch the pencil on the paint where the paint meets the wood.

Hold the eraser and twirl the pencil around.

Voilà! Correct grip.

Picking Up My Pencil

Use this song from the *Rock, Rap, Tap & Learn* music album to make your pencil grip lessons more memorable. You sing the first verse, and students will join in the second.

Materials
- "Picking Up My Pencil" from *Rock, Rap, Tap & Learn* music album

Activity

1. Listen to "Picking Up My Pencil" as background music a few times with your students.
2. For fun, review the names of the pencil grip fingers: thumb, pointer, tall man (middle finger).
3. Without the music, sing and demonstrate the first verse.
4. In the second verse, children will sing with you. They pick up their pencils, check their own grip, and their neighbor's too.

Note: The fast pace of the song is to encourage students to pick up the tune quickly, and to inspire them to sing it on their own.

ENRICHMENT

 Additional practice for Pencil Pick Ups.

SUPPORT/ELL

If a child struggles to position the pencil, place it in their fingers correctly. Name their fingers as you position them on the pencil.

Grasping Grip

Educators often have questions about pencil grip, such as why awkward pencil grips happen and how to correct them. We seldom hear about how to prevent them. A good pencil grip does not develop naturally. In fact, several factors affect how a child learns to hold a pencil correctly. Below are 10 things we often think about regarding grip:

1. **Experiences**
   We develop pencil grip habits while we are young. Children who are encouraged to feed themselves have more fine motor experiences than those who are spoon fed. Those who have early self-feeding experiences may have an easier time learning how to hold their crayons and pencils.

2. **Toys**
   Today's toys are very different from those with which we grew up. We should always encourage and remind families about non-battery operated toys because they help build hand strength.

3. **Imitation**
   Children are born imitators. When they are watching you write, always demonstrate a correct grip because they tend to do as you do.

4. **Early Instruction**
   Help children place their fingers. Teach Pre-K children and kindergartners their finger names and finger jobs and show them how their fingers should hold writing tools.

5. **Tool Size**
   Choose appropriate writing tools. We prefer little tools: Little Sponge Cubes, Little Chalk Bits, FLIP Crayons®, and Pencils for Little Hands. These tools promote using the finger tips naturally. Big tools elicit a fisted grip; little tools, a more mature grip. As adults, we write with pencils that are in proportion to our hands. Children should do the same.

6. **Timing**
   It is difficult to correct the grips of older children because we have to re-teach their motor patterns. Older children need time to get used to a new way of holding a pencil. It takes repetition, persistence, and practice.

7. **Blanket Rules**
   Avoid blanket rules about pencil grip devices. Some devices may work for a child. If they are motivating and work, use them. Use grip devices as a last resort and use them for older children who understand their purpose.

8. **Acceptance**
   Some awkward pencil grips are functional. If the child is comfortable and doesn't have speed or legibility issues, let it go.

9. **Joints**
   We are all made differently. Some of us have joints that are more relaxed. Therefore, expect slight variations in what is considered a standard grip. If a child is unable to use a standard grip, you may consider an altered grip.

10. **Summer**
    This is the perfect time to change an awkward grip. Take advantage of the child's down time to create new habits.

CAPITALS

Capitals are big, bold, and important. They deserve a very important place in developing strong handwriting skills. Teachers agree and task analysis shows that capitals are easier to learn than lowercase letters (NAEYC and IRA 1998).

In second grade, we review the capital letters as a group, separate from lowercase. Instead of reviewing 52 letter symbols with a mishmash of different sizes, positions, and confusing starting places, we divide and conquer.

In this section, children will:

- Build good habits for capital letter formation in a developmentally appropriate sequence

- Have many opportunities to self-check their letters

- Be provided with ways to enrich or support each lesson

We have carefully planned the curriculum to help you develop strong handwriting skills for every child, from the very first lesson.

Developmental Teaching

HANDWRITING SKILL PROGRESSION

When children learn to write their capitals, they develop a strong foundation for printing. Children learn to:
- Start letters at the top.
- Use the correct stroke sequence to form letters.
- Orient letters and numbers correctly—without reversals!

When we teach capitals first, learning lowercase letters is a breeze. Think about it: **c**, **o**, **s**, **v**, **w**, and **x**, **y**, and **z** are the same as their capitals; **j**, **k**, **t**, **p**, and **u** are also similar to their capital partners. If we teach capitals correctly, we have already prepared children for nearly half of the lowercase alphabet.

Some capitals are developmentally easier to write than others. Children gradually develop the ability to copy forms in a predictable order (Gesell 1940).

up to 3 years old   up to 4 years old   up to 6 years old

Developmental Analysis – Capitals Vs. Lowercase Letters

This is the capital/lowercase analysis that informs our developmental teaching order.

Capital Letters Are Easy
- All start at the top.
- All are the same height.
- All occupy the same vertical space.
- All are easy to recognize and identify (compare **A**, **B**, **D**, **G**, **P**, **Q** with **a**, **b**, **d**, **g**, **p**, **q**).
- All are big, bold, and familiar.

Lowercase Letters Are More Difficult
- Lowercase letters start in four different places (**a**, **b**, **e**, **f**).
- Lowercase letters are not all the same size:
    - 14 letters are half the size of capitals.
    - 12 are the same size as capitals.
- Lowercase letters occupy three different vertical positions: small, tall, descending.
- Lowercase letters are more difficult to recognize because of subtle differences (**a**, **b**, **d**, **g**, **p**, **q**).

Let's Do the Math
You can see at a glance that capitals are easier for children. Students have fewer chances to make mistakes when they write capital letters. They aim their pencil at the top and get it right. With lowercase, there are many more variables.

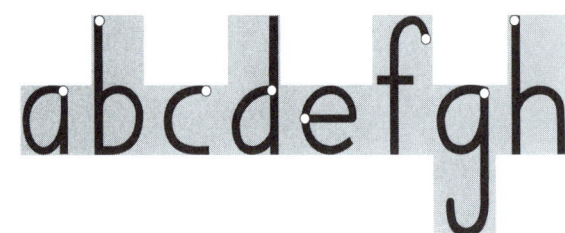

CAPITAL & LOWERCASE LETTER ANALYSIS		
	Capitals	Lowercase
Start	1	4
Size	1	2
Position	1	3
Appearance	• Familiar • Distinctive A, B, D, G, P, Q	• Many similar • Easy to confuse a, b, d, g, p, q

Student Edition Design

USING PRINTING POWER STUDENT EDITION
Our student editions use child-friendly language and large step-by-step models to promote excellence and efficient, effective practice for each letter.

Capital Letter
Children practice forming capital letters in Gray Blocks, triple lines, and single lines as they perfect their capital letter skills.

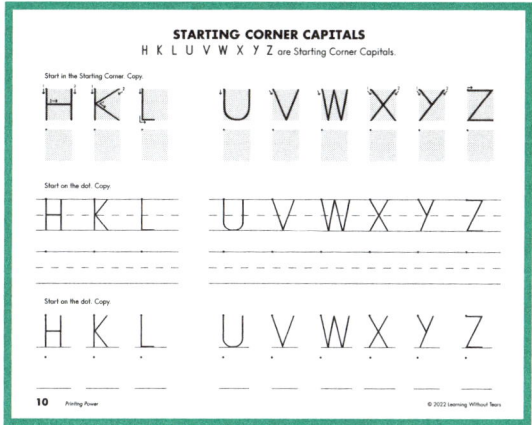
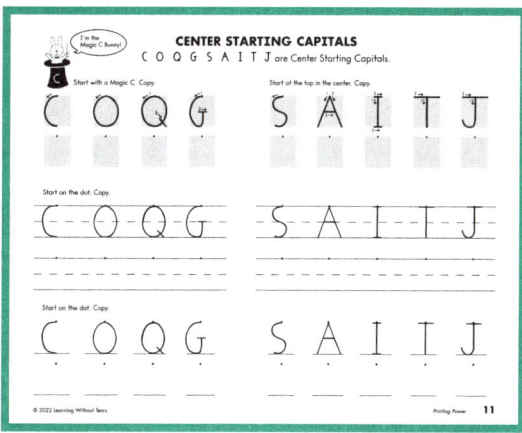

Gray Blocks and Simple Spatial Organization
We begin by teaching capitals and numbers with Gray Blocks to prevent reversals and help children learn how to place letters and numbers. The simple teaching strategies are reversal-proof and enable children to learn correct formation.

When children are learning to print, they need extra room to write. Many workbooks and worksheets are poorly designed, requiring students to cram their words into spaces that are too small. Our landscape style student editions give them ample space to write and develop good spacing habits.

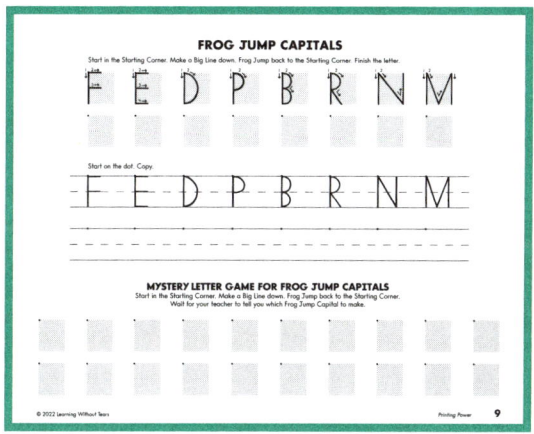

Capital Teaching Order/Learn & Check

DEVELOPMENTAL TEACHING ORDER

The Handwriting Without Tears® teaching order is planned to help children learn handwriting skills in the easiest, most efficient way. It's also developmentally planned to start with a review of the easy letters: the capitals. They are the first letters children should learn. Your kindergartners may know them, but you want to be sure they print them correctly. The capital teaching order will help you teach:

1. Correct formation: All capitals start at the top. Strokes are made in the correct sequence.
2. Correct orientation: No reversals.

To do this, start by teaching letters in groups on Gray Blocks:

Frog Jump Capitals

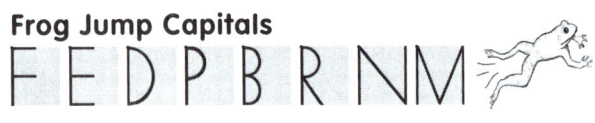

These letters start at the top left corner with a Big Line on the left. When the first line is on the left, the next part of the letter is on the right side. This prevents reversals and teaches good stroke habits.

Starting Corner Capitals

Reviewing these letters ensures that children start at the top left and use the left-to-right formation habit. The good habits children form with **U, V, W, X, Y, Z** will carry over to **u, v, w, x, y, z**.

Center Starting Capitals

C, O, Q, G start with a Magic C stroke. The good habits children learn here with **C, O, S, T, J** will make learning **c, o, s, t, j** much easier. There will be no problems with stroke direction or reversals.

LEARN & CHECK

Children need to know exactly what to do.

1. Start correctly.
2. Do each step in sequence.
3. Bump the line.

Set children up for success by pointing out in their student editions:

1. Start correctly. 2. Do each step. 3. Bump the line.

When you check their student edition letters, explain what they did right and help them correct any mistakes. After you have done this a few times, they'll begin to self-check with confidence.

p. 7

Pencil Pick-Ups

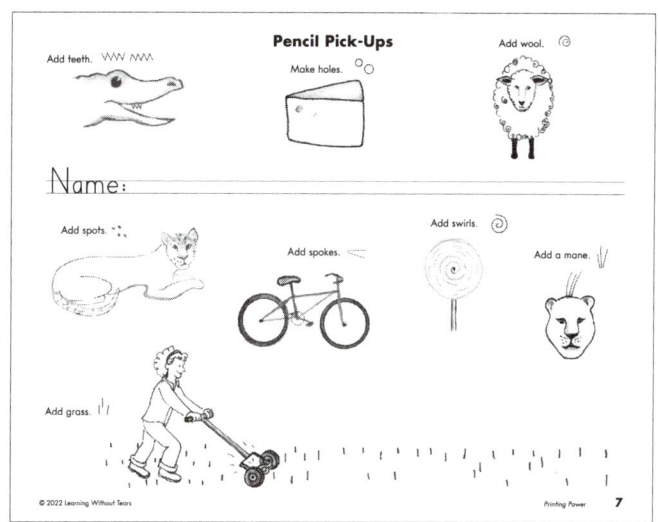

OBJECTIVES
To practice holding a pencil correctly.
To write Name in titlecase.

LESSON INTRODUCTION (Warm Up)
SONG: "Picking Up My Pencil" from *Rock, Rap, Tap & Learn* music album

Additional digital resources are available in the Interactive Digital Teaching Tool (IDTT).

LESSON PLAN

1. Direction Instruction (Demo)
Review names of the pencil grip fingers: thumb, pointer, and tall man (middle finger). Model Pencil Pick-Ups. Demonstrate how to write a proper name in title case.

2. Guided Practice
Children write their names on double lines.

3. Check Grip
Monitor as children use an appropriate grip during pencil pick-ups an if they write their name with correct size, placement and closeness.

ENRICHMENT

Use Pencil Pick-Ups for additional practice to reinforce good grip at home.

SUPPORT/ELL
Have children draw pictures with correct grip on a vertical surface to keep their wrist in a neutral position while drawing.

CROSS-CURRICULAR CONNECTIONS
Resources: For additional information about handedness or pencil grip refer to pages (pp. 33–39).

Frog Jump Capitals

Printing Power – p. 8

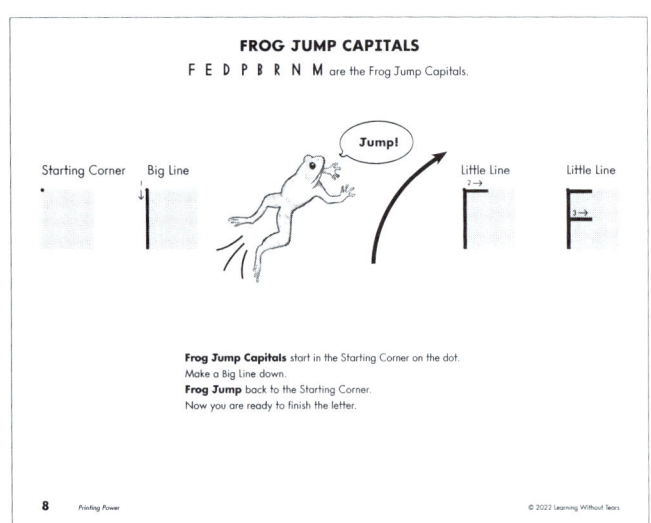

OBJECTIVE
To review the steps for writing Frog Jump Capitals:
F, **E**, **D**, **P**, **B**, **R**, **N**, and **M**.

LESSON INTRODUCTION (Warm Up)
Air Writing (p. 162)

Additional digital resources are available in the Interactive Digital Teaching Tool (IDTT).

LESSON PLAN

1. Direction Instruction (Demo)

Demonstrate **F** on the Slate Chalkboard or Gray Blocks.
Say the words for each step.

Lesson F:

 Start in the Starting Corner

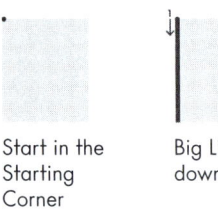 Big Line down

Frog Jump

 Little Line across the top

 Little Line across the middle

2. Guided Practice

Observe as children finger trace step-by-step models on the page while saying the words.

3. Check Letters

Monitor as children finger trace to see if they follow the steps correctly.

ENRICHMENT
Have children associate each Frog Jump letter with a word. For example, **F** is for Frog and **E** is for eagle.

SUPPORT/ELL
Have children practice Frog Jumps after the Big Line. Say "Ribbit" when it's time to jump to the top.

CROSS-CURRICULAR CONNECTIONS
Language Arts: Say the sounds for **F**, **E**, **D**, **P**, **B**, **R**, **N**, and **M**. Discuss the difference between alphabet knowledge and phonics.

Frog Jump Capitals

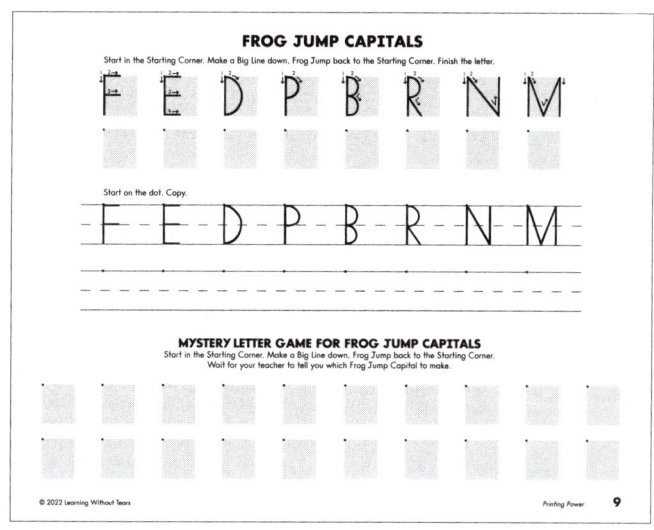

OBJECTIVE
To review and write Frog Jump Capitals with correct formation.

LESSON INTRODUCTION (Warm Up)
SONG: "Frog Jump Capitals" from *Rock, Rap, Tap & Learn* music album

Additional digital resources are available in the Interactive Digital Teaching Tool (IDTT).

LESSON PLAN

1. Direction Instruction (Demo)
Demonstrate **F**, **E**, **D**, **P**, **B**, **R**, **N**, and **M** on Gray Blocks. Say the words for each step.

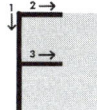 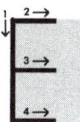 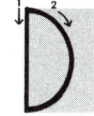 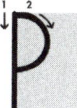 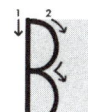  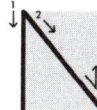 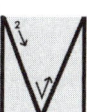

Demonstrate on triple lines.

Mystery Letter Game: Children follow your directions:
Put your pencil on the dot (starting corner). Make a Big Line down. Frog Jump back to the starting corner. Wait. Make letter **B** (or **N**, **P**, **E**, **F**, **M**, **R**, **D**).

2. Guided Practice
Observe as children copy the Frog Jump Capitals.

3. Check Letters
Monitor as children write the Frog Jump Letters with correct start and steps.

ENRICHMENT
 Frog Jump Capitals Group

SUPPORT/ELL
Have children say the steps out loud. Children like to say "ribbit" for the Frog Jump. Demonstrate the movement of the jump from the bottom of the Big Line to the top.

CROSS-CURRICULAR CONNECTIONS
Language Arts: As a class make a list of names that start with **F**, **E**, **D**, **P**, **B**, **R**, **N** and **M**.

Starting Corner Capitals

Printing Power – p. 10

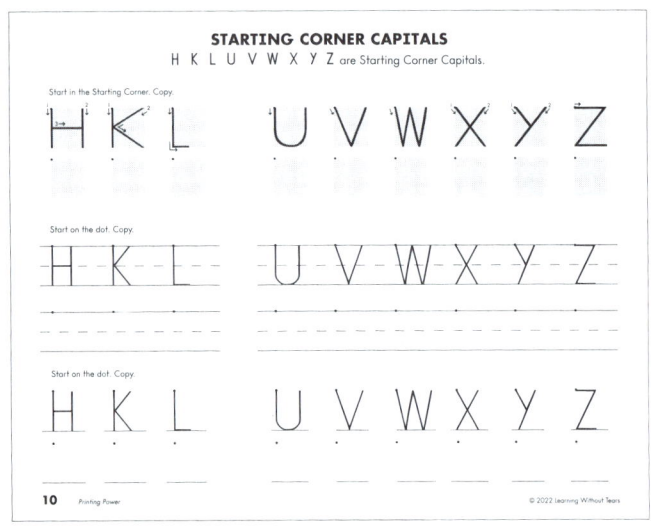

OBJECTIVE
To review and write the Starting Corner Capitals with correct formation.

LESSON INTRODUCTION (Warm Up)
Digital Letter and Number Formations (p. 164)

Additional digital resources are available in the Interactive Digital Teaching Tool (IDTT).

LESSON PLAN

1. Direction Instruction (Demo)

Demonstrate **H**, **K**, **L**, **U**, **V**, **W**, **X**, **Y**, and **Z** using Gray Blocks. Say the words for each step.

Demonstrate on triple lines.

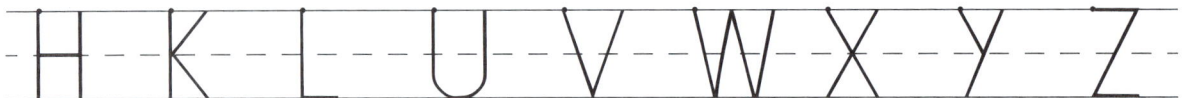

Demonstrate on single lines.

2. Guided Practice

Children copy Starting Corner Capitals: **H, K, L, U, V, W, X, Y,** and **Z**.
Observe as children copy the letters.

3. Check Letters

Monitor as children write the Starting Corner Capitals with correct start and steps.

ENRICHMENT

Starting Corner Capitals Group

SUPPORT/ELL

Some children may have been taught **Y** and that's fine. It's a style difference. We prefer **Y** because it uses the same strokes for the capital and lowercase letter.

CROSS-CURRICULAR CONNECTIONS

Language Arts: As a class, make a list of names that begin with **H, K, L, U, V, W, X, Y,** and **Z**.

Center Starting Capitals

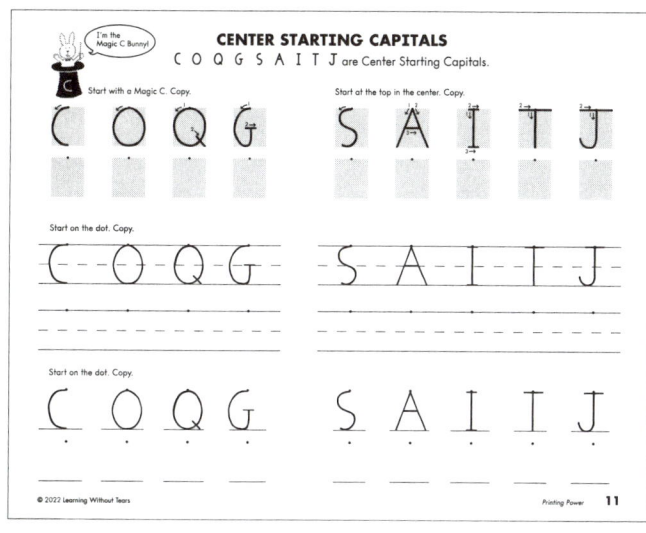

OBJECTIVE

To review and write Center Starting Capitals with correct formation.

LESSON INTRODUCTION (Warm Up)

Laser Letters (p. 163)

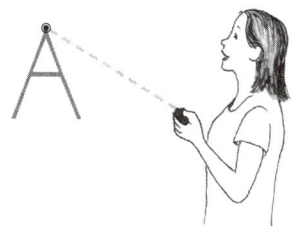

Additional digital resources are available in the Interactive Digital Teaching Tool (IDTT).

LESSON PLAN

1. Direction Instruction (Demo)

Demonstrate **C**, **O**, **Q**, **G**, **S**, **A**, **I**, **T**, and **J** using Gray Blocks. Say the words for each step.

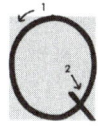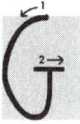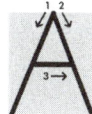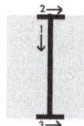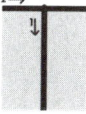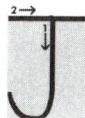

Demonstrate on triple lines.

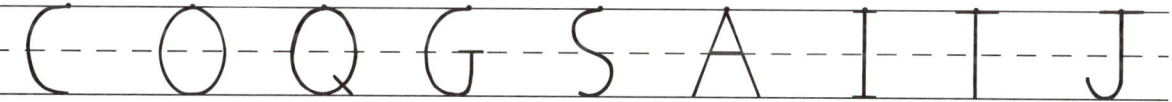

Demonstrate on single lines.

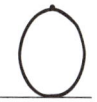

2. Guided Practice

Children copy Center Starting Capitals: **C**, **O**, **Q**, **G**, **S**, **A**, **I**, **T**, and **J**. Observe as children copy the letters.

3. Check Letters

Monitor as children write the Center Starting Capitals with correct start and steps.

ENRICHMENT

 Center Starting Capitals Group

SUPPORT/ELL

You may choose to use the center (top) of a slate chalkboard (or a door) with a small mark to orient children to the center.

CROSS-CURRICULAR CONNECTIONS

Language Arts: Identify informational labels with capitals. Examples include: STOP, EXIT, BOYS, and GIRLS.

CAPITAL REVIEW

Printing Power – p. 12

OBJECTIVE
To review and write all capitals with correct formation.

LESSON INTRODUCTION (Warm Up)
SONG: "Alphabet Boogie" from *Rock, Rap, Tap & Learn* music album

> Additional digital resources are available in the Interactive Digital Teaching Tool (IDTT).

LESSON PLAN

1. Direction Instruction (Demo)
Demonstrate **A**, **B**, and **C** on the Slate Chalkboard or Gray Blocks. Say the words for each step.

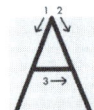 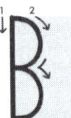 

2. Guided Practice
Children copy **A**, **B**, and **C**.
Observe as children copy the rest of the alphabet on their own.

3. Check Letters
Monitor as children write the capitals with correct start and steps.

ENRICHMENT
Write the alphabet and leave letters missing for children to fill in the missing capitals.

SUPPORT/ELL
If a child is having difficulty forming a letter, model correct formation on the slate chalkboard.

CROSS-CURRICULAR CONNECTIONS
Language Arts: Have children find the vowels in each row: the beginning, middle, and end of the alphabet. Say the long and short sounds.

Number Review

p. 13

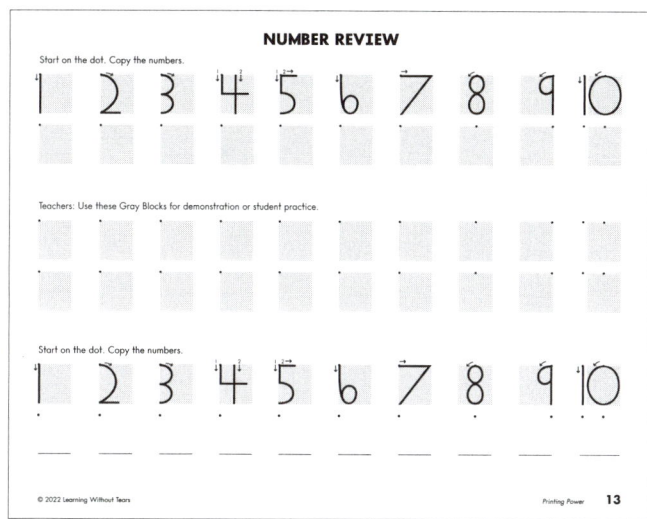

OBJECTIVE
To review and write the numbers 1–10 with correct formation.

LESSON INTRODUCTION (Warm Up)
SONG: "Number Song" from *Rock, Rap, Tap & Learn* music album

Additional digital resources are available in the Interactive Digital Teaching Tool (IDTT).

LESSON PLAN

1. Direction Instruction (Demo)
Demonstrate 1–10 on the Slate Chalkboard or Gray Blocks. Say the words for each step.

   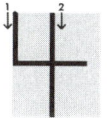      

2. Guided Practice
Children copy 1–10.
Observe as children copy 1–10 on their own.

3. Check Numbers
Monitor as children write their numbers with correct start and steps.

NOTE: Numbers are placed at the back of *Printing Power*, however, the teaching guidelines suggest you teach and review numbers at the beginning of the year during math activities.

ENRICHMENT
Encourage children to say the directions for number formations out loud, either as a class or individually.

SUPPORT/ELL
The middle section of the page is designed for you to give individual help as needed.

CROSS-CURRICULAR CONNECTIONS
Math: It's easy to learn counting by twos. Just have children turn pages and read the left page numbers aloud.

LOWERCASE LETTERS, WORDS & SENTENCES

It's time for all the letters, words, and sentences. The 26 capitals you've taught already give your students an excellent start for lowercase letters. Lowercase lessons begin with letters your students already know. We start with **c**, **o**, **s**, **v**, and **w**—five letters that are exactly the same as capitals just smaller. That's not all. Beginning with those five letters gives another opportunity for you to be sure every child has good habits for **c**, **o**, **s**, **v**, and **w**. That's an excellent lowercase start.

Because only familiar and previously taught letters are used in our word practice, children typically use correct habits for writing every letter. With word practice, these habits become automatic and lead directly to fluency. At first, every new letter takes care and conscious effort, but gradually, more letters are written both correctly and automatically.

In this section, children will:

- Build good habits for lowercase letter formation in a developmentally appropriate sequence

- Have many opportunities to self-check their letters

- Be provided with ways to enrich or support each lesson

- Use recently used letters in words to extend their learning

Student Edition Design

LOWERCASE LETTER, WORDS & SENTENCE PAGES
Children practice newly taught letters in words and sentences. These pages model good spacing and review capitals. The ☑ teaches children to self-check their work, reinforcing letter formation and sentence skills.

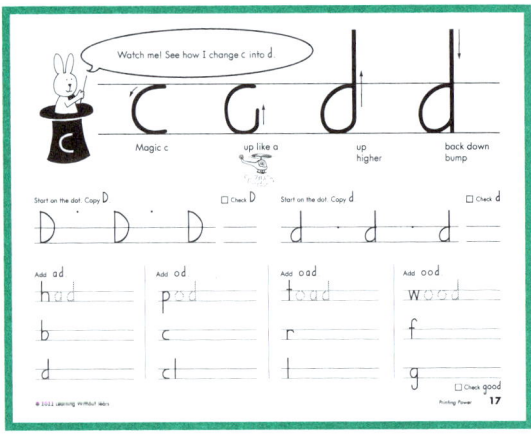

As children move to lowercase, our double lines foster handwriting success. The mid line is for size. The base line is for placement. Small letters fit in the middle space. Tall letters go in the top space. Descending letters go in the bottom space. Double lines make it easy for children to place letters and to make them the right size.

Children will never have to write a letter before they learn it, but our student edition will expose children to reading letters before they learn to write them.

The Words & Sentences for Me pages contain printing practice with onsets and rimes, comparative words, and suffixes. For these activities, we have children write words that contain letters the students have already learned. By using familiar letters, they are able to better understand concepts and learn to write more efficiently. Reading comprehension is strengthened page by page as students add new letters to their skill set.

The Words & Sentences writing activities serve a dual purpose: they promote correct letter placement and formation while also developing foundational reading skills. Students have fun with engaging and fun letter and reading practice instead of rote copy work.

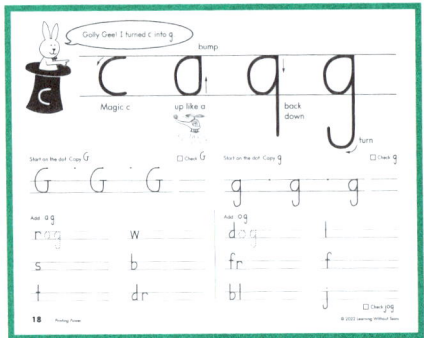  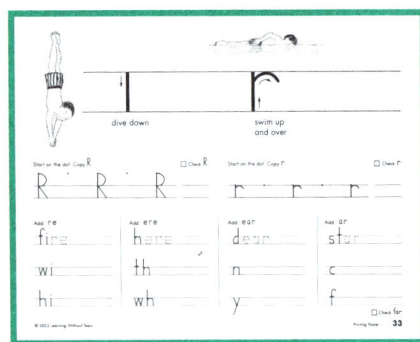

Onsets and Rimes
Children practice printing the first and last parts of words. In doing so, they also build foundational phonics and reading skills.

Suffixes
Students practice adding suffixes to words to practice fluency.

Comparative Words
Students learn the comparative suffixes -er and -est, which simultaneously build handwriting, grammar skills, and critical thinking skills.

Double Line Success

LINE CONFUSION: DOUBLE LINES ENABLE SUCCESS

For children to become well-rounded in handwriting, they must be able to write efficiently on all types of lined paper. When it comes to choosing a style of paper, there are certainly many options: single lines, double lines, triple lines, dotted or straight. But which type is best for students who are new to writing

Have you seen this in your classroom?

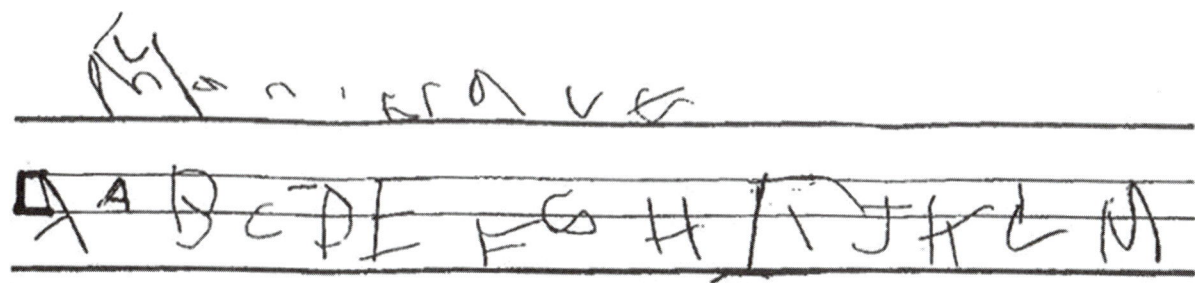

Many children have trouble understanding multiple lines. Giving children a blue line, a dotted line, a red line, and another blue line and then asking them to start at "2 o'clock between the dotted line and the red line" is too confusing.

Become a Line Leader in Double Lines

Our double lines quickly teach children how to place letters: small letters fit in the middle space, tall letters go in the top space, descending letters go in the bottom space. Without having to spend extra time deciding how to orient their letters on the paper, children can launch right in to printing their ABCs or putting the poem in their heads onto the paper.

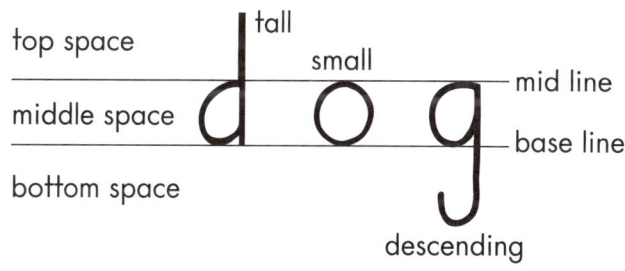

Double lines help children place letters correctly, eliminating line confusion. The base line guides placement, and the mid line controls the size of letters. Students who struggle with start and placement on other styles of paper succeed on double lines.

One, Two, Red, or Blue: Line Generalization

Although we advocate double line paper, our student editions provide activities for children to experience different types of lined paper. We begin with simple double line paper and work up to mastering all line types. Having your students experiment with and learn a variety of paper styles poises them for success in handwriting.

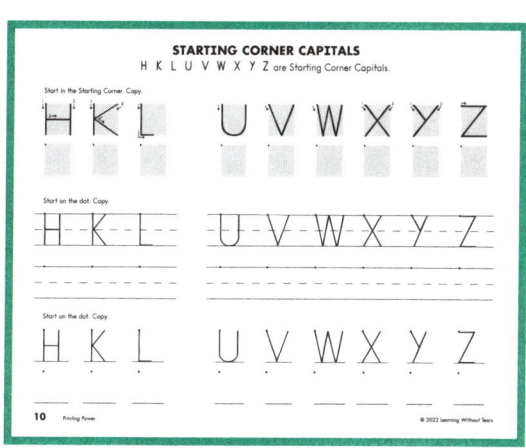

Lowercase Teaching Order

LETTER GROUPS

Our lowercase teaching order promotes good habits for letter formation and writing success. This is done by grouping letters to facilitate:

1. Easy start: All lowercase letters (except **d** and **e**) begin at the top.
2. Correct placement: The tall, small, and descending letters are in proportion and placed correctly.
3. Correct orientation: No **b** and **d** confusion, no **g** and **q** confusion, no reversed letters!

LOWERCASE LETTERS ARE TAUGHT IN FIVE GROUPS

Same as Capitals and t

c o s v w   t

The first five letters are exactly like their capitals, just smaller. What an easy start—just bring your good habits from capitals! Lowercase **t** is made like **T**. It's just crossed lower.

Magic c

a d g

These high frequency letters begin with the familiar Magic c. Starting with **c** placed correctly helps children make and place the **d** tall and **g** descending.

Transition Group

u i e l k y j

Here are the rest of the vowels: **u**, **i**, **e**. Letters **u**, **k**, **y**, **j** are familiar from capitals. The focus will be on careful placement and size.

Diver Letters

p r n m h b

These letters all start with the same pattern: they dive down, swim up, swim over! We avoid **b** and **d** confusion by separating the letters and teaching them in different groups based on formation habits.

Final Group

f q x z

Lowercase **f** has a tricky start. Letter **q** is taught here to avoid **g** and **q** confusion. Letters **x** and **z** are familiar, but infrequently used.

Learn & Check

At the board and in the student edition, the focus of your teaching will be on letters, words, and sentences. You are teaching letter formation as well as word and sentence skills. You will teach in easy, small steps so your students know exactly what to do. Then, you'll help them develop their ability to ☑ letter, word, and sentence skills. Use p. 5 of *Printing Power* to explain what is expected when they self-check.

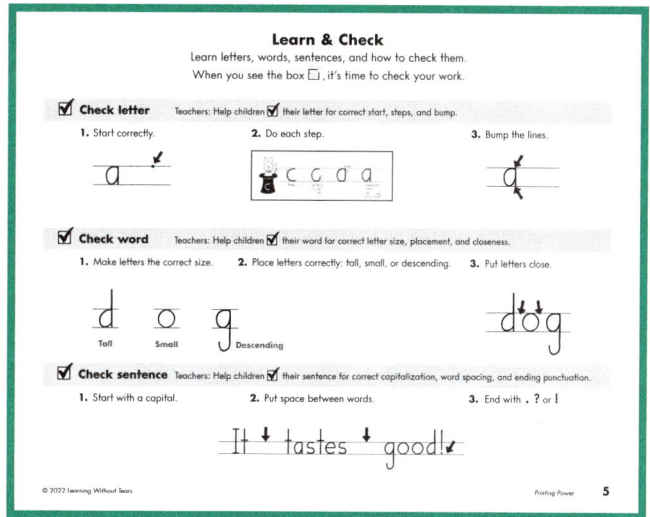

Throughout the student edition you will see opportunities for children to self-check their handwriting. Self-checking helps students understand where they are doing well and where they need improvement. They will put extra effort into making the checked letters and sentences correctly. This also leads to an informal self-checking process in daily writing. When children struggle here, you will know where they need extra attention.

Below is an example of how *Printing Power* is designed to promote self-checking skills.
We have highlighted a letter, word, and sentence and the area where your students will self-check.

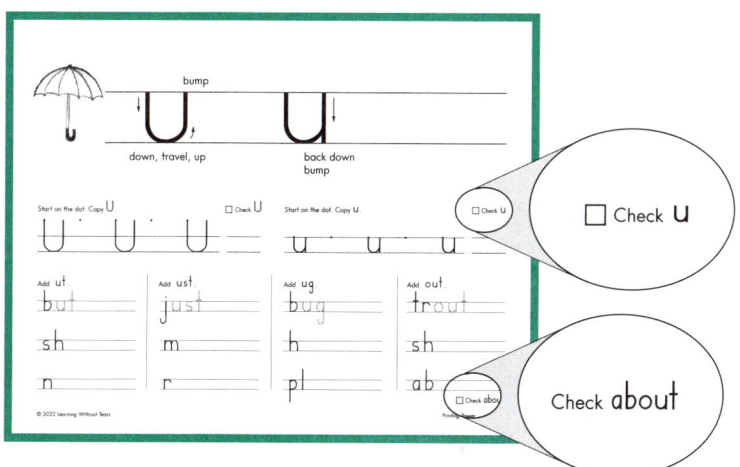

Check Letter and Word Skills

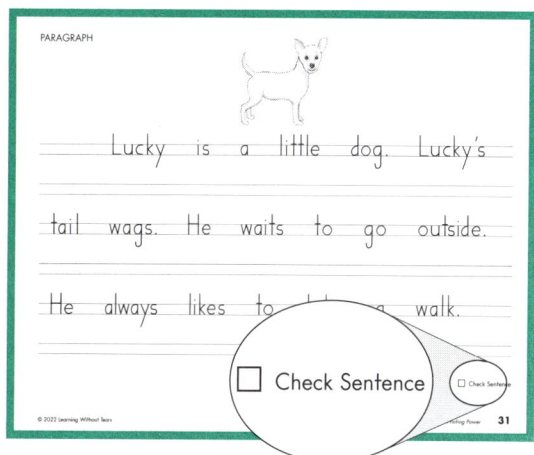

Check Sentence Skills

Same as Capitals

Printing Power – p. 14

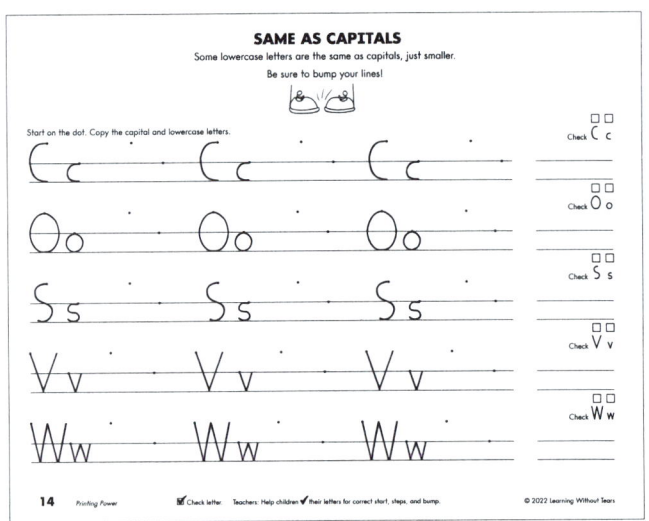

OBJECTIVE

To write capital and lowercase **C c**, **O o**, **S s**, **V v**, and **W w** with correct formation.

LESSON INTRODUCTION (Warm Up)

Hand Activity (p. 167)

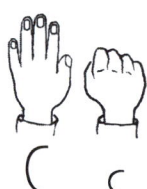

Additional digital resources are available in the Interactive Digital Teaching Tool (IDTT).

LESSON PLAN

1. Direction Instruction (Demo)

Demonstrate **Cc**, **Oo**, **Ss**, **Vv**, and **Ww** on double lines.
Say the words for each letter.

2. Guided Practice

Children copy letters.
Monitor as children complete the letters on their own.

3. Check Letters

Help children ✓ their letters for correct start, steps, and bump.

READ & DISCUSS

Read the letters together. Discuss their similarities in appearance and differences in size.

ENRICHMENT

Have children write the word **cows** on double line paper.

SUPPORT/ELL

Preview lowercase **c** with Wet-Dry-Try on the Blackboard with Double Lines (p. 168). In the student edition, write each **c** with a highlighter for children to trace with a pencil.

CROSS-CURRICULAR CONNECTIONS

Language Arts: Discuss other capitals and lowercase letters that look alike.

p. 15 — T t

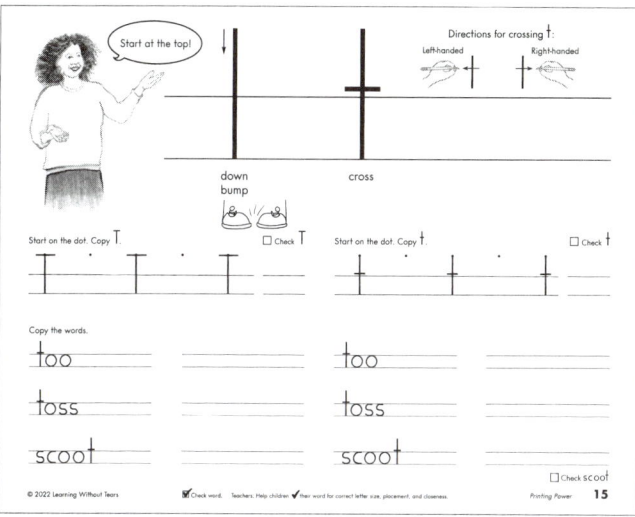

OBJECTIVES
To use correct habits for writing capital **T** and lowercase **t**; to build fluency by practicing previously learned letters.

LESSON INTRODUCTION (Warm Up)
Wet-Dry-Try on Blackboard with Double Lines (p. 168)

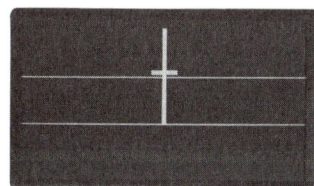

Additional digital resources are available in the Interactive Digital Teaching Tool (IDTT).

LESSON PLAN

1. Direction Instruction (Demo)
Demonstrate **T**, **t** on double lines.
Say the words for each step.
Demonstrate the words **too** and **toss**.

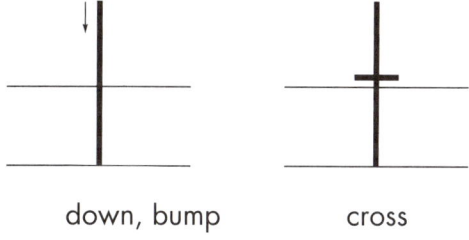

down, bump   cross

2. Guided Practice
Children copy: **T**, **t**, **too**, and **toss**.
Monitor as children write the other words on their own.

3. Check Letter & Word
Help children ✓ their letter for correct start, steps, and bump.
Help children ✓ their word for correct size, placement, and closeness.

READ & DISCUSS
Read the words together and discuss.

ENRICHMENT
Home Link: Same as Capitals Group
c, **o**, **s**, **v**, **w**, and **t**.

SUPPORT/ELL
Use Letter Story: **T** is tall, **t** is Tall to reinforce correct formation of **t** (p. 161).

CROSS-CURRICULAR CONNECTIONS
Language Arts: Talk to children about homophones. Use "to," "too," and "two" as an example. Use each word correctly in a sentence.

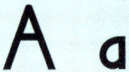 *Printing Power* – p. 16

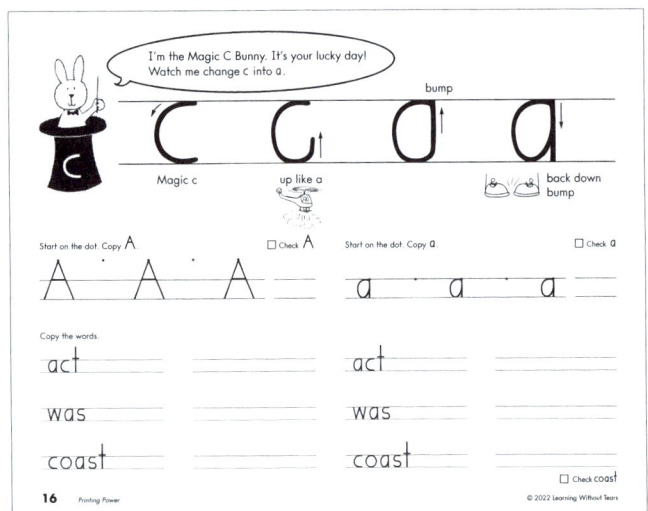

OBJECTIVES
To use correct habits for writing capital **A** and lowercase **a**; to build fluency by practicing previously learned letters.

LESSON INTRODUCTION (Warm Up)
Introduce Magic C Bunny

> Additional digital resources are available in the Interactive Digital Teaching Tool (IDTT).

LESSON PLAN

1. Direction Instruction (Demo)
Demonstrate **A**, **a** on double lines.
Say the words for each step.
Demonstrate the words **act** and **was**.

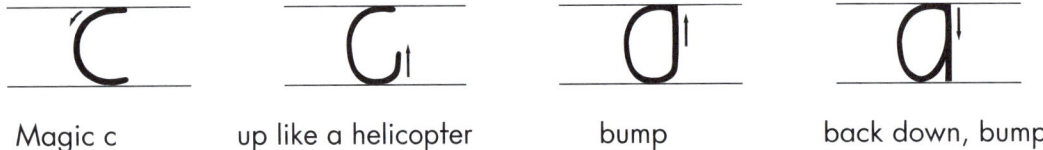

Magic c up like a helicopter bump back down, bump

2. Guided Practice
Children copy: **A**, **a**, **act**, and **was**.
Monitor as children write the other words on their own.

3. Check Letter & Word
Help children ✓ their letter for correct start, steps, and bump.
Help children ✓ their word for correct size, placement, and closeness.

READ & DISCUSS
Read the words together and discuss.

ENRICHMENT
Have children write **C c**, **O o**, and **A a** on double line paper. Discuss how **C c** and **O o** are Magic C Letters, but **A** is not even though **a** is a Magic c letter.

SUPPORT/ELL
If children write lowercase **a** too skinny, encourage them to start on the dot and travel on the mid line before curving down.

CROSS-CURRICULAR CONNECTIONS
Language Arts: Look around the room to find things that have the short /a/ sound in them. Make a class list of the things you find.

p. 17 D d

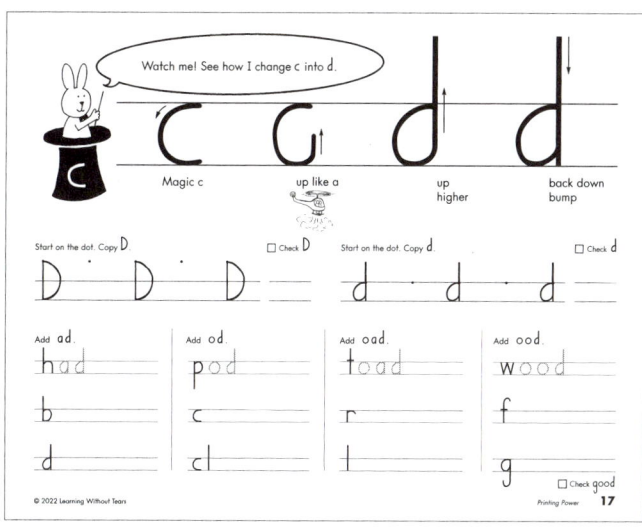

OBJECTIVES
To use correct habits for writing capital **D** and lowercase **d**; to build fluency by practicing previously learned letters.

LESSON INTRODUCTION (Warm Up)
Wet-Dry-Try on Blackboard with Double Lines (p. 168)

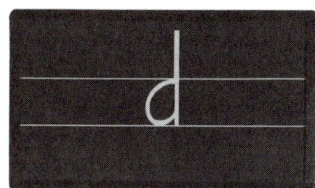

Additional digital resources are available in the Interactive Digital Teaching Tool (IDTT).

LESSON PLAN

1. Direction Instruction (Demo)
Demonstrate **D**, **d** on double lines.
Say the words for each step.
Demonstrate adding rimes to onsets in the words **had**, **pod**, **toad**, and **wood**.

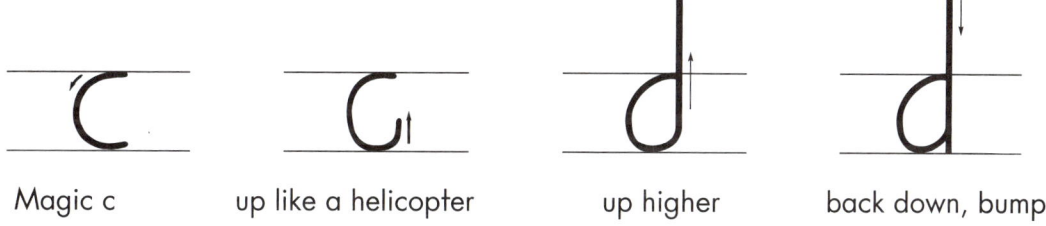

Magic c   up like a helicopter   up higher   back down, bump

2. Guided Practice
Children copy: **D**, **d** and add rimes.
Monitor as children complete words.

3. Check Letter & Word
Help children ☑ their letter for correct start, steps, and bump.
Help children ☑ their word for correct size, placement, and closeness.

READ & DISCUSS
Read the words together and discuss.

ENRICHMENT
A+ Worksheet Maker: Create a spelling worksheet with words using lowercase **d**.

SUPPORT/ELL
Teach an alphabet rhyme to remember how to make **d**. Say, "**a**, **b**, **c**. Magic c turns into **d**." Point to a visual as you repeat the rhyme.

CROSS-CURRICULAR CONNECTIONS
Language Arts: Go on a scavenger hunt inside or outside the classroom to look for letter **d**. As a class, write a list of the things you find.

G g

Printing Power – p. 18

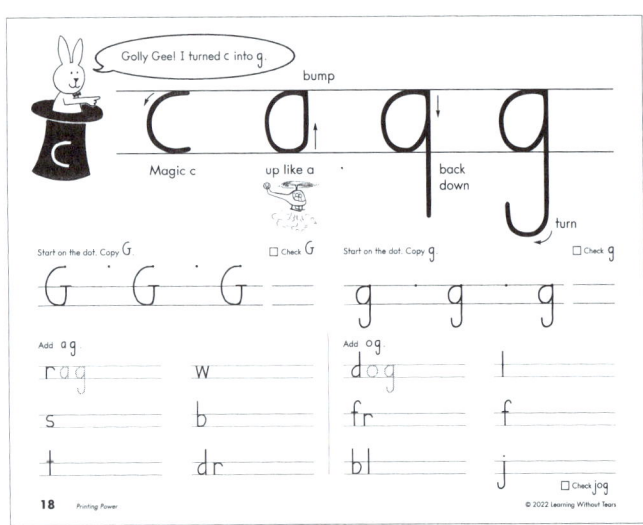

OBJECTIVES

To use correct habits for writing capital **G** and lowercase **g**; to build fluency by practicing previously learned letters.

LESSON INTRODUCTION (Warm Up)

Air Writing (p. 162)

Additional digital resources are available in the Interactive Digital Teaching Tool (IDTT).

LESSON PLAN

1. Direction Instruction (Demo)

Demonstrate **G**, **g** on double lines.
Say the words for each step.
Demonstrate adding rimes to onsets in the words **rag** and **dog**.

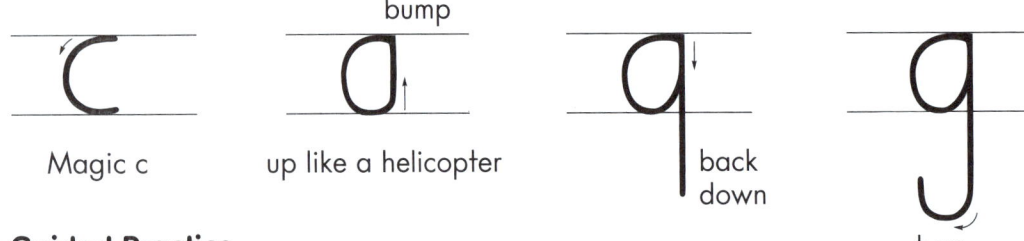

2. Guided Practice

Children copy: **G**, **g** and add rimes.
Monitor as children complete words.

3. Check Letter & Word

Help children ✓ their letter for correct start, steps, and bump.
Help children ✓ their word for correct size, placement, and closeness.

READ & DISCUSS

Read the words together and discuss.

ENRICHMENT

Home Link: Magic C Letters Group **c**, **a**, **d**, and **g**.

SUPPORT/ELL

Use Letter Story: *If George Fails* to reinforce correct formation of **g** (p. 160).

CROSS-CURRICULAR CONNECTIONS

Language Arts: Discuss how rhyming words have the same ending sounds. Challenge children to come up with additional rhyming words.

p. 19

Magic c Mystery Letters

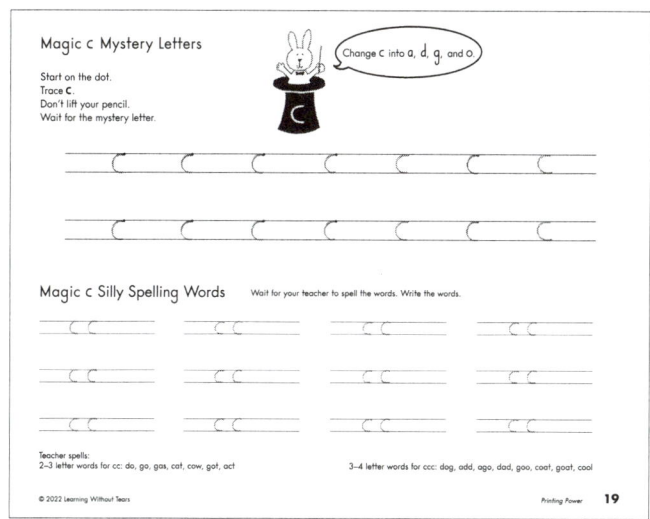

OBJECTIVE
To reinforce good habits for Magic c Letters (**c, a, d, g, o**).

LESSON INTRODUCTION (Warm Up)
SONG: "Magic c Rap" from *Rock, Rap, Tap & Learn* music album

> Additional digital resources are available in the Interactive Digital Teaching Tool (IDTT).

LESSON PLAN

1. Direction Instruction (Demo)

Demonstrate magic **c**'s turning into **a**'s, **d**'s, **g**'s, and **o**'s on double lines.

Magic c Mystery Letters: Children follow your directions: **Start on the dot. Trace c. Don't lift your pencil. Wait for the mystery letter. Make letter a (or d, g, o).**

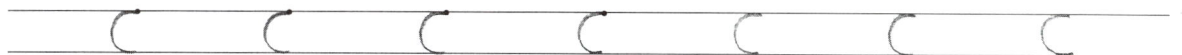

Magic c Silly Spelling Words: Dictate each word for children to write letter by letter. For Magic c letters say: **Magic c. Wait. Change c into (either c, o, a, d, g).**

2. Guided Practice

Observe as children follow your directions and write the Magic c Mystery words.
Sample words: do, go, dot, cat, gas, act.

3. Check Letters & Words

Monitor as children write the Magic c letters and Magic c words.

ENRICHMENT
Children write five **c**'s on the Blackboard with Double Lines. In pairs, they take turns turning the **c**'s into **o, a, d,** and **g**.

SUPPORT/ELL
Begin with two-letter silly spelling words until children demonstrate understanding.

CROSS-CURRICULAR CONNECTIONS
Language Arts: Discuss how Magic c changes **c** into other letters just as the seasons change during the year.

Punctuation

Printing Power – p. 20

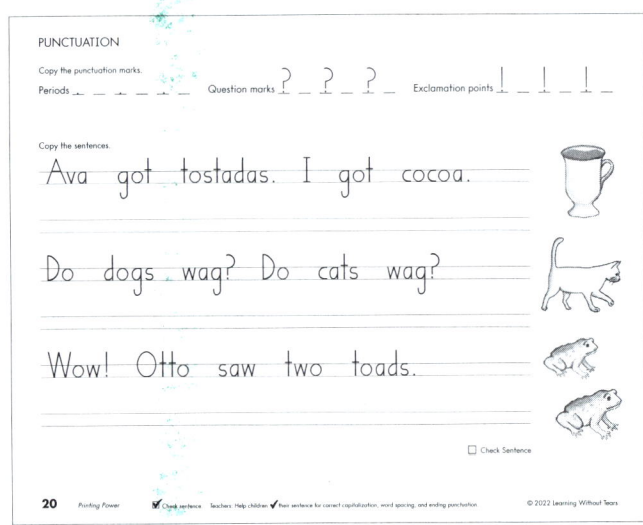

OBJECTIVE
To write and use periods, question marks, and exclamation points correctly.

LESSON INTRODUCTION (Warm Up)
SONG: "Sentence Song" from *Rock, Rap, Tap & Learn* music album

Additional digital resources are available in the Interactive Digital Teaching Tool (IDTT).

LESSON PLAN

1. Direction Instruction (Demo)

Demonstrate punctuation marks for children to copy.
Demonstrate on double lines: **Ava got tostadas.**
Remind children to start with a capital, put space between words, and end with a period.

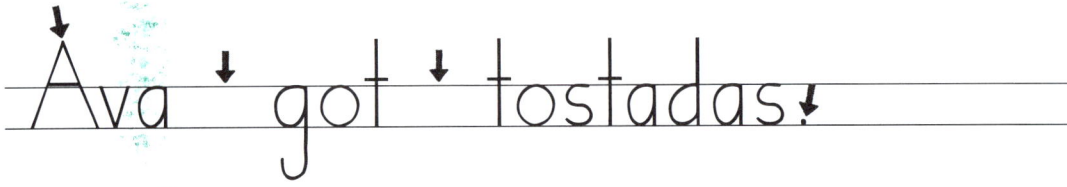

2. Guided Practice

Children copy: **Ava got tostadas. I got cocoa.**
Monitor as children copy other sentences on their own.

3. Check Sentence

Help children ✓ their sentence for correct capitalization, word spacing, and ending punctuation.

ENRICHMENT
Dictate two sentences for children to write on double line paper with one sentence using a question mark and the other using an exclamation point.

SUPPORT/ELL
Use facial expressions and gestures in addition to words to help children understand whether the sentence is a question, statement, or exclamation.

CROSS-CURRICULAR CONNECTIONS
Language Arts: Discuss how punctuation helps us read and write. Ending punctuation shows where the sentences stop.

p. 21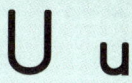

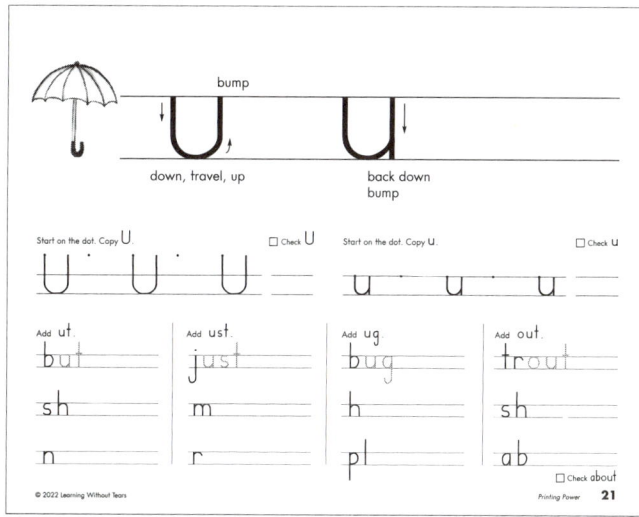

OBJECTIVES

To use correct habits for writing capital **U** and lowercase **u**; to build fluency by practicing previously learned letters.

LESSON INTRODUCTION (Warm Up)

Wet-Dry-Try on Blackboard with Double Lines (p. 168)

Additional digital resources are available in the Interactive Digital Teaching Tool (IDTT).

LESSON PLAN

1. Direction Instruction (Demo)

Demonstrate **U**, **u** on double lines.
Say the words for each step.
Demonstrate adding rimes to onsets in the words **but**, **just**, **bug**, and **trout**.

down, travel, up, bump   back down, bump

2. Guided Practice

Children copy: **U**, **u** and add rimes.
Monitor as children complete words.

3. Check Letter & Word

Help children ✓ their letter for correct start, steps, and bump.
Help children ✓ their word for correct size, placement, and closeness.

READ & DISCUSS

Read the words together and discuss.

ENRICHMENT

A+ Worksheet Maker: Create a spelling list using words ending in **-ug** and **-ut**.

SUPPORT/ELL

Help children find the subtle difference between **U** and **u**. Encourage children to travel on the bottom line before going up if they are making the **u** too pointed.

CROSS-CURRICULAR CONNECTIONS

Science: Discuss rain. Have children research the water cycle and write a report.

I i

Printing Power – p. 22

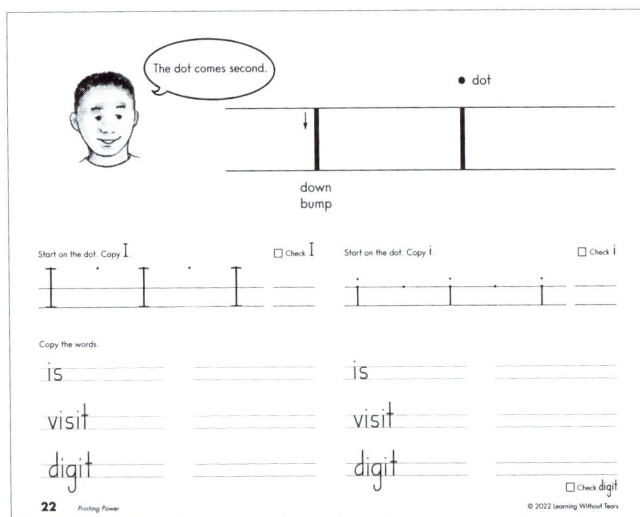

OBJECTIVES
To use correct habits for writing capital **I** and lowercase **i**; to build fluency by practicing previously learned letters.

LESSON INTRODUCTION (Warm Up)
Laser Letters (p. 163)

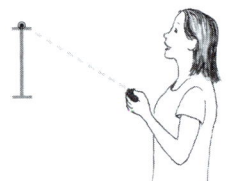

Additional digital resources are available in the Interactive Digital Teaching Tool (IDTT).

LESSON PLAN

1. Direction Instruction (Demo)
Demonstrate **I**, **i** on double lines.
Say the words for each letter.
Demonstrate the words **is** and **visit**.

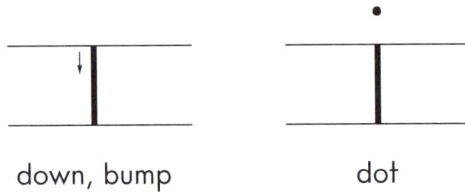

down, bump   dot

2. Guided Practice
Children copy: **I**, **i**, **is**, and **visit**.
Monitor as children write the other words on their own.

3. Check Letter & Word
Help children ✓ their letter for correct start, steps, and bump.
Help children ✓ their word for correct size, placement, and closeness.

READ & DISCUSS
Read the words together and discuss.

ENRICHMENT
Dictate words with the letters **c**, **o**, **s**, **v**, **w**, **t**, **a**, **d**, **g**, **u**, and **i** for children to write on double line paper. Examples include: dig, it, dust, and out.

SUPPORT/ELL
Teach children how to make a dot. Have children practice making dots at the top of the page. Dots shouldn't be too big and shouldn't sit on the mid line.

CROSS-CURRICULAR CONNECTIONS
Language Arts: The boy at the top of the student edition page has a quote bubble. Quotations are the exact words out of a person's mouth.

p. 23 E e

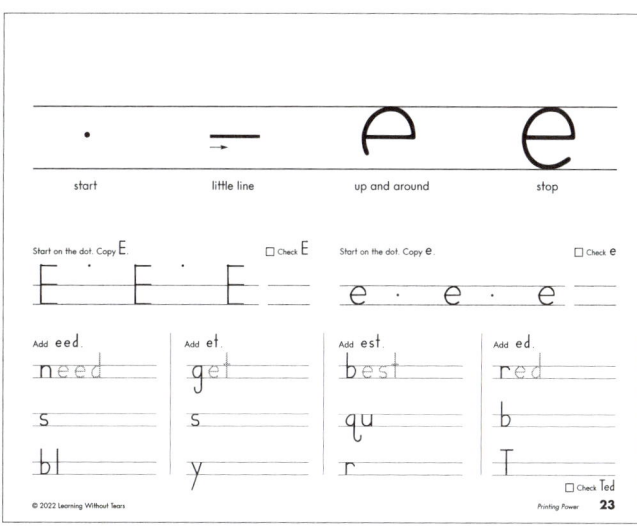

OBJECTIVES
To use correct habits for writing capital **E** and lowercase **e**; to build fluency by practicing previously learned letters.

LESSON INTRODUCTION (Warm Up)
SONG: "Vowels" from *Rock, Rap, Tap & Learn* music album

Additional digital resources are available in the Interactive Digital Teaching Tool (IDTT).

LESSON PLAN

1. Direction Instruction (Demo)
Demonstrate **E**, **e** on double lines.
Say the words for each step.
Demonstrate the words **need**, **get**, **best**, and **red**.

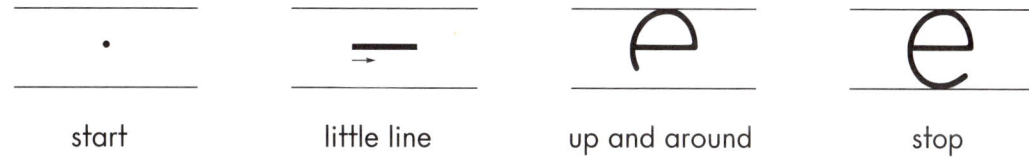

2. Guided Practice
Children copy: **E**, **e** and complete words.
Monitor as children complete words.

3. Check Letter & Word
Help children ✓ their letter for correct start, steps, and bump.
Help children ✓ their word for correct size, placement, and closeness.

READ & DISCUSS
Read the words together and discuss.

ENRICHMENT
Vowels are the glue that hold words together. Have children write a sentence on double line paper and then circle the vowels in the words.

SUPPORT/ELL
Use Letter Story: *Run the Bases* to reinforce correct formation of **e** (p. 160).

CROSS-CURRICULAR CONNECTIONS
Science: Talk about different types of seeds that can grow and what supplies children would need to grow their own garden.

Letter Size & Place

Printing Power – p. 24

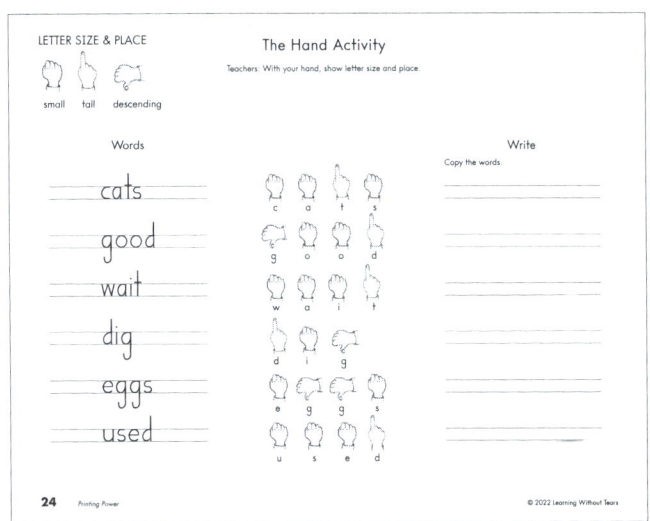

OBJECTIVES

To recognize the size and position of small, tall, and descending letters; to write words on double lines.

LESSON INTRODUCTION (Warm Up)

Hand Activity (p. 167)

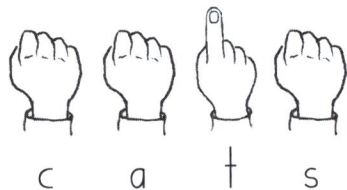

Additional digital resources are available in the Interactive Digital Teaching Tool (IDTT).

LESSON PLAN

1. Direction Instruction (Demo)

Demonstrate **cats**, **good**, and **wait** on double lines.
Move hands to show tall, small, or descending letters.

2. Guided Practice

Children imitate tall, small, and descending hand positions for each letter.
Children copy: **cats**, **good**, and **wait**.
Observe as children copy other words on their own.

3. Check Words

Monitor as children write their words for correct size, placement, and closeness.

ENRICHMENT

Children demonstrate their names using the Hand Activity.

SUPPORT/ELL

Have children focus on the individual letter and movement. Only add letters to build words when children are comfortable with the hand movements.

CROSS-CURRICULAR CONNECTIONS

Language Arts: Children practice silly sentences using the words wait, cat, and eggs.

p. 25

Rhymes

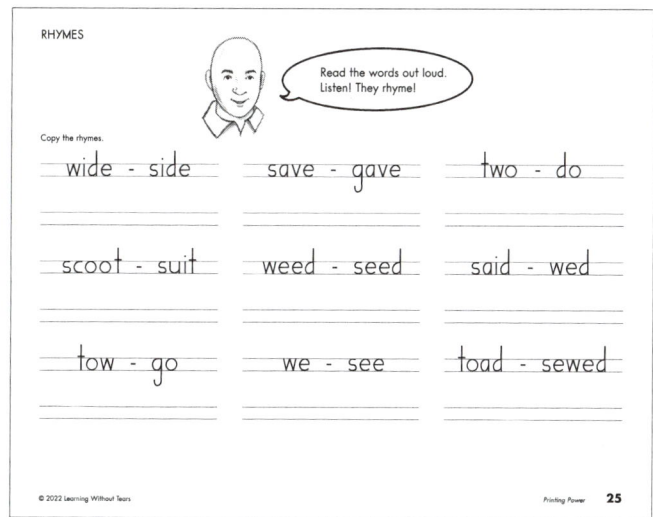

OBJECTIVES
To build writing fluency; to practice rhyme awareness.

LESSON INTRODUCTION (Warm Up)
Hand Activity (p. 167)

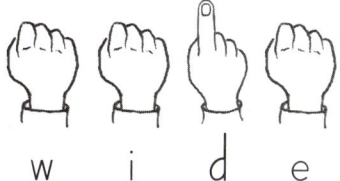

Additional digital resources are available in the Interactive Digital Teaching Tool (IDTT).

LESSON PLAN

1. Direction Instruction (Demo)

Rhymes end with the same sounds.
Demonstrate **wide - side** and **save - gave** on double lines.

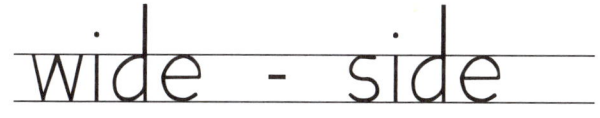

2. Guided Practice

Children copy: **wide - side** and **save - gave**.
Observe as children copy other words on their own.

3. Check Words

Monitor as children write their words for correct size, placement, and closeness.

ENRICHMENT
Have children write rhyming words or a poem on double line paper.

SUPPORT/ELL
Have children practice reading the words left to right, top to bottom. The rhyming makes it easier for children to connect one word to another.

CROSS-CURRICULAR CONNECTIONS
Language Arts: Use wide-side and save-gave to teach that the silent e makes the vowels say its name.

© 2022 Learning Without Tears — Printing Power Teacher's Guide: Lowercase Letters, Words & Sentences — **69**

L l

Printing Power – p. 26

OBJECTIVES
To use correct habits for writing capital **L** and lowercase **l**; to build fluency by practicing previously learned letters.

LESSON INTRODUCTION (Warm Up)
Digital Letter and Number Formations (p. 164)

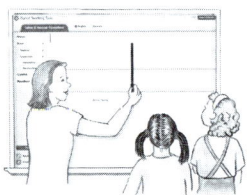

Additional digital resources are available in the Interactive Digital Teaching Tool (IDTT).

LESSON PLAN

1. Direction Instruction (Demo)
Demonstrate **L**, **l** on double lines.
Say the words for each step.
Demonstrate the words **late** and **gold**.

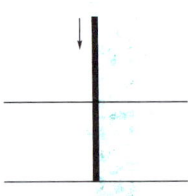

down, bump

2. Guided Practice
Children copy: **L**, **l**, **late**, and **gold**.
Monitor as children write the other words on their own.

3. Check Letter & Word
Help children ☑ their letter for correct start, steps, and bump.
Help children ☑ their word for correct size, placement, and closeness.

READ & DISCUSS
Read the words together and discuss.

ENRICHMENT
Make a list of words using **l** blends. Examples include: slide, class, glad, and glove. Have children write sentences with these words.

SUPPORT/ELL
Have children make a capital **L** with their index finger and thumb. Have children hold up their right hand to make a lowercase **l** with their index finger to recognize the differences.

CROSS-CURRICULAR CONNECTIONS
Language Arts: Learn and use different tenses for both regular and irregular verbs. Examples include: I jump, I jumped, and I will jump.

p. 27 — K k

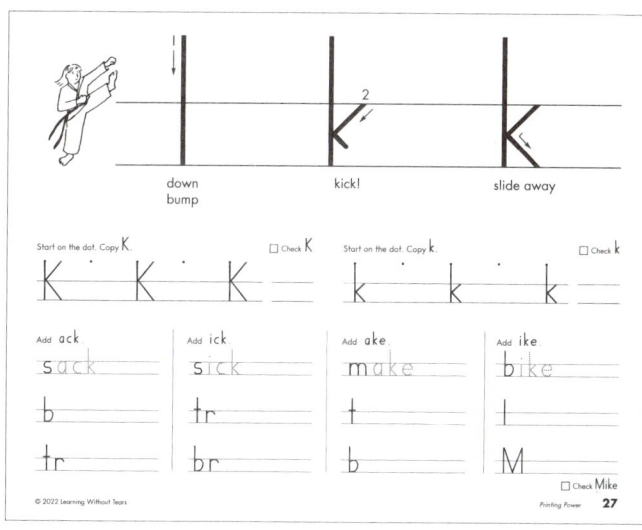

OBJECTIVES
To use correct habits for writing capital **K** and lowercase **k**; to build fluency by practicing previously learned letters.

LESSON INTRODUCTION (Warm Up)
Wet-Dry-Try on Blackboard with Double Lines (p. 168)

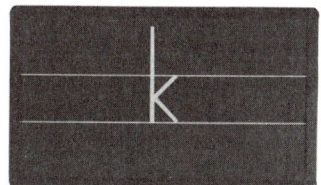

Additional digital resources are available in the Interactive Digital Teaching Tool (IDTT).

LESSON PLAN

1. Direction Instruction (Demo)

Demonstrate **K**, **k** on double lines.
Say the words for each step.
Demonstrate adding rimes to onsets in the words **sack**, **sick**, **make**, and **bike**.

 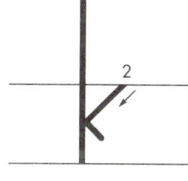 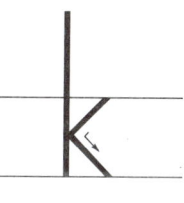

down, bump   kick!   slide away

2. Guided Practice

Children copy: **K**, **k** and add rimes.
Monitor as children complete words.

3. Check Letter & Word

Help children ✓ their letter for correct start, steps, and bump.
Help children ✓ their word for correct size, placement, and closeness.

READ & DISCUSS
Read the words together and discuss.

ENRICHMENT
Use A+ Worksheet Maker to create words with the digraph: **ck** (tack, sack, tick, clock).

SUPPORT/ELL
Use Letter Story: *karate k* to reinforce correct formation of **k** (p. 160).

CROSS-CURRICULAR CONNECTIONS
Social Studies: Discuss that Karate was invented in Japan. Find Japan on a map or globe.

Y y

Printing Power – p. 28

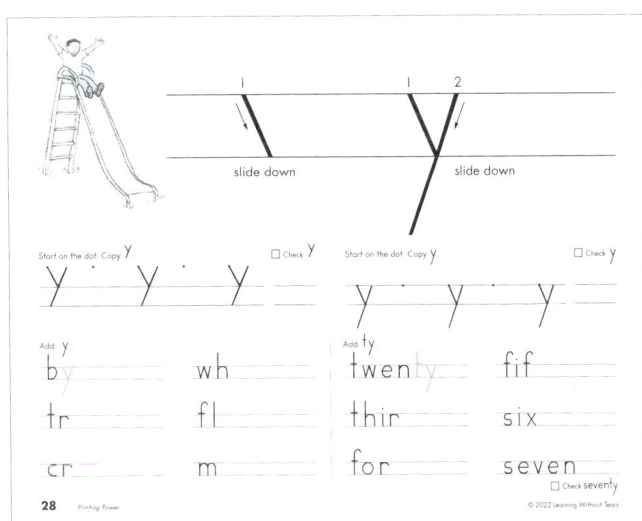

OBJECTIVES
To use correct habits for writing capital **Y** and lowercase **y**; to build fluency by practicing previously learned letters.

LESSON INTRODUCTION (Warm Up)
SONG: "Descending Letters" from *Rock, Rap, Tap & Learn* music album

Additional digital resources are available in the Interactive Digital Teaching Tool (IDTT).

LESSON PLAN

1. Direction Instruction (Demo)
Demonstrate **Y**, **y** on double lines.
Say the words for each step.
Demonstrate the words **by** and **twenty**.

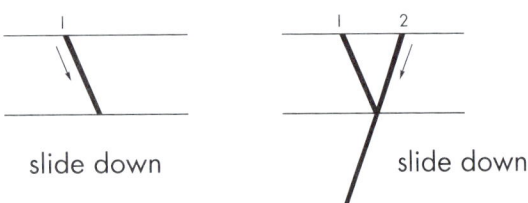

2. Guided Practice
Children copy: **Y**, **y** and complete words.
Monitor as children complete words.

3. Check Letter & Word
Help children ✓ their letter for correct start, steps, and bump.
Help children ✓ their word for correct size, placement, and closeness.

READ & DISCUSS
Read the words together and discuss.

ENRICHMENT
A+ Worksheet Maker: Create a worksheet incorporating words children have already learned. Examples include: silly, yes, yak, day, say, and lolly.

SUPPORT/ELL
Use Wet-Dry-Try for **y** on Blackboard with Double Lines (p. 168).

CROSS-CURRICULAR CONNECTIONS
Science: As a class, make a list of living or non-living items that begin with **y**.

p. 29   J j

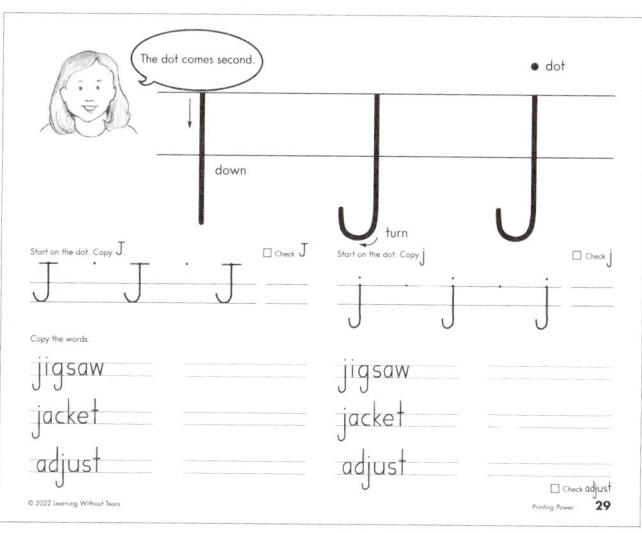

OBJECTIVE

To use correct habits for writing capital **J** and lowercase **j**; to build fluency by practicing previously learned letters.

LESSON INTRODUCTION (Warm Up)

Air Writing (p. 162)

> Additional digital resources are available in the Interactive Digital Teaching Tool (IDTT).

LESSON PLAN

1. Direction Instruction (Demo)

Demonstrate **J**, **j** on double lines.
Say the words for each step.
Demonstrate the words **jigsaw** and **jacket**.

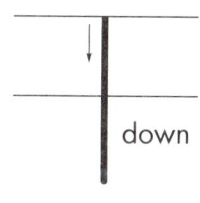 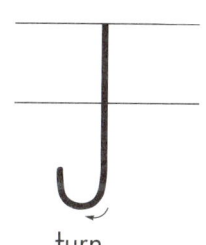 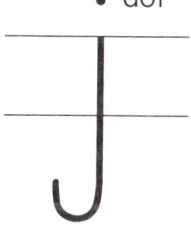

2. Guided Practice

Children copy: **J**, **j**, **jigsaw**, and **jacket**.
Monitor as children write the other words on their own.

3. Check Letter & Word

Help children ☑ their letter for correct start, steps, and bump.
Help children ☑ their word for correct size, placement, and closeness.

READ & DISCUSS

Read the words together and discuss.

ENRICHMENT

Transition Letters Group **u**, **i**, **e**, **l**, **k**, **y**, and **j**.

SUPPORT/ELL

Lowercase **j** is a low frequency letter. Children are likely to forget how to make it. Remember to point out **j** in words.

CROSS-CURRICULAR CONNECTIONS

Social Studies: Using poster paper, have children decorate a puzzle piece about something they value. Put together the puzzle and discuss.

Singular & Plural

Printing Power – p. 30

OBJECTIVE
To write singular and plural nouns.

LESSON INTRODUCTION (Warm Up)
Hand Activity (p. 167)

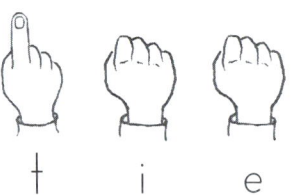

Additional digital resources are available in the Interactive Digital Teaching Tool (IDTT).

LESSON PLAN

1. Direction Instruction (Demo)

Explain that singular means one. Plural means two.
Demonstrate **leg - legs** and **goose - geese** on double lines.
Say the words for each letter.

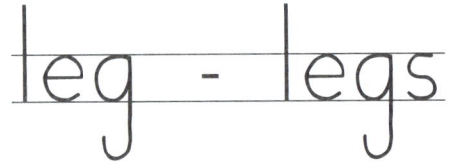 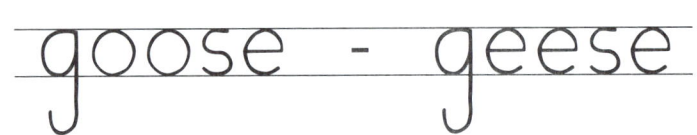

2. Guided Practice

Children copy: **leg - legs** and **goose - geese**.
Monitor as children copy the other singular and plural words on their own.

3. Check Word

Help children ✓ their word for size, placement, and closeness.

ENRICHMENT
Make a class list of irregular nouns. Say the singular noun and help children say the plural noun. Children pick two words from the list and write sentences on double line paper.

SUPPORT/ELL
Teach children the irregular body part plurals: foot and feet, tooth and teeth.

CROSS-CURRICULAR CONNECTIONS
Language Arts: Teach regular and irregular plurals with these two columns.

Paragraph

p. 31

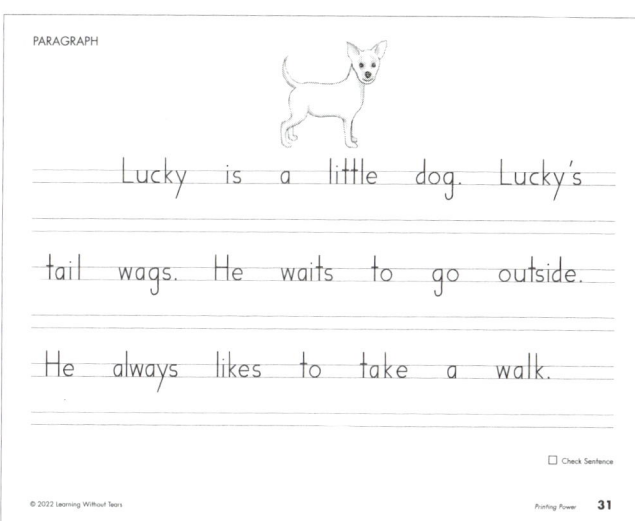

OBJECTIVES
To build writing fluency; to build paragraph skills.

LESSON INTRODUCTION (Warm Up)
Wet-Dry-Try on Blackboard with Double Lines (p. 168)

Additional digital resources are available in the Interactive Digital Teaching Tool (IDTT).

LESSON PLAN

1. Direction Instruction (Demo)
Demonstrate on double lines: **Lucky is a little dog.**
Remind children to start with a capital, put space between words, and end with a period.

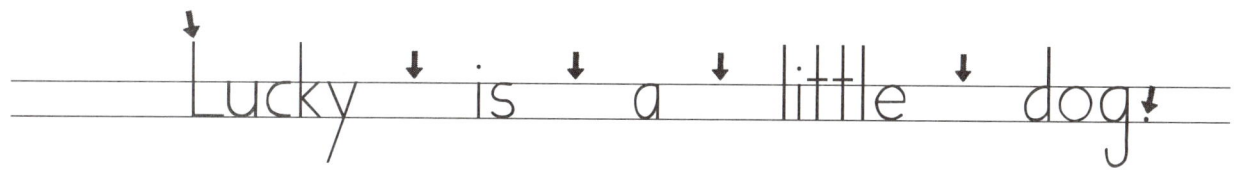

2. Guided Practice
Children copy: **Lucky is a little dog.**
Monitor as children complete the paragraph.

3. Check Sentence
Help children ✓ their sentence for correct capitalization, word spacing, and ending punctuation.

ENRICHMENT
Help children notice the apostrophe in "Lucky's." Explain that an apostrophe ('s) shows possession or ownership. List other examples. Children copy examples on double line paper.

SUPPORT/ELL
Show children how to leave room for an indent by using their pinky finger (horizontally) to measure the space. Reiterate that paragraphs start with an indent.

CROSS-CURRICULAR CONNECTIONS
Social Studies: Chihuahua is a dog breed and a Mexican state that borders Texas and New Mexico. Have children locate it on a map.

P p

Printing Power – p. 32

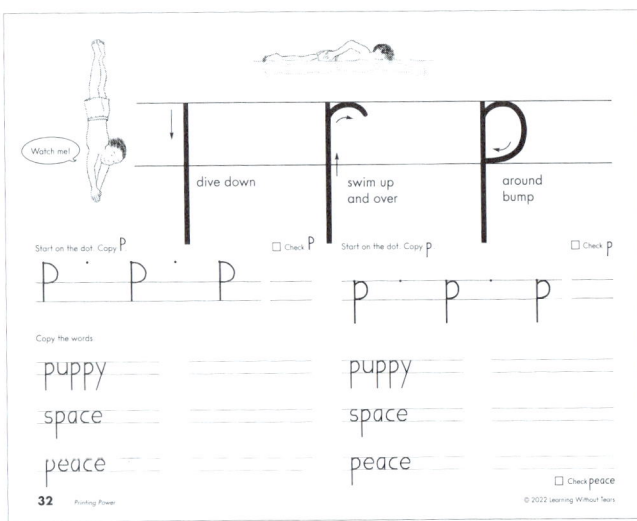

OBJECTIVES

To use correct habits for writing capital **P** and lowercase **p**; to build fluency by practicing previously learned letters.

LESSON INTRODUCTION (Warm Up)

SONG: "Diver Letters' School" from *Rock, Rap, Tap & Learn* music album

Additional digital resources are available in the Interactive Digital Teaching Tool (IDTT).

LESSON PLAN

1. **Direction Instruction (Demo)**

   Demonstrate **P**, **p** on double lines.
   Say the words for each step.
   Demonstrate the words **puppy** and **space**.

2. **Guided Practice**

   Children copy: **P**, **p**, **puppy**, and **space**.
   Monitor as children write the other words on their own.

3. **Check Letter & Word**

   Help children ✓ their letter for correct start, steps, and bump.
   Help children ✓ their word for correct size, placement, and closeness.

READ & DISCUSS

Read the words together and discuss.

ENRICHMENT

Place six starting dots on the mid line of double line paper. Randomly call out letters that are descending such as the **p**. Ask children to write three words using **p**.

SUPPORT/ELL

Help children retrace neatly by highlighting the descending line of each **p**. Tell children to stay on your highlighted line as they trace down and up to begin **p**.

CROSS-CURRICULAR CONNECTIONS

Science: Talk about outer space. Ask children which planets they know. Read informational texts on the solar system.

p. 33   R r

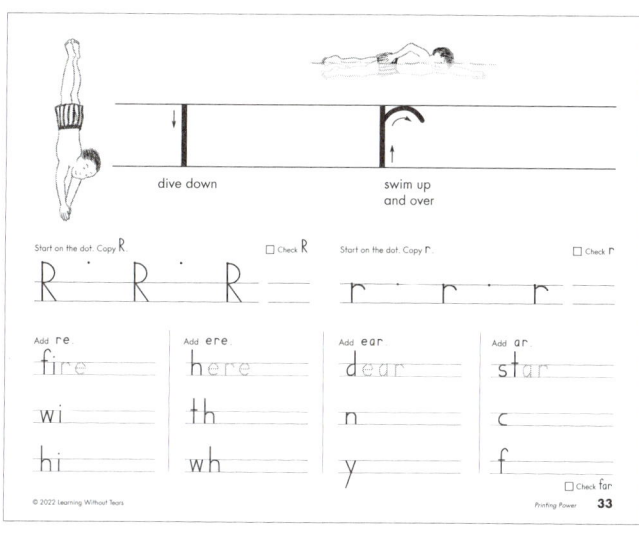

OBJECTIVES
To use correct habits for writing capital **R** and lowercase **r**; to build fluency by practicing previously learned letters.

LESSON INTRODUCTION (Warm Up)
Laser Letters (p. 163)

Additional digital resources are available in the Interactive Digital Teaching Tool (IDTT).

LESSON PLAN

1. Direction Instruction (Demo)

Demonstrate **R**, **r** on double lines.
Say the words for each step.
Demonstrate the words **fire**, **here**, **dear**, and **star**.

2. Guided Practice

Children copy: **R**, **r** and complete words.
Monitor as children complete words.

3. Check Letter & Word

Help children ✓ their letter for correct start, steps, and bump.
Help children ✓ their word for correct size, placement, and closeness.

READ & DISCUSS

Read the words together and discuss.

ENRICHMENT
Play with alliterative sentences. Examples include: "Richard ran with a red racquet." Have children write the sentence on double line paper.

SUPPORT/ELL
Have children act out Diver Letters to reinforce start and sequence.

CROSS-CURRICULAR CONNECTIONS
Language Arts: Discuss alliterative poems that use **r**. Have children write and present their poems to the class.

Printing Power – p. 34

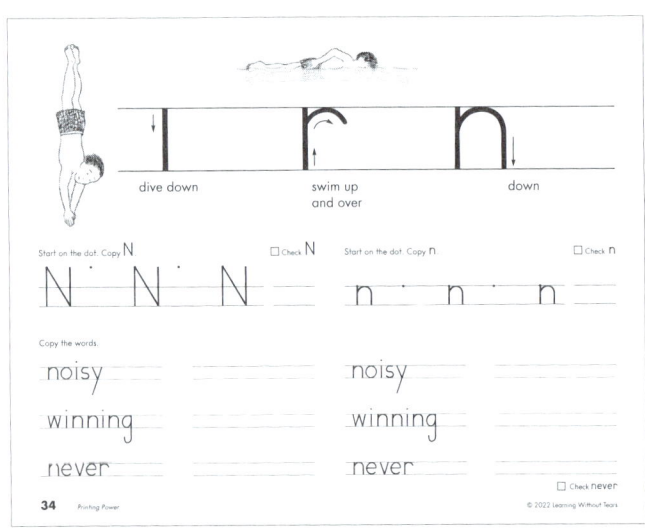

OBJECTIVES
To use correct habits for writing capital **N** and lowercase **n**; to build fluency by practicing previously learned letters.

LESSON INTRODUCTION (Warm Up)
Wet-Dry-Try on Blackboard with Double Lines (p. 168)

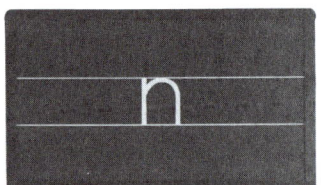

Additional digital resources are available in the Interactive Digital Teaching Tool (IDTT).

LESSON PLAN

1. **Direction Instruction (Demo)**

    Demonstrate **N**, **n**.
    Say the words for each step.
    Demonstrate the words **noisy** and **winning**.

    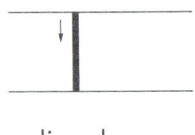 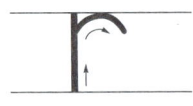 

    dive down   swim up and over   down

2. **Guided Practice**

    Children copy: **N**, **n**, **noisy**, and **winning**.
    Monitor as children write the other words on their own.

3. **Check Letter & Word**

    Help children ☑ their letter for correct start, steps, and bump.
    Help children ☑ their word for correct size, placement, and closeness.

READ & DISCUSS
Read the words together and discuss.

ENRICHMENT
A+ Worksheet Maker: Create a worksheet incorporating words with **n**.

SUPPORT/ELL
For lowercase **n**, show children how to travel on the mid line before turning down (this also works for **m**, **h**, and **b**).

CROSS-CURRICULAR CONNECTIONS
Language Arts: Practice vowel team /oi/. Ask students if they know any words with the /oi/ sound. Have children spell these words.

p. 35

M m

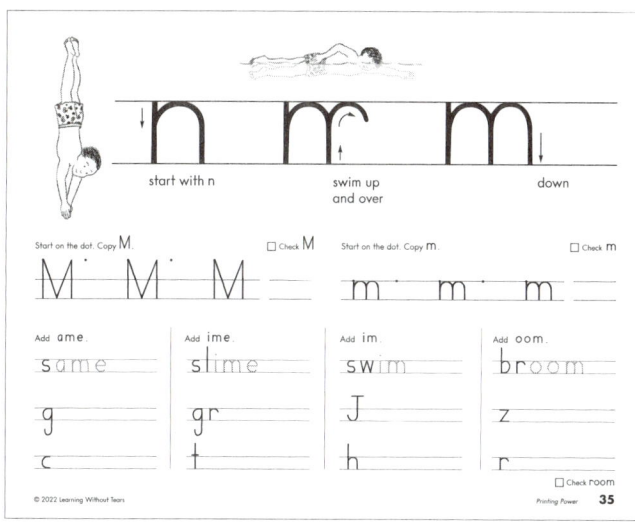

OBJECTIVES

To use correct habits for writing capital **M** and lowercase **m**; to build fluency by practicing previously learned letters.

LESSON INTRODUCTION (Warm Up)

Voices (p. 169)

Additional digital resources are available in the Interactive Digital Teaching Tool (IDTT).

LESSON PLAN

1. **Direction Instruction (Demo)**

    Demonstrate **M**, **m** on double lines.
    Say the words for each step.
    Demonstrate adding rimes to onsets in the words **same**, **slime**, **swim**, and **broom**.

    start with n   swim up and over   down

2. **Guided Practice**

    Children copy: **M**, **m** and add rimes.
    Monitor as children complete words by adding rimes to onsets.

3. **Check Letter & Word**

    Help children ☑ their letter for correct start, steps, and bump.
    Help children ☑ their word for correct size, placement, and closeness.

READ & DISCUSS

Read the words together and discuss.

ENRICHMENT

Have children choose two **m** words and write two sentences using the **m** words they chose on double line paper.

SUPPORT/ELL

Use Letter Story: *Stinky m* to reinforce correct formation of **m** (p. 161).

CROSS-CURRICULAR CONNECTIONS

Language Arts: Discuss different places where children can swim and describe the different swimming strokes.

H h

Printing Power – p. 36

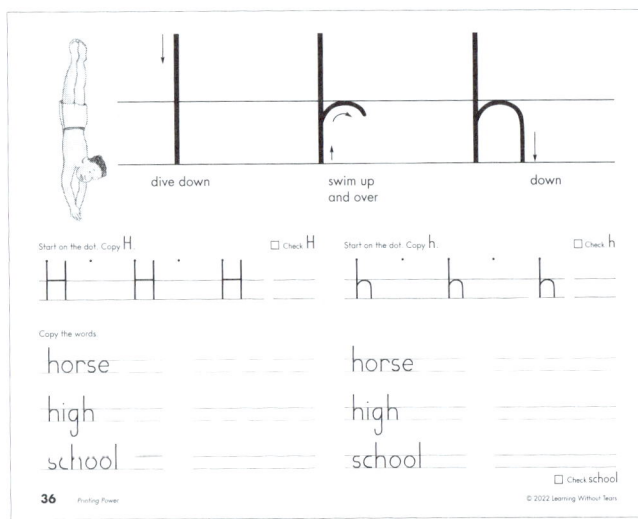

OBJECTIVES

To use correct habits for writing capital **H** and lowercase **h**; to build fluency by practicing previously learned letters.

LESSON INTRODUCTION (Warm Up)

Air Writing (p. 162)

> Additional digital resources are available in the Interactive Digital Teaching Tool (IDTT).

LESSON PLAN

1. Direction Instruction (Demo)

Demonstrate **H**, **h** on double lines.
Say the words for each step.
Demonstrate the words **horse** and **high**.

dive down   swim up and over   down

2. Guided Practice

Children copy: **H**, **h**, **horse**, and **high**.
Monitor as children write the other words on their own.

3. Check Letter & Word

Help children ☑ their letter for correct start, steps, and bump.
Help children ☑ their word for correct size, placement, and closeness.

READ & DISCUSS

Read the words together and discuss.

ENRICHMENT

Have children write words using Diver Letters on double line paper. Examples include: hat, mat, man, same, and his.

SUPPORT/ELL

For lowercase **h**, show children how to travel on the mid line before turning down. (this also works for **m**, **n**, and **b**).

CROSS-CURRICULAR CONNECTIONS

Math: Have children take turns writing the school schedule for the day. Children write the time and subject or activity on the board.

p. 37 — B b

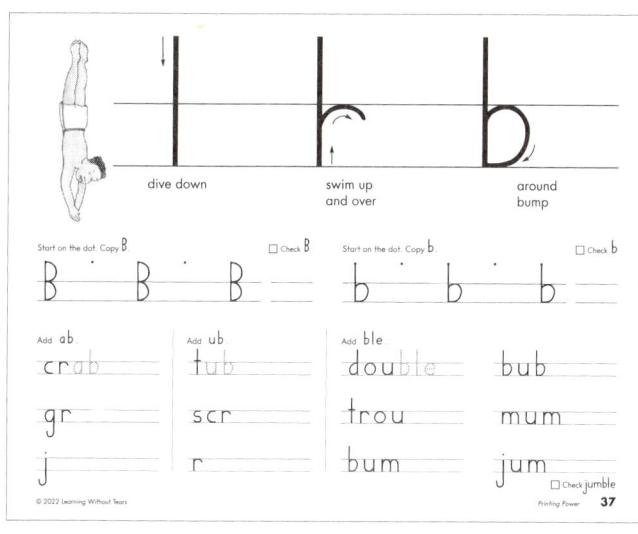

OBJECTIVES
To use correct habits for writing capital **B** and lowercase **b**; to build fluency by practicing previously learned letters.

LESSON INTRODUCTION (Warm Up)
Digital Letter and Number Formations (p. 164)

Additional digital resources are available in the Interactive Digital Teaching Tool (IDTT).

LESSON PLAN

1. Direction Instruction (Demo)
Demonstrate **B**, **b** on double lines.
Say the words for each step.
Demonstrate the words **crab**, **tub**, and **double**.

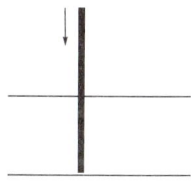      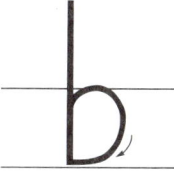

dive down   swim up and over   around, bump

2. Guided Practice
Children copy: **B**, **b** and complete the words.
Monitor as children complete words.

3. Check Letter & Word
Help children ✓ their letter for correct start, steps, and bump.
Help children ✓ their word for correct size, placement, and closeness.

READ & DISCUSS
Read the words together and discuss.

ENRICHMENT
Home Link: Diver Letters Group
p, **r**, **n**, **m**, **h**, and **b**.

SUPPORT/ELL
Use Letter Story: *Honeybee* to reinforce correct formation of **b** (p. 160).

CROSS-CURRICULAR CONNECTIONS
Science: Research and discuss crabs to discover their habitat and fun facts about crabs.

Turn h into b

Printing Power – p. 38

OBJECTIVES
To develop word fluency with rhyming words; to practice letter formations for **h** and **b**.

LESSON INTRODUCTION (Warm Up)
SONG: "Sentence Song" from *Rock, Rap, Tap & Learn* music album

Additional digital resources are available in the Interactive Digital Teaching Tool (IDTT).

LESSON PLAN

1. Direction Instruction (Demo)
Demonstrate turning **h** into **b**. Demonstrate on double lines: **Here is an h for a honeybee**.

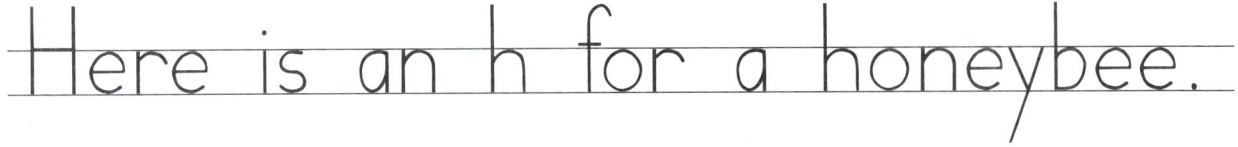

2. Guided Practice
Children trace the **h** into **b**.
Children copy: **Here is an h for a honeybee**.
Monitor as children copy rhyming words on their own.

3. Check Sentence
Help children ✓ their sentence for correct capitalization, word spacing, and ending punctuation.

ENRICHMENT
Have children write more **h** and **b** onset-rime words: hulk-bulk, hut-but, hand-band, and hoot-boot.

SUPPORT/ELL
This activity helps eliminate **b** and **d** confusion. Teach children to write **h** before **b** and magic **c** before **d**.

CROSS-CURRICULAR CONNECTIONS
Language Arts: Identify long and short vowels in words. Then, remind children how some long and short vowel sounds use vowel teams.

p. 39

Word Search

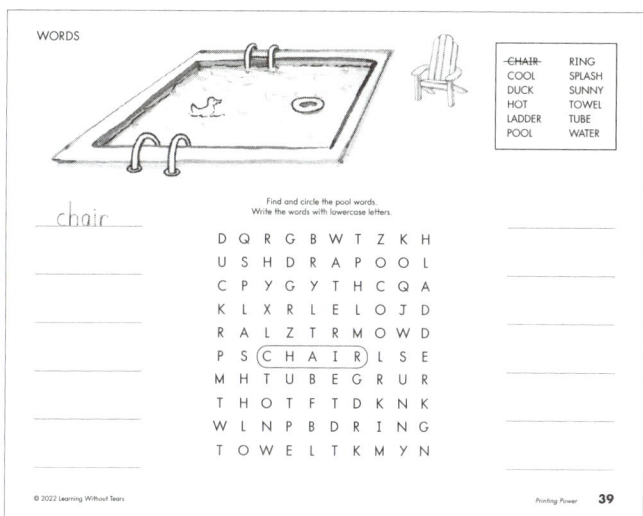

OBJECTIVES

To find words; to use a word bank; to change capitals into lowercase letters.

LESSON INTRODUCTION (Warm Up)

Wet-Dry-Try on Blackboard with Double Lines (p. 168)

Additional digital resources are available in the Interactive Digital Teaching Tool (IDTT).

LESSON PLAN

1. Direction Instruction (Demo)

Read the title and words in the word bank. Use CHAIR as an example. Tell children to look for hidden words, circle them, and write them on the single line in lowercase.

2. Guided Practice

Children circle the words in the word search and write them on the single line using lowercase letters. Remind children to cross out the word in the word bank.

3. Check Words

Monitor as children write their words for correct size, placement, and closeness.

ENRICHMENT

Teach children how to make their own word search. Have them switch with a partner to complete.

SUPPORT/ELL

For children who can't find the words in the word search, help them by tracing over the word with a highlighter before they circle the word.

CROSS-CURRICULAR CONNECTIONS

Language Arts: Write a persuasive letter when summer vacation is canceled and the only way to bring it back is to write a letter.

F f

Printing Power – p. 40

OBJECTIVES

To use correct habits for writing capital **F** and lowercase **f**; to build fluency by practicing previously learned letters.

LESSON INTRODUCTION (Warm Up)

Laser Letters (p. 163)

> Additional digital resources are available in the Interactive Digital Teaching Tool (IDTT).

LESSON PLAN

1. Direction Instruction (Demo)

Demonstrate **F**, **f** on double lines.
Say the words for each step.
Demonstrate the words **raft**, **lift**, and **raffle**.

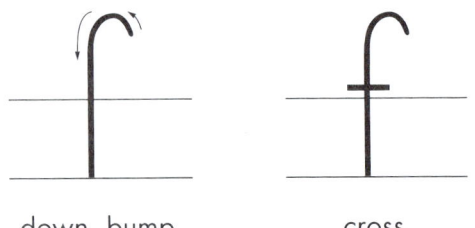

down, bump   cross

2. Guided Practice

Children copy: **F, f** and complete words.
Monitor as children complete words.

3. Check Letter & Word

Help children ✓ their letter for correct start, steps, and bump.
Help children ✓ their word for correct size, placement, and closeness.

READ & DISCUSS

Read the words together and discuss.

ENRICHMENT

Have children create and write real and silly words ending in **-ffle**.

SUPPORT/ELL

Use the Letter Story: *Fire Hose Squirts* to reinforce correct formation of **f** (p. 160).

CROSS-CURRICULAR CONNECTIONS

Social Studies: Discuss firemen and other people who help in the community.

p. 41   Q q

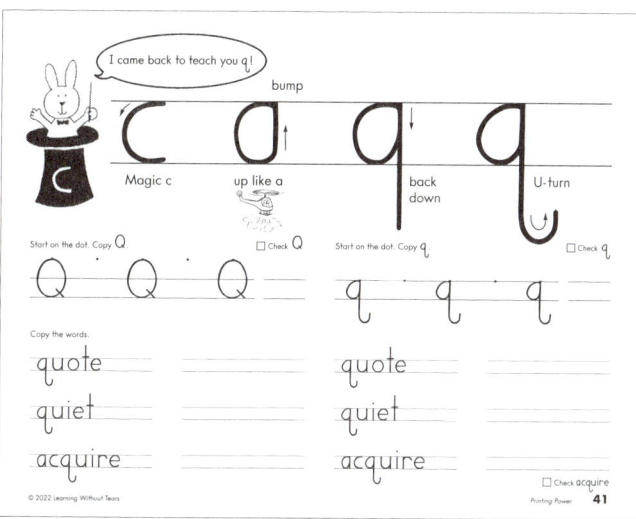

OBJECTIVES
To use correct habits for writing capital **Q** and lowercase **q**; to build fluency by practicing previously learned letters.

LESSON INTRODUCTION (Warm Up)
Voices (p. 169)

Additional digital resources are available in the Interactive Digital Teaching Tool (IDTT).

LESSON PLAN

1. Direction Instruction (Demo)

Demonstrate **Q**, **q** on double lines.
Say the words for each step.
Demonstrate the words **quote** and **quiet**.

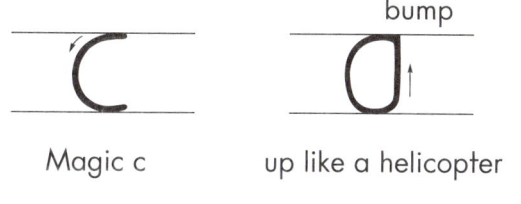
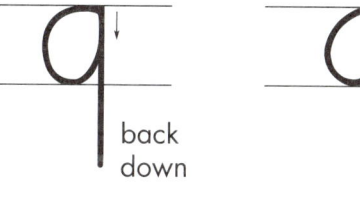

2. Guided Practice

Children copy: **Q**, **q**, **quote**, and **quiet**.
Observe as children copy words on their own.

3. Check Letter & Word

Help children ☑ their letter for correct start, steps, and bump.
Help children ☑ their word for correct size, placement, and closeness.

READ & DISCUSS

Read the words together and discuss.

ENRICHMENT
Give a **q** quiz. Have children practice spelling and writing **q** words. Talk about how **u** always follows **q** in English.

SUPPORT/ELL
Use Letter Story: *U-Turn* to reinforce correct formation of **q** (p. 161).

CROSS-CURRICULAR CONNECTIONS
Language Arts: Encourage children to write stories using dialogue and quotation marks.

Greek and Latin

Printing Power – p. 42

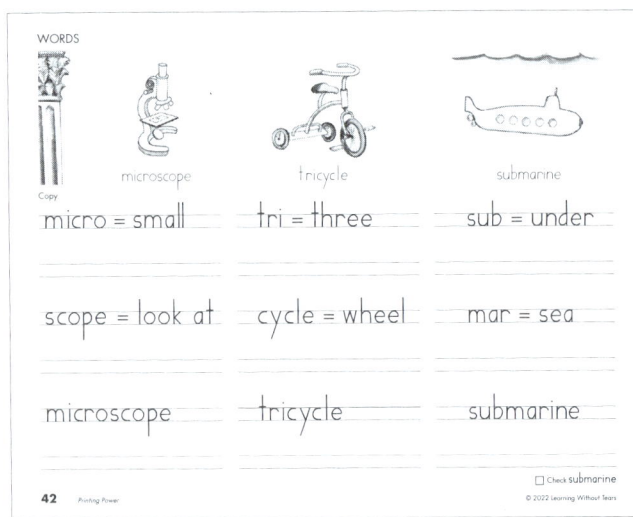

OBJECTIVES
To learn prefixes and root words; to use Greek and Latin clues to figure out words.

LESSON INTRODUCTION (Warm Up)
Hand Activity (p. 167)

Additional digital resources are available in the Interactive Digital Teaching Tool (IDTT).

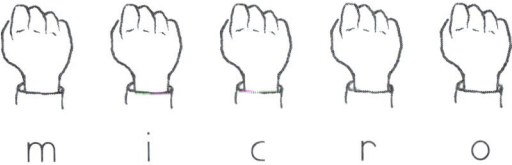

LESSON PLAN

1. Direction Instruction (Demo)
Knowing Greek and Latin helps children figure out big English words. Demonstrate on double lines **micro = small** and **scope = look at**.

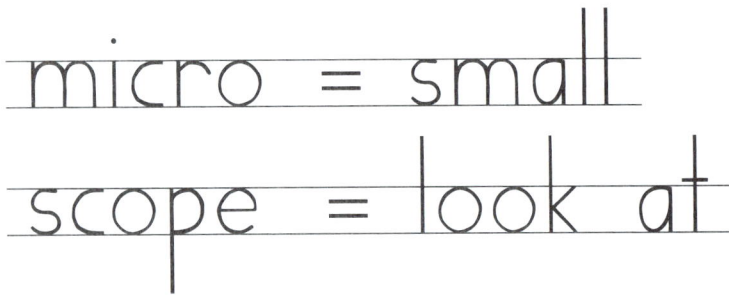

2. Guided Practice
Children copy: **micro = small** and **scope = look at**.
Monitor as children copy words on their own after you explain the meanings.

3. Check Word
Help children ✓ their word for size, placement, and closeness.

ENRICHMENT
Introduce other prefixes to figure out big words. Examples include: **peri** (around for periscope) and **tele** (far for telescope). Have children write prefixes on double line paper.

SUPPORT/ELL
Highlight the prefixes by themselves and then again in the big words for children to connect.

CROSS-CURRICULAR CONNECTIONS
Language Arts: Have children look in a dictionary for words that begin with the prefixes: **micro-**, **tri-**, and **sub-**.

p. 43 # Paragraph

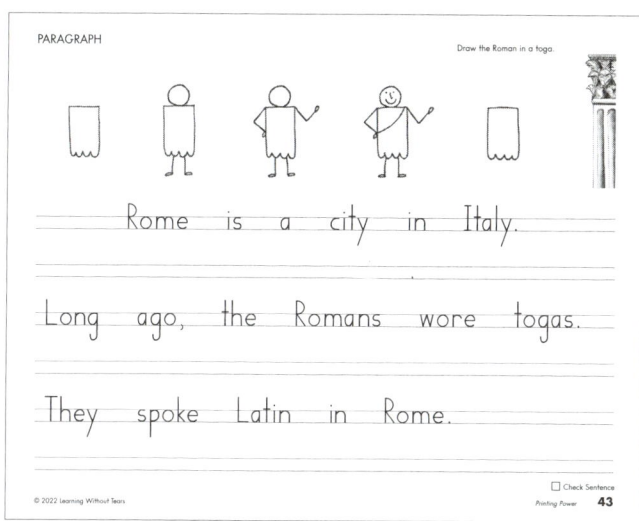

OBJECTIVES

To build paragraph skills; to indent and write sentences about a topic.

LESSON INTRODUCTION (Warm Up)

Show books with paragraphs. Find the indents and paragraphs.

> Additional digital resources are available in the Interactive Digital Teaching Tool (IDTT).

LESSON PLAN

1. Direction Instruction (Demo)

Demonstrate on double lines: **Rome is a city in Italy.**
Remind children to start with a capital, put space between words, and end with a period.

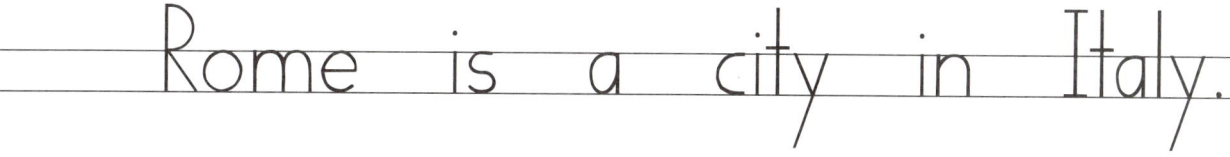

2. Guided Practice

Children copy: **Rome is a city in Italy.**
Monitor as children copy the paragraph

3. Check Sentence

Help children ✓ their sentence for correct capitalization, word spacing, and ending punctuation.
Note: Children may complete the illustration at the top of the page.

ENRICHMENT

Teach children to capitalize the first word in a sentence and proper nouns. Examples include: countries (Italy), nationalities (Romans), etc. Write these examples on double line paper.

SUPPORT/ELL

Show children how to leave room for an indent by using their pinky finger (horizontally) to measure the space. Reiterate that paragraphs start with an indent.

CROSS-CURRICULAR CONNECTIONS

Social Studies: A major event in ancient Rome was the eruption of Mount Vesuvius. Have children research and write a paragraph.

Printing Power – p. 44

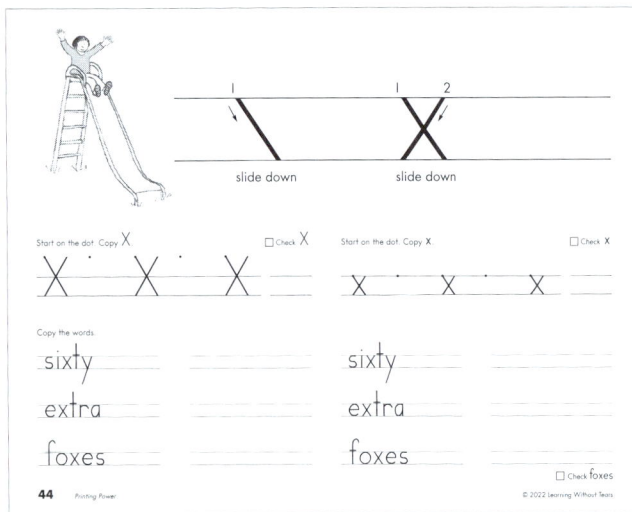

OBJECTIVES
To use correct habits for writing capital **X** and lowercase **x**; to build fluency by practicing previously learned letters.

LESSON INTRODUCTION (Warm Up)
SONG: "Diagonals" from *Rock, Rap, Tap & Learn* music album

Additional digital resources are available in the Interactive Digital Teaching Tool (IDTT).

LESSON PLAN

1. Direction Instruction (Demo)
Demonstrate **X**, **x** on double lines.
Say the words for each step.
Demonstrate the words **sixty** and **extra**.

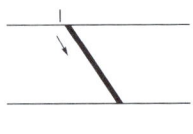

slide down

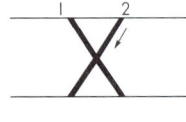

slide down

2. Guided Practice
Children copy: **X**, **x**, **is**, and **visit**.
Monitor as children write the other words on their own.

3. Check Letter & Word
Help children ✓ their letter for correct start, steps, and bump.
Help children ✓ their word for correct size, placement, and closeness.

READ & DISCUSS
Read the words together and discuss.

ENRICHMENT
Have children write two to three sentences about **60** foxes! It can be funny or silly.

SUPPORT/ELL
Left-handed children often need support to begin **x** at the top left. Highlight the first slide down stroke for children to trace.

CROSS-CURRICULAR CONNECTIONS
Math: Using only four numbers, ask students how many ways they can add to **60**.

p. 45   Z z

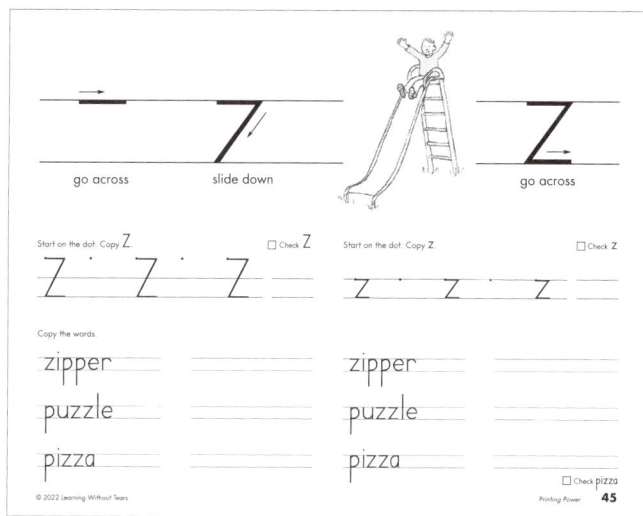

OBJECTIVES
To use correct habits for writing capital **Z** and lowercase **z**; to build fluency by practicing previously learned letters.

LESSON INTRODUCTION (Warm Up)
Wet-Dry-Try on Blackboard with Double Lines (p. 168)

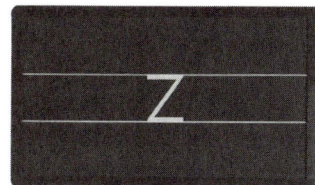

Additional digital resources are available in the Interactive Digital Teaching Tool (IDTT).

LESSON PLAN

1. Direction Instruction (Demo)
Demonstrate **Z**, **z** on double lines.
Say the words for each step.
Demonstrate the words **zipper** and **puzzle**.

go across   slide down   go across

2. Guided Practice
Children copy: **Z**, **z**, **zipper**, and **puzzle**.
Monitor as children write the other words on their own.

3. Check Letter & Word
Help children ☑ their letter for correct start, steps, and bump.
Help children ☑ their word for correct size, placement, and closeness.

READ & DISCUSS
Read the words together and discuss.

ENRICHMENT
Home Link: Final Letters Group **f**, **q**, **x**, and **z**.

SUPPORT/ELL
Use Letter Story: *Z Chase* to reinforce correct formation of **z**. (p. 161).

CROSS-CURRICULAR CONNECTIONS
Math: Draw a pizza to talk about geometry. Divide the pizza into two, three, or four equal parts and discuss halves, thirds, fourths, etc.

Lowercase Review

Printng Power – p. 46

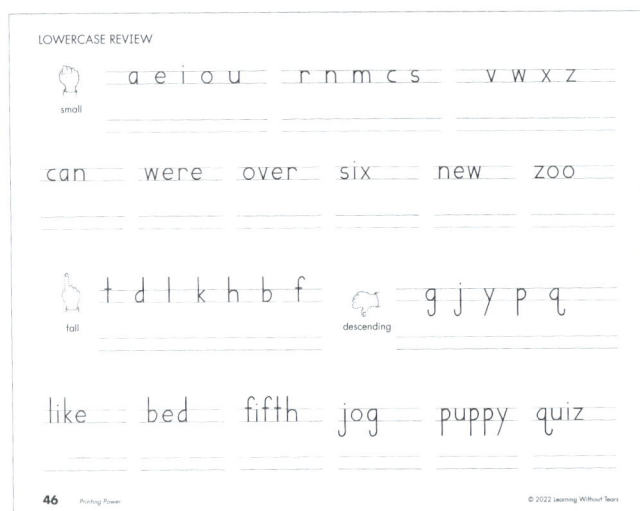

OBJECTIVE
To write letters with correct size and placement.

LESSON INTRODUCTION (Warm Up)
Hand Activity (p. 167)

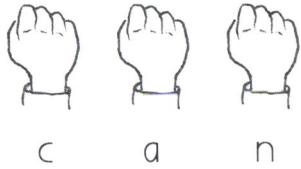

Additional digital resources are available in the Interactive Digital Teaching Tool (IDTT).

LESSON PLAN

1. Direction Instruction (Demo)

Demonstrate on double lines: **can**, **like**, and **jog**.
Move hands to show tall, small, or descending letters.

  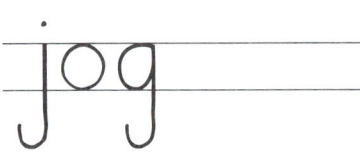

2. Guided Practice

Children imitate tall, small, and descending hand positions for each letter.
Children copy: **can**, **like**, and **jog**.
Observe as children copy letters and words on their own.

3. Check Letters & Words

Monitor as children write their letters for correct start, steps, and bump and check their words for correct size, placement and closeness.

ENRICHMENT
Have children take turns in pairs demonstrating the Hand Activity for a designated word list.

SUPPORT/ELL
Have children point and touch the top space on paper for tall letters such as the lowercase **t**, before they start writing.

CROSS-CURRICULAR CONNECTIONS
Language Arts: Write a class story incorporating all the words from the activity. For example: My puppy likes to sleep on my bed.

p. 47

Capital & Lowercase

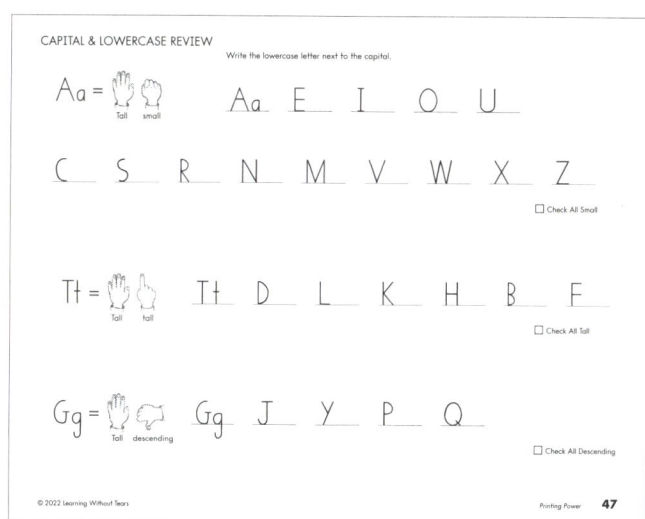

OBJECTIVES
To write lowercase letters from memory; to place letters correctly beside capitals.

LESSON INTRODUCTION (Warm Up)
Hand Activity (p. 167)

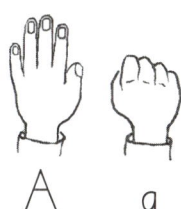

Additional digital resources are available in the Interactive Digital Teaching Tool (IDTT).

LESSON PLAN

1. Direction Instruction (Demo)
Demonstrate on a single line: **a**, **e**, **t**, **d**, **g**, and **j**.
Move hands to show tall, small, or descending letters.

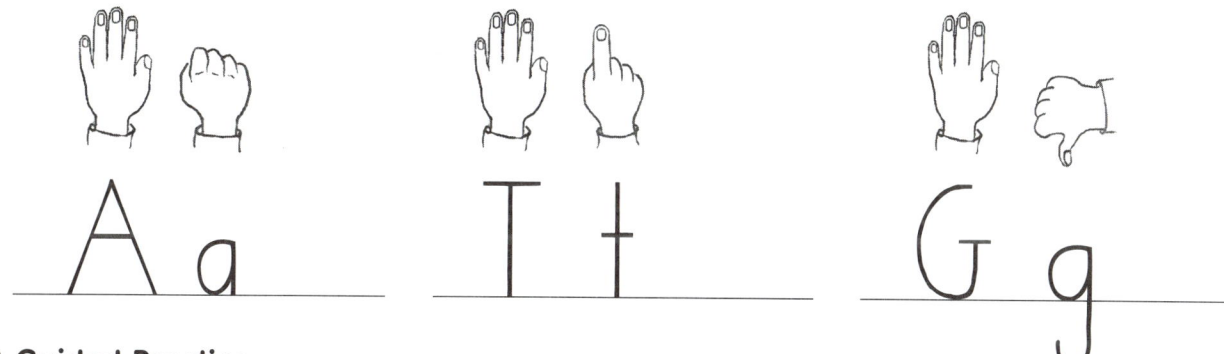

2. Guided Practice
Children write the corresponding lowercase letter beside each capital.

3. Check Letters
Help children ✓ their letters for correct start, steps, and bump.

ENRICHMENT
Have children use the Hand Activity to recite the entire alphabet.

SUPPORT/ELL
If children have difficulty with writing letters on a single line, review letter size and placement using double line paper.

CROSS-CURRICULAR CONNECTIONS
Language Arts: Discuss the different sizes of lowercase letters. Compare how the tall lowercase letters and capital letters are the same size.

WRITING ACTIVITIES

Today's second graders are expected to write more than ever. They take spelling tests, write stories, use daily writing journals, and even use sentences to explain math problems. This is the year of self-expression. In second grade, handwriting fluency will have an impact on academic performance.

Fluency is showing mastery of a subject or skill. Handwriting fluency is being able to automatically write letters and form them correctly without thinking. Reading fluency encompasses the speed or rate of reading, as well as the ability to read materials with expression and comprehension. Meyer and Felton defined reading fluency as "the ability to read connected text rapidly, smoothly, effortlessly, and automatically with little conscious attention to the mechanics of reading, such as decoding" (quoted in Mather and Goldstein 2001).

In the section children will:

- Continue to build letter and word skills
- Practice correct punctuation and sentence formation
- Get a taste of rhyming, poetry, and paragraphs

Sentence Spacing

Printing Power – p. 48

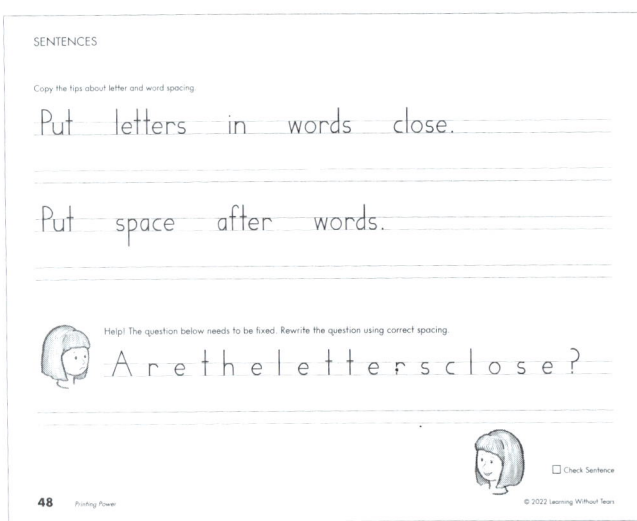

OBJECTIVE
To practice sentence spacing.

LESSON INTRODUCTION (Warm Up)
SONG: "Sentence Song" from *Rock, Rap, Tap & Learn* music album

Additional digital resources are available in the Interactive Digital Teaching Tool (IDTT).

LESSON PLAN

1. Direction Instruction (Demo)

Have children point their index fingertips together, almost touching. Say, "Letters in words must be close but not touching."
Demonstrate on double lines: **Put letters in words close.**
Remind children to start with a capital, put space between words, and end with a period.

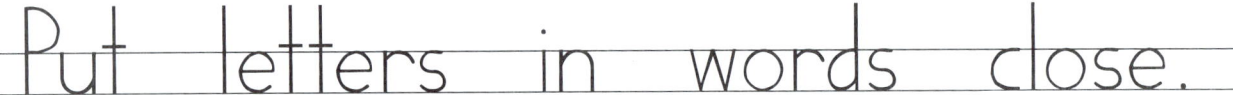

2. Guided Practice

Children copy: **Put letters in words close.**
Monitor as children write the other sentences on their own.

3. Check Sentence

Help children ✓ their sentence for correct capitalization, word spacing, and ending punctuation.

ENRICHMENT
Make other sentences "all better" by writing more sick sentences for the children to correct. Allow children to take turns making up sentences for their classmates.

SUPPORT/ELL
Draw two fingers almost touching each other to illustrate word spacing (p. 191).

CROSS-CURRICULAR CONNECTIONS
Language Arts: Practice spacing while writing a narrative about an event. Encourage children to use descriptive words.

p. 49

Sentence Spacing

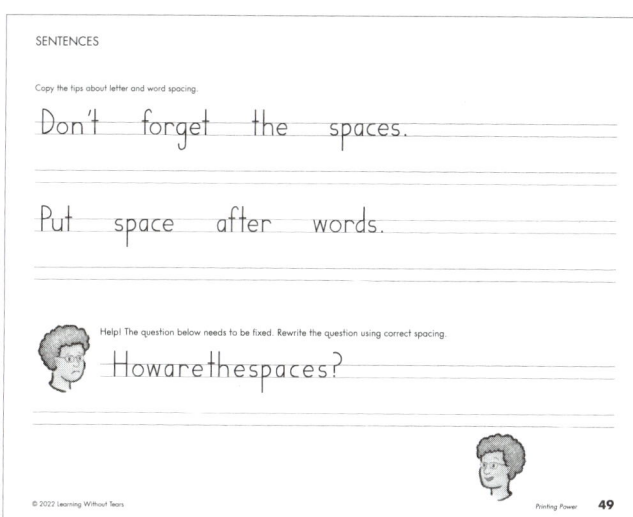

OBJECTIVE
To practice sentence spacing.

LESSON INTRODUCTION (Warm Up)
Bottle of Nothing (p. 191)

Additional digital resources are available in the Interactive Digital Teaching Tool (IDTT).

LESSON PLAN

1. Direction Instruction (Demo)

Demonstrate on double lines: **Don't forget the spaces**.
Tell children there is "nothing" after each word before they write the next word.
Remind children to start with a capital, put space between words, and end with a period.

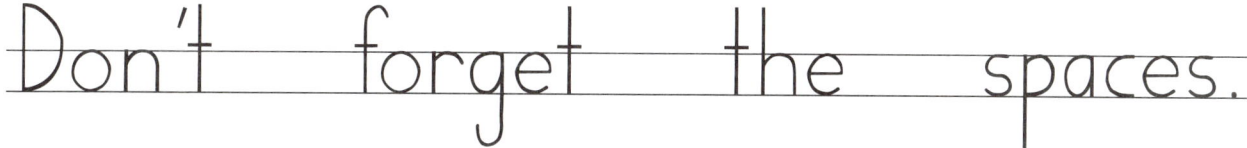

2. Guided Practice

Children copy: **Don't forget the spaces.**
Observe as children copy the other sentences on their own.

3. Check Sentence

Monitor children as they copy their sentence for correct capitalization, word spacing, and ending punctuation.

ENRICHMENT
Make other sentences "all better" by writing more sick sentences for the children to correct. Allow children to take turns making up sentences for their classmates.

SUPPORT/ELL
Play the Sick Sentence Clinic (p 191).

CROSS-CURRICULAR CONNECTIONS
Language Arts: Practice spacing while writing a narrative about an event. Encourage the use of descriptive words.

Paragraph

Printing Power – p. 50

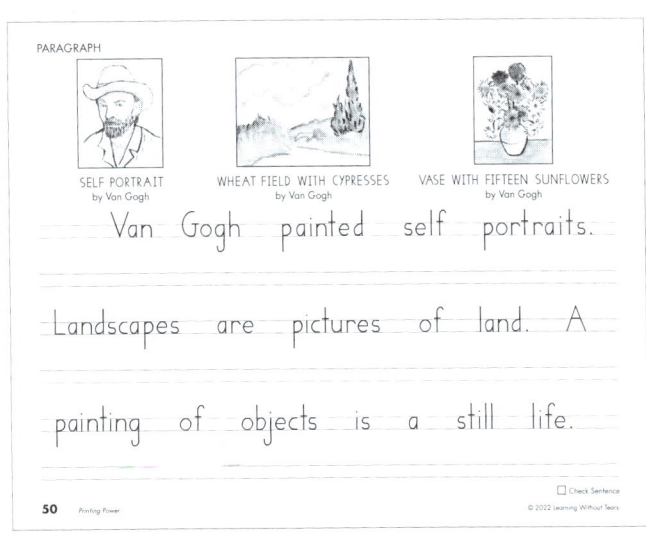

OBJECTIVE
To practice paragraph skills.

LESSON INTRODUCTION (Warm Up)
Wet-Dry-Try on Blackboard with Double Lines (p. 168)

Additional digital resources are available in the Interactive Digital Teaching Tool (IDTT).

LESSON PLAN

Handwriting

1. Direction Instruction (Demo)

Demonstrate on double lines: **Van Gogh painted self portraits.**
Remind children to start with an indent and a capital, put space between words, and end with a period.

2. Guided Practice

Children copy: **Van Gogh painted self portraits.**
Monitor as children copy the rest of the paragraph on their own.

3. Check Sentence

Help children ✓ their sentence for correct capitalization, word spacing, and ending punctuation.

Writing

Children begin writing by drawing pictures. In second grade, children will still enjoy drawing pictures to help illustrate their writing.

ENRICHMENT
Give children experience with drawing people, places, or things. Let them draw each other for a portrait, go outside to draw a landscape, or set up a still life drawing opportunity.

SUPPORT/ELL
Show children how to leave room for an indent by using their pinky finger (horizontally) to measure the space. Reiterate that paragraphs start with an indent.

CROSS-CURRICULAR CONNECTIONS
Social Studies: Have children read informational texts about Vincent Van Gogh and share their findings in a report to the class.

Self-Portrait & Writing

p. 51

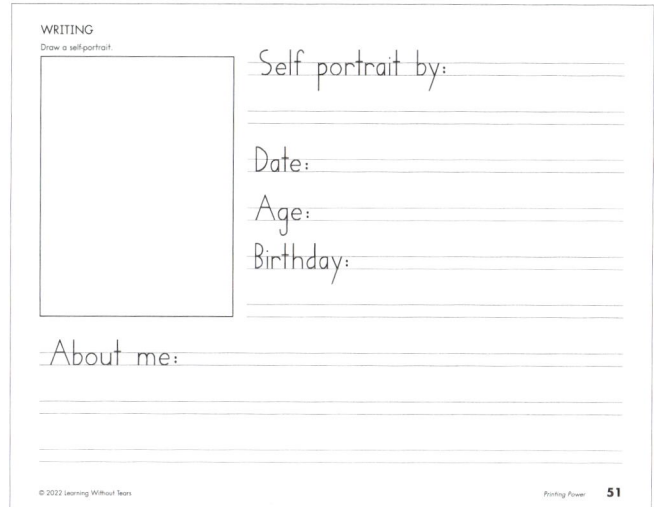

OBJECTIVE
To practice writing informational text.

LESSON INTRODUCTION (Warm Up)
Have children share fun facts about themselves in small groups before activity.

> Additional digital resources are available in the Interactive Digital Teaching Tool (IDTT).

LESSON PLAN

Handwriting

1. Direction Instruction (Demo)

Demonstrate on double lines: **Self Portrait by: (insert name)**.

2. Guided Practice

Children copy: **Self Portrait by_____**
Observe as children write information about themselves.

3. Check Sentences

Monitor as children write sentences for correct capitalization, word spacing, and ending punctuation.

Writing

Children like to write about themselves. To expand this type of writing have them write about another family member.

ENRICHMENT
Have children learn new facts about each other and write them on double line paper.

SUPPORT/ELL
Ask children to tell you about themselves and write the information in a sentence. Have children copy the sentence.

CROSS-CURRICULAR CONNECTIONS
Language Arts: Discuss self portraits. Have children research famous self portraits from around the world.

Homophones

Printing Power – p. 52

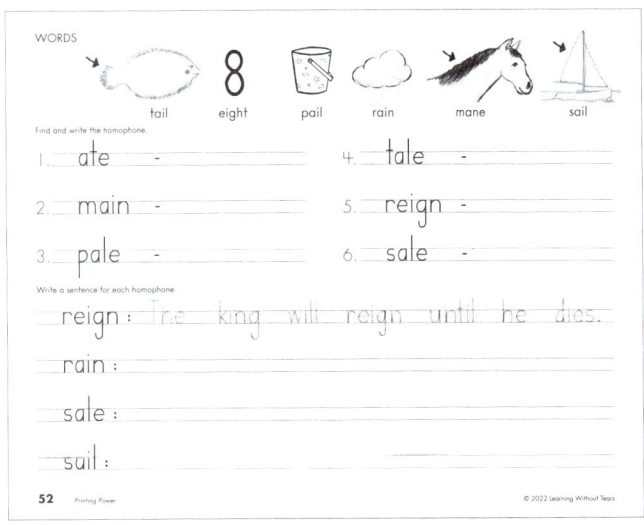

OBJECTIVE
To develop vocabulary and practice sentences to understand homophones.

LESSON INTRODUCTION (Warm Up)
Have children act out the different homophones. For example, hold up eight fingers to show **eight**, and rub stomach to indicate that you **ate** something.

> Additional digital resources are available in the Interactive Digital Teaching Tool (IDTT).

LESSON PLAN

Handwriting

1. Direction Instruction (Demo)
Discuss how homophones sound the same, but have different meanings and spellings. Demonstrate on double lines: **ate - eight** and **main - mane**.

2. Guided Practice
Children copy: **ate - eight** and **main - mane**.
Observe as children complete the homophones and sentences on their own.

3. Check Words & Sentences
Monitor as children write their words for correct size, placement, and closeness, and check their sentences for correct capitalization, word spacing, and ending punctuation.

Writing
Did you notice the homophones all have a long **a** sound? The words use four different spellings of long **a**: a_e, ai, eigh, and eign. You might even teach ay and ey too!

ENRICHMENT
Have children practice writing more homophones, such as knew-new and witch-which in sentences.

SUPPORT/ELL
Pair children in teams so they can help each other with reading and finding the words. Have them check each other's writing, too.

CROSS-CURRICULAR CONNECTIONS
Social Studies: Discuss what the word "reign" means. Provide examples about the history of kings and queens who have reigned.

p. 53

Paragraph – Sign Language

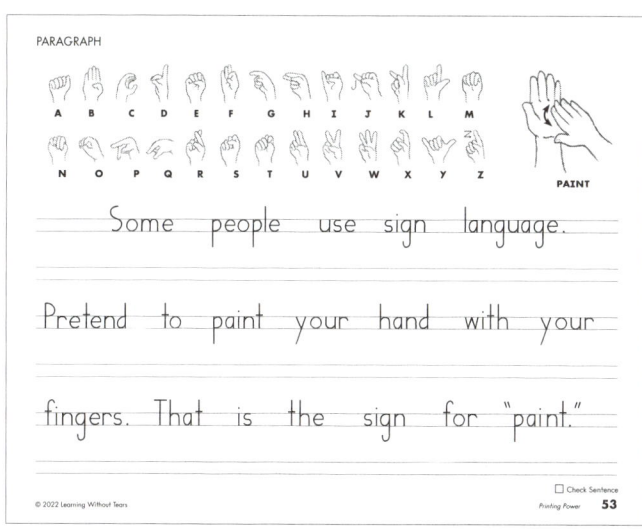

OBJECTIVES
To practice paragraph skills; to try fingerspelling and American Sign Language (ASL).

LESSON INTRODUCTION (Warm Up)
Have children make a letter using ASL.

> Additional digital resources are available in the Interactive Digital Teaching Tool (IDTT).

LESSON PLAN

Handwriting

1. Direction Instruction (Demo)
Demonstrate on double lines: **Some people use sign language.**
Remind children to start with an indent and a capital, put space between words, and end with a period.

2. Guided Practice
Children copy: **Some people use sign language.**
Monitor as children copy the rest of the paragraph on their own.

3. Check Sentence
Help children ✓ their sentence for capitalization, word spacing, and ending punctuation.

Writing
Did you know that deaf babies learn to communicate before hearing babies do? That's why signs (like "more") are popular with parents. Discuss the topic of sign language and discover other ASL signs.

ENRICHMENT
Demonstrate fingerspelling with your palm facing another child. Have children fingerspell the first letter in their names.

SUPPORT/ELL
This paragraph features three descending letters (**p**, **g**, and **y**). Preview these three letters before starting the lesson.

CROSS-CURRICULAR CONNECTIONS
Social Studies: Discuss American Sign Language. Practice spelling names and familiar words in sign language.

Quotations

Printing Power – p. 54

OBJECTIVE
To practice writing speech with quotation marks.

LESSON INTRODUCTION (Warm Up)
Have children stand up and use different voices when saying these quotes.

Additional digital resources are available in the Interactive Digital Teaching Tool (IDTT).

LESSON PLAN

Handwriting

1. Direction Instruction (Demo)

Discuss speech bubbles and show them in comic books. Demonstrate on double lines: **"Can you swim?"**

2. Guided Practice

Observe children as they copy the first quotation and write the others on their own.

3. Check Sentence

Monitor as children write their sentences for correct capitalization, word spacing, and ending punctuation.

Writing

This is the best way to teach direct quotes or the words that someone directly says. It's easy when children understand that the "quotation marks" work like speech bubbles. Everything that someone says, including the ending punctuation is in the speech bubbles!

ENRICHMENT
Have children look in books, find sentences with quotation marks, and copy these sentences on double line paper.

SUPPORT/ELL
Highlight the ending punctuation inside the speech bubbles to help children remember to include it.

CROSS-CURRICULAR CONNECTIONS
Social Studies: Look at famous quotations throughout history. Discuss the meaning and who said the quotation.

Paragraph – Julie Trains Boo

OBJECTIVE
To practice writing quotations within a paragraph.

LESSON INTRODUCTION (Warm Up)
Show books with paragraphs. Find the indents and paragraphs.

> Additional digital resources are available in the Interactive Digital Teaching Tool (IDTT).

LESSON PLAN

Handwriting

1. Direction Instruction (Demo)

Demonstrate on double lines: **Julie trains Boo. She says, "Sit."**
Remind children to start with an indent and a capital, put space between words, and end with a period.

2. Guided Practice

Children copy: **Julie trains Boo. She says, "Sit."**
Monitor as children copy the paragraph on their own.

3. Check Sentence

Help children ✓ their sentence for capitalization, word spacing, and ending punctuation.

Writing

This is a narrative paragraph. It has a topic sentence and sentences about the sequence of events. The previous page prepares children to copy the quotations within paragraphs.

ENRICHMENT
Have children write a paragraph with a conversation between two people using quotation marks correctly.

SUPPORT/ELL
Model for children in their student editions where to put the quotation marks within the paragraph.

CROSS-CURRICULAR CONNECTIONS
Social Studies: Discuss service dogs and how they can help children. Explain the appropriate behavior around a service dog.

Compound Words

Printing Power – p. 56

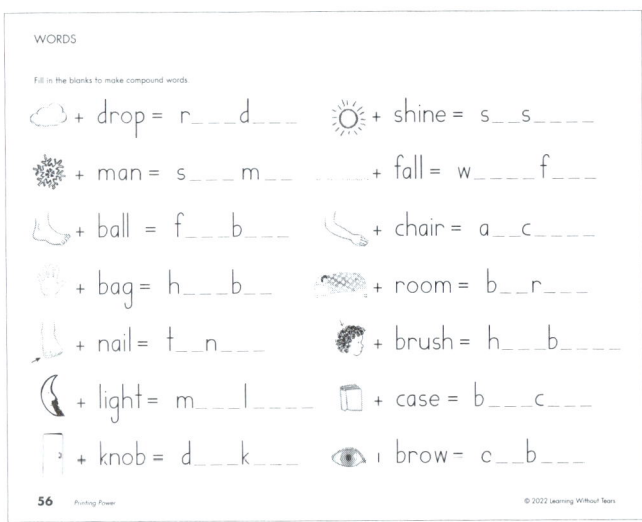

OBJECTIVES
To build compound words; to gain confidence writing long words.

LESSON INTRODUCTION (Warm Up)
Use real objects to illustrate compound words. Examples include: paperclip, toothbrush, etc.

> Additional digital resources are available in the Interactive Digital Teaching Tool (IDTT).

LESSON PLAN

Handwriting

1. Direction Instruction (Demo)

Discuss how compound words are made from two little words. Demonstrate on single lines: **raindrop** and **sunshine**.

2. Guided Practice

Children copy: **raindrop** and **sunshine**.
Observe as children copy the other compound words on their own.

3. Check Words

Monitor as children write their words for correct size, placement, and closeness.

Writing

Pictures and one-syllable words are easy and fun. By turning them into compound words, children develop confidence in reading and writing longer words.

ENRICHMENT
Have children write three sentences using different compound words.

SUPPORT/ELL
Show children pictures of the final compounds words to improve vocabulary and understanding. Use the words in a sentence: "I brush my hair with a hairbrush."

CROSS-CURRICULAR CONNECTIONS
Language Arts: Have children find out the meaning of compound words with knowledge of the individual words (i.e., horsefly and lighthouse).

p. 57

Syllables

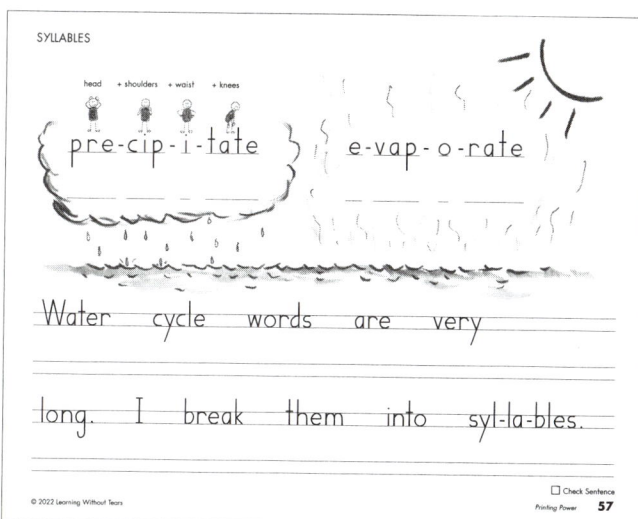

OBJECTIVES
To practice breaking down words into syllables; to develop sentence writing.

LESSON INTRODUCTION (Warm Up)
Syllable Activity (p. 171)

Additional digital resources are available in the Interactive Digital Teaching Tool (IDTT).

LESSON PLAN

Handwriting

1. Direction Instruction (Demo)

Demonstrate syllables in words **pre-cip-i-tate** and **e-vap-o-rate** using the Syllable Activity. Demonstrate on double lines: **Water cycle words are very long.**

2. Guided Practice

Children copy: **Water cycle words are very long.**
Monitor as children copy the other sentence on their own.

3. Check Sentence

Help children ✓ their sentence for correct capitalization, word spacing, and ending punctuation.

Writing

The Syllable Activity teaches children syllables through movement, clear hearing, and counting. Your second graders will love it and you can even use it to teach syllable spelling.

ENRICHMENT
Have children think of other words that have three or more syllables and put them in sentences on double line paper.

SUPPORT/ELL
Have children begin with two to three syllables engaging in the Syllable Activity. When children feel comfortable then have them identify four or more syllable words.

CROSS-CURRICULAR CONNECTIONS
Science: Discuss common tools that are used to measure weather.

Words – Sea & Land

Printing Power – p. 58

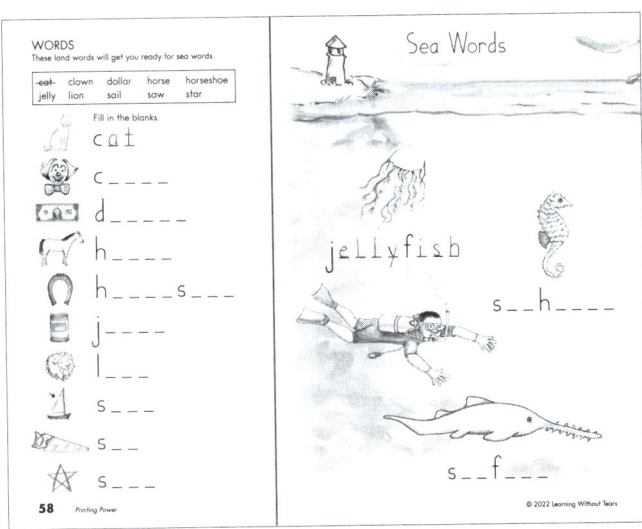

OBJECTIVES
To use a word bank; to label pictures; to develop vocabulary.

LESSON INTRODUCTION (Warm Up)
Hand Activity (p. 167)

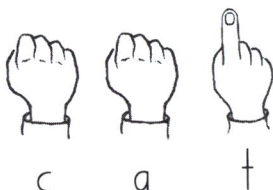

Additional digital resources are available in the Interactive Digital Teaching Tool (IDTT).

LESSON PLAN

Handwriting

1. Direction Instruction (Demo)
Demonstrate on single lines: **cat**, **clown**, and **dollar**.

2. Guided Practice
Children copy: **cat**, **clown**, **dollar**.
Observe as they write the other letters to complete the words on their own.
Remind them to cross out the words in the word bank.

3. Check Words
Observe as children copy and complete the words on their own.

Writing
Finding words in a word bank is a skill your second graders need to learn. This page motivates children to complete the section by tracking and finding the word to match the picture icon.

ENRICHMENT
Have children write a short paragraph using the land words.

SUPPORT/ELL
Have children highlight the first letter of the words in the word bank. This will help them associate the label with the word in the word bank.

CROSS-CURRICULAR CONNECTIONS
Science: Discuss why land words were used to name things in the sea (cat and catfish whiskers).

p. 59

Words – Sea & Land

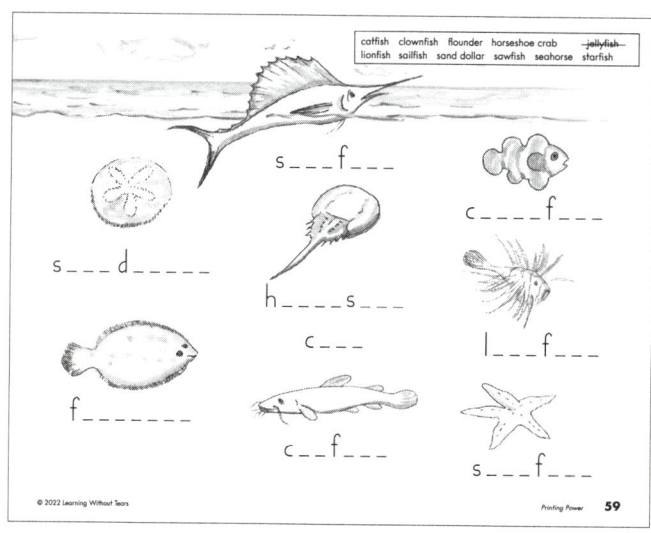

OBJECTIVES
To use a word bank; to label pictures; to develop vocabulary.

LESSON INTRODUCTION (Warm Up)
Hand Activity (p. 167)

Additional digital resources are available in the Interactive Digital Teaching Tool (IDTT).

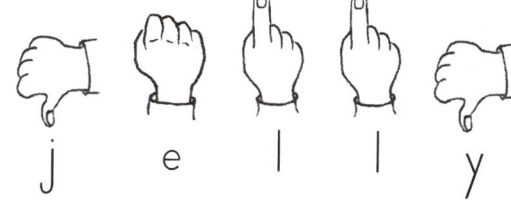

LESSON PLAN

Handwriting

1. Direction Instruction (Demo)
Demonstrate on single lines: **sailfish**, and **sanddollar**.

2. Guided Practice
Children copy: **sailfish**, and **sanddollar**.
Observe as they write the other letters to complete the words on their own.
Remind them to cross out the words in the word bank.

3. Check Words
Observe as children copy and complete the words on their own.

Writing
Find the flounder and write this poem:
  The Flounder
  The Flounder is a funny fish,
  Sort of flat, like a dish,
  One side up, the other down,
  Eyes on top to look around.

ENRICHMENT
Have children write a paragraph about the following topic: What would I do if I could live underwater?

SUPPORT/ELL
Teacher points to each letter of the sea creature and children point to each letter in the word bank to discover the correct answer.

CROSS-CURRICULAR CONNECTIONS
Science: Discuss different types of sharks. Have children research one particular shark and discuss facts about it.

Continents & Oceans

Printing Power – p. 60

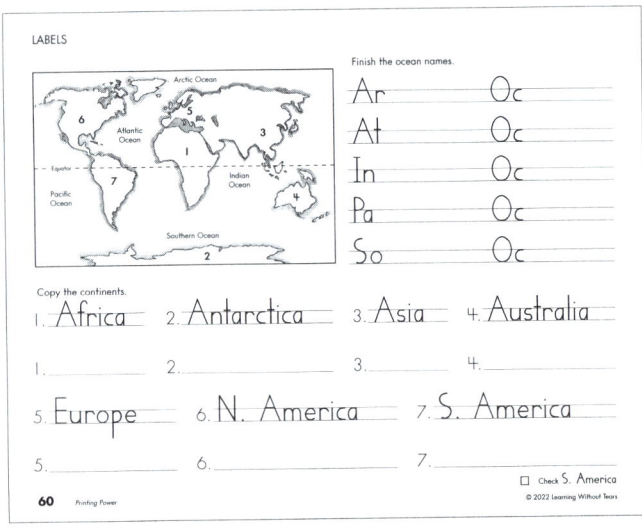

OBJECTIVES
To capitalize proper nouns related to geography; to write on single lines.

LESSON INTRODUCTION (Warm Up)
Use a real globe to point out the continents.

> Additional digital resources are available in the Interactive Digital Teaching Tool (IDTT).

LESSON PLAN

Handwriting

1. Direction Instruction (Demo)

Demonstrate on double lines: **Arctic Ocean**
Demonstrate on single lines: **Africa** and **Antarctica**.

2. Guided Practice

Children copy: **Arctic Ocean**, **Africa**, and **Antarctica**.
Observe children as they finish the ocean names and copy the continents on their own.

3. Check Words

Help children ☑ their word for correct size, placement, and closeness.

Writing

Do syl-la-ble spelling and write the continents using syllable spelling: Af-ri-ca, Ant-arc-ti-ca, A-sia, Aus-tra-li-a, Eu-rope, North A-mer-i-ca, and South A-mer-i-ca.

ENRICHMENT
Have children write a sentence about an ocean and a continent.

SUPPORT/ELL
Help children locate the continent name and find it on a map before writing the next continent. Have children use colored pencils to color the oceans.

CROSS-CURRICULAR CONNECTIONS
Social Studies: Have children research and write about an ocean or continent. They can present their information to the class.

List – Places

p. 61

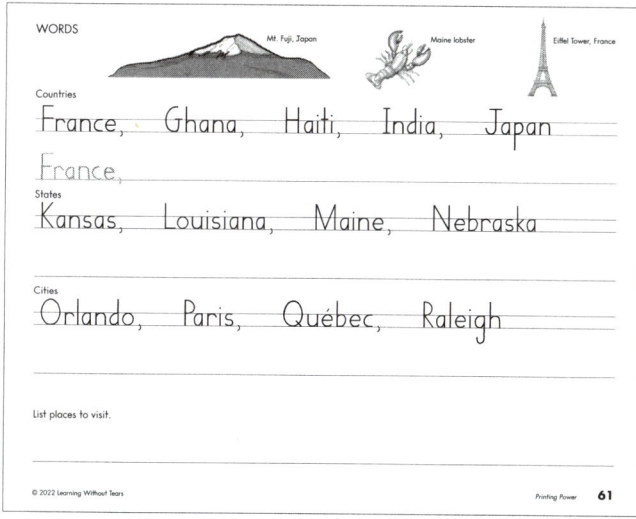

OBJECTIVES

To capitalize proper nouns; to use serial commas.

LESSON INTRODUCTION (Warm Up)

Use a real globe and map to show countries, states, and cities.

> Additional digital resources are available in the Interactive Digital Teaching Tool (IDTT).

LESSON PLAN

Handwriting

1. Direction Instruction (Demo)

Discuss how proper nouns are always capitalized.
Demonstrate on a single line: **France, Ghana,** and **Haiti**.
Discuss places that children may want to visit.

2. Guided Practice

Children copy: **France, Ghana,** and **Haiti**.
Observe as children copy the remaining proper nouns and list places to visit on their own.

3. Check Words

Observe as children copy and write the proper nouns and list places they would like to visit.

Writing

This is a list in a series. Use a comma to separate listed items. We call a comma like this a serial or series comma. On the last line, children may also use commas to separate city from state or country. Examples include: Paris, France.

ENRICHMENT

Have children make a list of other things using a serial comma.

SUPPORT/ELL

Highlight the capital letters and commas to make them noticeable and to encourage children to correctly copy them.

CROSS-CURRICULAR CONNECTIONS

Social Studies/Science: Mount Fuji is a volcano, but it hasn't erupted more than 300 years. Discuss why volcanoes erupt.

Poem – Apostrophe

Printing Power – p. 62

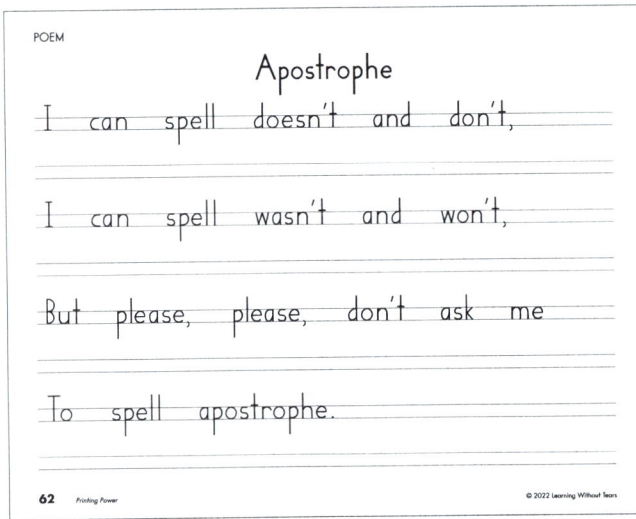

OBJECTIVES
To use poetry conventions; to write contractions with apostrophes.

LESSON INTRODUCTION (Warm Up)
Split class into two groups and have one group say, "you are" (as two words) and have the other group say, "you're" (as a contraction). Repeat for other similar words.

> Additional digital resources are available in the Interactive Digital Teaching Tool (IDTT).

LESSON PLAN

Handwriting

1. Direction Instruction (Demo)

Discuss how poems are structured.
Demonstrate on double lines: **I can spell doesn't and don't,**
Remind children to start lines with a capital, put space between words, and use poem punctuation.

2. Guided Practice

Observe as children copy the first line and complete the poem on their own.

3. Check Poem

Monitor children as they write their poem for correct capitalization, word spacing, and poem punctuation.

Writing

A contraction is a shortened form of a word. The omitted letters are replaced with an apostrophe. Present other contractions to children so they learn various words.

ENRICHMENT
Give children a list of words and have them write the contractions for those words. Examples include: can not = can't; you have = you've; and they are = they're.

SUPPORT/ELL
Highlight the apostrophes for children to notice. Take more time to discuss contractions. Show children that will not = won't. Show other examples.

CROSS-CURRICULAR CONNECTIONS
Language Arts: Look in books to find examples of contractions in text and show children.

Antonyms

p. 63

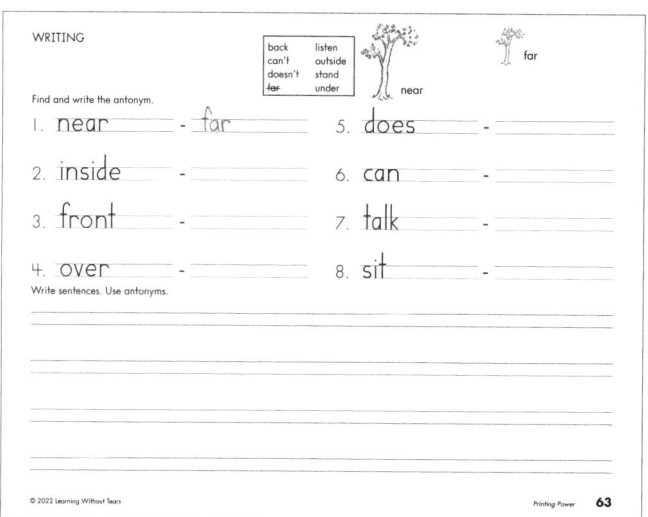

OBJECTIVE
To write antonyms using a word bank.

LESSON INTRODUCTION (Warm Up)
Take turns acting out antonyms. For example, show that you can **talk** by putting your hands around your mouth and that you can **listen** by putting your hands to your ears.

> Additional digital resources are available in the Interactive Digital Teaching Tool (IDTT).

LESSON PLAN

Handwriting

1. Direction Instruction (Demo)
Discuss that an antonym means the opposite.
Demonstrate the first word and its opposite on double lines: **near - far** and **inside - outside**.

2. Guided Practice
Observe as children copy and write the antonyms on their own.

3. Check Words & Sentences
Monitor as children write the words for correct size, placement, and closeness and sentences for correct capitalization, word spacing, and ending punctuation.

Writing

Antonyms are words that mean the opposite. We want children to use antonyms to contrast two different things. The prefix **anti-** or **ant-** means against. The word root **nym** means name.

ENRICHMENT
What's the opposite of an antonym? A synonym is a word that means "the same." Have children make a list of synonyms.

SUPPORT/ELL
Be sure children cross out words after they use them. That makes the next words easier to find. The words in the word bank are in alphabetical order.

CROSS-CURRICULAR CONNECTIONS
Language Arts: Use the prefix **un** and its meaning (not) to talk about antonyms (i.e., happy/unhappy, finished/unfinished).

Question & Answer – Strange Sleepers   *Printing Power* – p. 64

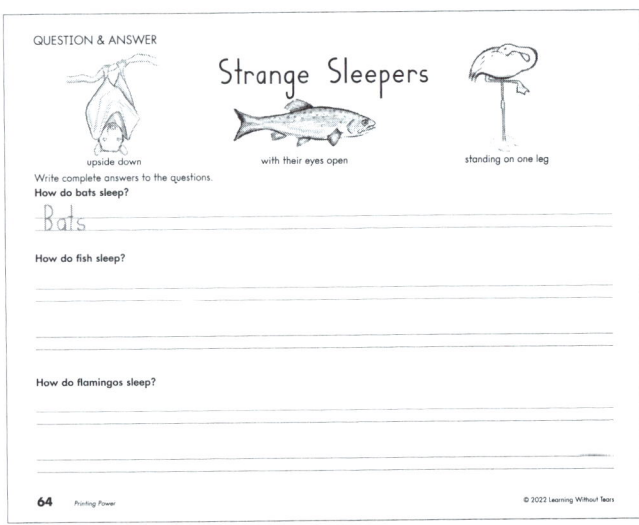

OBJECTIVE
To build writing fluency; to write answers with complete sentences.

LESSON INTRODUCTION (Warm Up)
Syllable Activity (p. 171)

Additional digital resources are available in the Interactive Digital Teaching Tool (IDTT).

LESSON PLAN

Handwriting

1. Direction Instruction (Demo)
Practice answering each question with a complete sentence.
Demonstrate on double lines: **Bats sleep upside down.**
Remind children to start with a capital, put space between words, and end with a period.

2. Guided Practice
Observe as children copy the first answer and write the answers to the other questions on their own.

3. Check Sentences
Monitor as children write their sentences for correct capitalization, word spacing, and ending punctuation.

Writing
This is informational text. Besides learning about strange sleepers, children are learning to use the resources (words and pictures) at the top of the page. Children use part of each question and their resources to write complete answers.

ENRICHMENT
Children choose one of the animals on this page and write some interesting facts about it on double line paper.

SUPPORT/ELL
Dictate the answer to children who are having difficulty with forming an answer to the question.

CROSS-CURRICULAR CONNECTIONS
Science: Discuss other animals that have unique sleep habits (i.e., sharks have to constantly swim, dolphins sleep with one eye open, etc.).

Question & Answer – Picky Eaters

p. 65

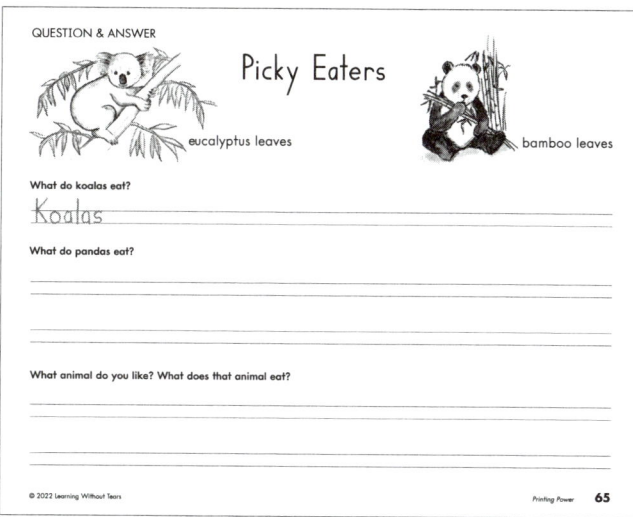

OBJECTIVE
To build writing fluency; to write answers with complete sentences.

LESSON INTRODUCTION (Warm Up)
Syallable Activity (p. 191)

Additional digital resources are available in the Interactive Digital Teaching Tool (IDTT).

LESSON PLAN

Handwriting

1. Direction Instruction (Demo)
Practice answering each question with a complete sentence.
Demonstrate on double lines: **Koalas eat eucalyptus leaves.**
Remind children to start with a capital, put space between words, and end with a period.

2. Guided Practice
Observe as children copy the first answer and write the answers to the other questions on their own.

3. Check Sentences
Monitor as children write their sentences for correct capitalization, word spacing, and ending punctuation.

Writing
This informational text is about two animals with very restricted diets. Children use the resources and the pictures to write complete answers. At the bottom of the page, children may answer the questions differently. Use this same format with other topics.

ENRICHMENT
Children expand writing about their favorite animal on double line paper.

SUPPORT/ELL
Dictate the answer to children who are having difficulty with forming an answer to the question.

CROSS-CURRICULAR CONNECTIONS
Science: These are the only foods that a panda or koala will eat. Compare that to all the foods that they like to eat.

Dates

Printing Power – p. 66

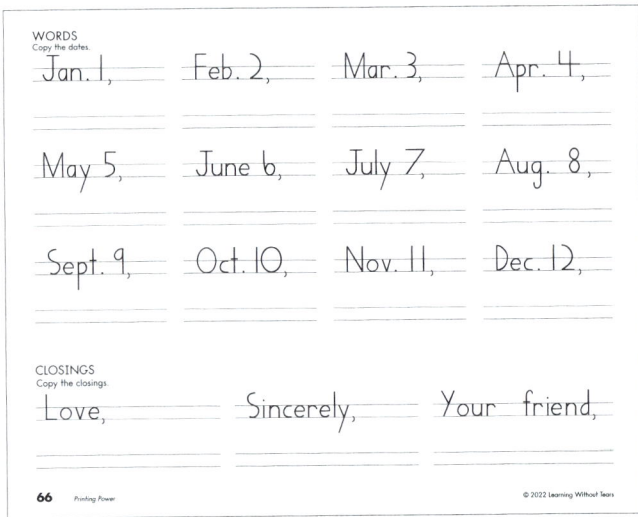

OBJECTIVES
To write dates, abbreviations, and letter closings; to prepare for letter writing.

LESSON INTRODUCTION (Warm Up)
Sing a calendar and/or day of the week song.

> Additional digital resources are available in the Interactive Digital Teaching Tool (IDTT).

LESSON PLAN

Handwriting

1. Direction Instruction (Demo)

Discuss abbreviations and how they are used.
Demonstrate on double lines: **Jan. 1, Feb. 2, Mar. 3,** and **Apr. 4,**

2. Guided Practice

Children copy: **Jan. 1, Feb. 2, Mar. 3,** and **Apr. 4,**
Observe as children copy the abbreviations and the letter closings.

3. Check Words

Monitor as children write their words for correct size, placement, and closeness.

Writing

Writing name and date on papers is an important skill for children to learn. Three months—May, June, and July—aren't abbreviated because they are short already. The comma is used between day and year.

ENRICHMENT
Children write the abbreviations for days of the week.

SUPPORT/ELL
Cut out the months of old calendars for sorting activities. Have children match the months and put them in order.

CROSS-CURRICULAR CONNECTIONS
Language Arts: Create cards (birthday, holiday, etc.) for family and friends. Remind children to write the date and a letter closing.

Thank You Letter

p. 67

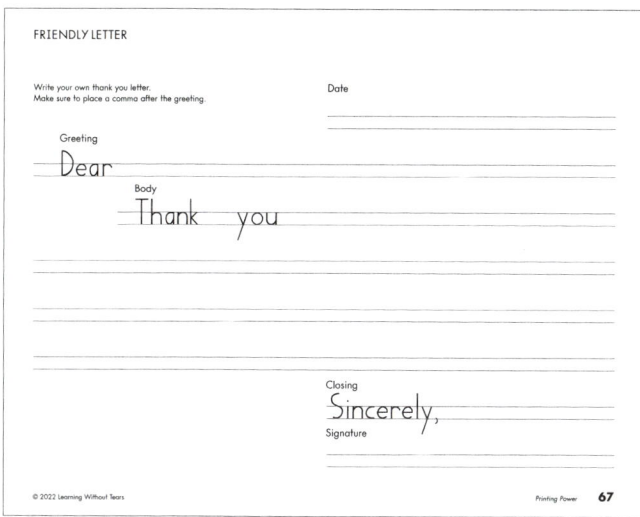

OBJECTIVE
To write a personal thank you letter with a friendly format.

LESSON INTRODUCTION (Warm Up)
Have children share what they are thankful for with the class.

> Additional digital resources are available in the Interactive Digital Teaching Tool (IDTT).

LESSON PLAN

Handwriting

1. Direction Instruction (Demo)
Discuss and demonstrate how to write a sample letter on double lines. Read the parts of a letter from top to bottom: date, greeting, body, closing, signature.
Ask children to write their own letter.

2. Guided Practice
Observe as children write the date, greeting, body, and letter closing.

3. Check Letter Format
Monitor as children write their letter for correct format.

Writing
When technology takes over the world, the personal handwritten thank you letter or note will survive. Advice books about manners, job applications, and career success recommend handwriting thank you letters.

ENRICHMENT

Children write another letter format using a letter template.

SUPPORT/ELL
Tell children to refer to the dates on the facing page to help them with the format of writing a date.

CROSS-CURRICULAR CONNECTIONS
Social Studies: Participate in a pen pal program with students from another country. Students can write letters to individuals or another class.

Vowels

Printing Power – p. 68

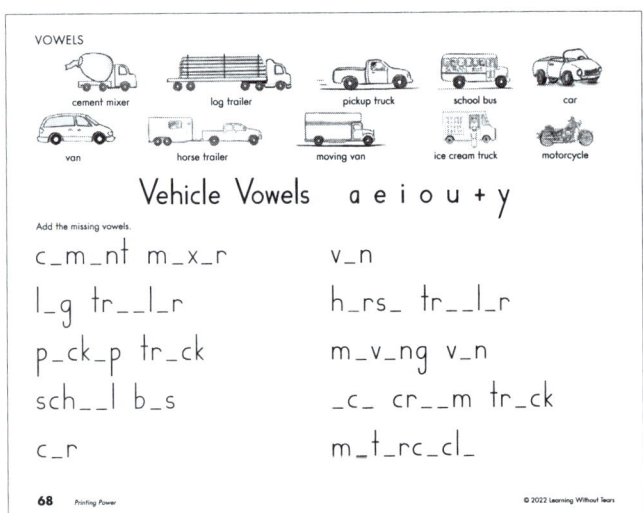

OBJECTIVE
To add and write the missing vowels correctly.

LESSON INTRODUCTION (Warm Up)
SONG: "Vowels" from *Rock, Rap, Tap & Learn* music album

> Additional digital resources are available in the Interactive Digital Teaching Tool (IDTT).

LESSON PLAN

Handwriting

1. Direction Instruction (Demo)
Demonstrate vowels in the following words: **cement mixer** and **log trailer**.

2. Guided Practice
Children copy: **cement mixer** and **log trailer**.
Observe as children write the other vowels to complete the words on their own.

3. Check Letters
Monitor as children write their letters for correct start, steps, and bump.

Writing
Before you let children start writing, have them search for the consonant digraphs: ck, cr, and tr and the only trigraph: sch. Then, look for the vowel digraphs: ai, ea, and oo and the one silent **e**.

ENRICHMENT
Children write complete sentences using two of the vehicle words.

SUPPORT/ELL
Show children how to find the vowel in each word. Demonstrate other words as needed.

CROSS-CURRICULAR CONNECTIONS
Language Arts: Compare and contrast the motorcycle to the car. As a class, create a Venn diagram.

p. 69

Poem – Four Wheel Drive

OBJECTIVES

To build writing fluency; to learn poem basics such as title, lines, and rhyme.

LESSON INTRODUCTION (Warm Up)

Have children stand up every time they hear a rhyming word in the poem.

> Additional digital resources are available in the Interactive Digital Teaching Tool (IDTT).

LESSON PLAN

Handwriting

1. Direction Instruction (Demo)

Demonstrate on double lines: **Four-wheel drive,**
Remind children to start lines with a capital, put space between words, and use poem punctuation. Once children have copied the first three lines, dictate the final lines, **Or through the snow.**

2. Guided Practice

Observe as children copy the poem and write the last line from dictation.

3. Check Poem

Monitor as children write their poem for correct capitalization, word spacing, and ending punctuation.

Writing

Use the poem to contrast paragraphs and poems. Paragraphs have topics. Poems have titles. Paragraphs have sentences. Poems have lines. Sentences start one after another. Each line starts on a new line, etc.

ENRICHMENT

Discuss ideas on how to write poems. Have children write their own poem on double line paper.

SUPPORT/ELL

Dictate to children to prepare them for independent writing and to help children who are struggling with spelling.

CROSS-CURRICULAR CONNECTIONS

Language Arts: Discuss the difference between four-wheel drive and two-wheel drive.

Labels – Guitar

Printing Power – p. 70

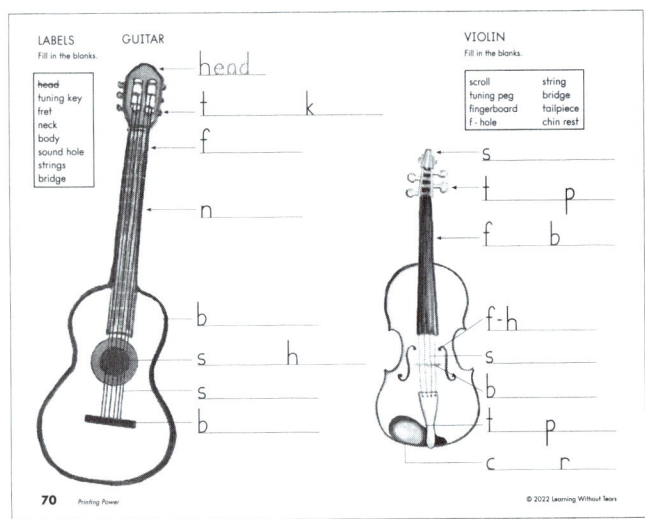

OBJECTIVES
To use word banks; to label a guitar and violin; to develop vocabulary.

LESSON INTRODUCTION (Warm Up)
Listen and compare guitar and violin music.

> Additional digital resources are available in the Interactive Digital Teaching Tool (IDTT).

LESSON PLAN

Handwriting

1. Direction Instruction (Demo)
Discuss and identify the parts of a guitar and violin.
Demonstrate the following parts of a guitar: **turning key**, **fret**, and **neck**.
Label the parts of a guitar on a single line.

2. Guided Practice
Observe as children copy, find, and write the words to label the guitar and violin on their own. Remind them to cross out the words in the word bank.

3. Check Words
Monitor as children write their words for correct size, placement and closeness.

Writing
Labels provide information about people, places, or objects. In this example, we can use the labels to compare two stringed instruments.

ENRICHMENT
Say complete sentences using the label words to describe the parts of a guitar. Have children write one of the sentences using the label words.

SUPPORT/ELL
Bring in a real guitar and/or violin to help children connect the words to the instrument.

CROSS-CURRICULAR CONNECTIONS
Language Arts/Music: Compare guitars and violins. Count the tuning pegs to know how many strings are on both.

p. 71

Paragraph – Violin

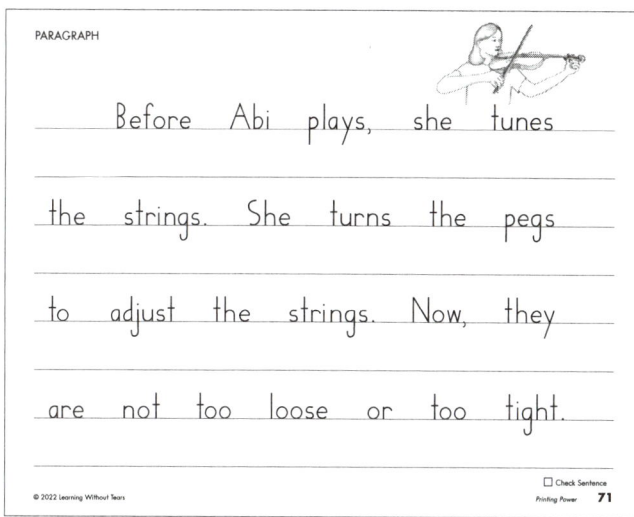

OBJECTIVES
To build writing fluency; to build paragraph skills.

LESSON INTRODUCTION (Warm Up)
Show books with paragraphs. Find the indents and paragraphs.

Additional digital resources are available in the Interactive Digital Teaching Tool (IDTT).

LESSON PLAN

Handwriting

1. Direction Instruction (Demo)
Demonstrate on double lines: **Before Abi plays, she tunes the strings.**
Remind children to start with an indent and a capital, put space between words, and end with a period.

2. Guided Practice
Observe as children indent, copy the first sentence, and complete the paragraph on their own.

3. Check Sentence
Help children ✓ their sentence for correct capitalization, word spacing, and ending punctuation.

Writing
Use this paragraph as a model for writing a narrative about other sequences and steps, in preparing for something.

ENRICHMENT
Have children write their own paragraph describing a time they either played a musical instrument or watched someone play an instrument.

SUPPORT/ELL
Remind children to "bump" the lines and start each new word directly under the first letter of the model. Demonstrate as needed in the student edition.

CROSS-CURRICULAR CONNECTIONS
Language Arts: Read the Caldecott Honors book, *Zin! Zin! Zin! A Violin* by Lloyd Moss and discuss musical instruments.

QWERTY

Printing Power – p. 72

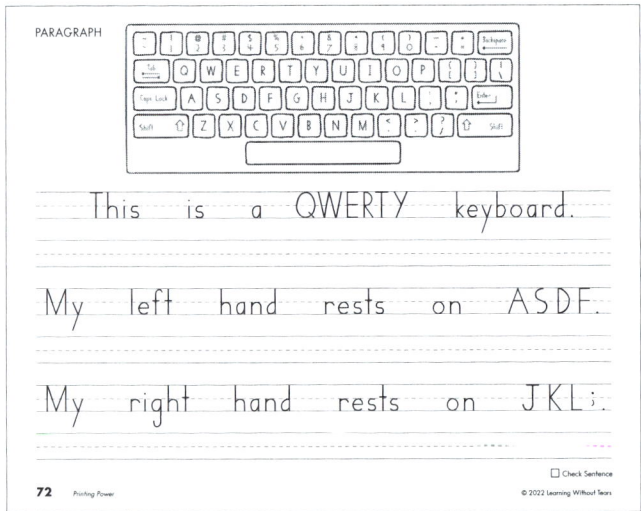

OBJECTIVES

To build writing fluency; to build paragraph skills.

LESSON INTRODUCTION (Warm Up)

Explore a real keyboard to identify the QWERTY layout.

> Additional digital resources are available in the Interactive Digital Teaching Tool (IDTT).

LESSON PLAN

Handwriting

1. Direction Instruction (Demo)

Discuss why a keyboard is in a QWERTY layout.
Demonstrate on triple lines: **This is a QWERTY keyboard.**
Remind children to start with an indent and a capital, put space between words, and end with a period.

2. Guided Practice

Children copy: **This is a QWERTY keyboard.**
Monitor as children copy the paragraph on their own.

3. Check Sentence

Help children ✓ their sentence for capitalization, word spacing, and ending punctuation.

Writing

Today's children learn to express themselves with handwriting and keyboarding. As a teacher, make sure to address both methods of communication in your classroom.

ENRICHMENT

Have children copy this paragraph on a tablet or computer.

SUPPORT/ELL

Use a real keyboard to demonstrate the QWERTY layout and show how fingers are placed.

CROSS-CURRICULAR CONNECTIONS

Social Studies: Discuss how the QWERTY layout was invented to actually prevent the hammers of a typewriter from jamming.

Calendar Surprise

p. 73

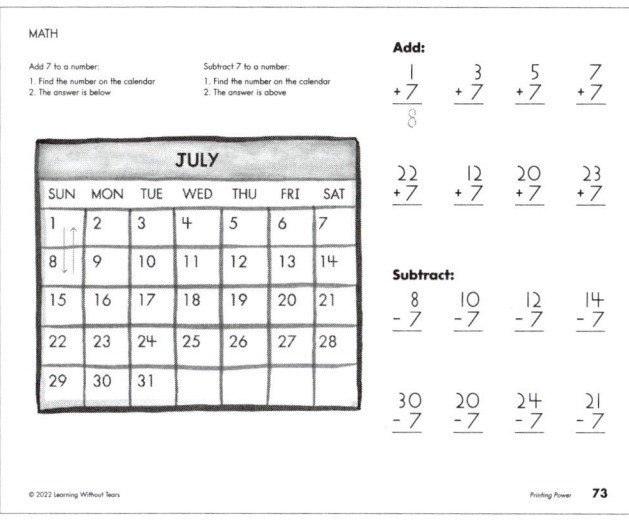

OBJECTIVE
To use numerals to write solutions for addition and subtraction problems.

LESSON INTRODUCTION (Warm Up)
Complete this activity using a real calendar.

> Additional digital resources are available in the Interactive Digital Teaching Tool (IDTT).

LESSON PLAN

Handwriting

1. Direction Instruction (Demo)
Demonstrate how to add 7 and subtract 7 using a calendar.

2. Guided Practice
Monitor as children complete the addition and subtraction problems.

3. Check Numbers
Check to see if students solve the problems and write the answers correctly.

Writing
Children remember calendar activities, but this one has a surprise. Show children how to do this with a calendar. Start by adding 7 to numbers 1–21. Then subtract 7 from numbers 8–28. They'll love being right and they'll learn their "7" facts.

ENRICHMENT
Give children a blank calendar and have them write in the numbers for the week of the appropriate month.

SUPPORT/ELL
Have children point to each day of the week as they add or subtract 7 from each column.

CROSS-CURRICULAR CONNECTIONS
Math: Make a table that goes beyond 28 to demonstrate how the concept will continue to work with larger numbers.

Irregular Nouns & Verbs

Printing Power – p. 74

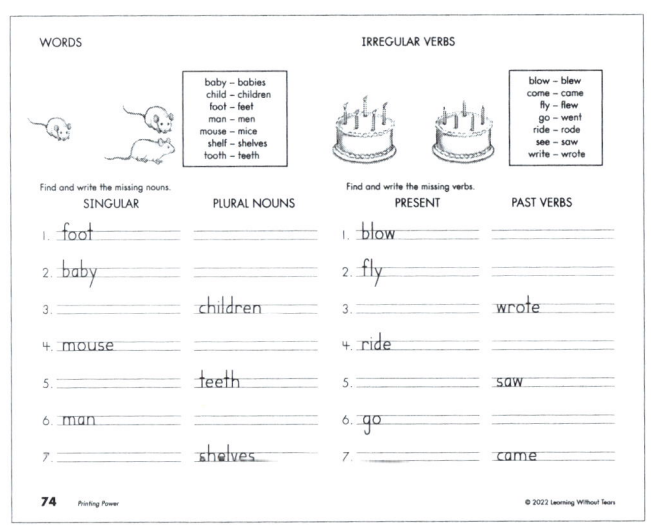

OBJECTIVES

To write singular and plural irregular nouns; to write present and past irregular verbs.

LESSON INTRODUCTION (Warm Up)

Take turns saying a sentence using a singular or plural noun. For example, give children the singular noun foot and have them use feet in a sentence.

Additional digital resources are available in the Interactive Digital Teaching Tool (IDTT).

LESSON PLAN

Handwriting

1. Direction Instruction (Demo)

Discuss regular and irregular plural nouns and regular and irregular verbs. Demonstrate on a double lines: **foot - feet** and **blow - blew**.

2. Guided Practice

Children copy: **foot - feet** and **blow - blew**.
Observe as children find and write the missing nouns and verbs on their own.
Remind children to cross out the words in the word bank.

3. Check Words

Monitor as children write their words for correct size, placement and closeness.

Writing

How many? The regular way to make plural nouns is to add **s**: one hand, two hands. Nouns like foot don't follow the rule. They're irregular.

The regular way to make past tense is to add **d** or **ed**: I skate today. I skated yesterday. Verbs like bow don't follow the rule. They're irregular.

ENRICHMENT

Have children write two sentences using a word pair on double line paper.

SUPPORT/ELL

To make the verb examples easier, add time references and use sentences. Examples include: "Today, I skate." and "Yesterday, I skated."

CROSS-CURRICULAR CONNECTIONS

Language Arts: Nouns are names of people, places, and things. Verbs show action. As a class, identify a list of nouns and/or verbs.

Sentence Building

p. 75

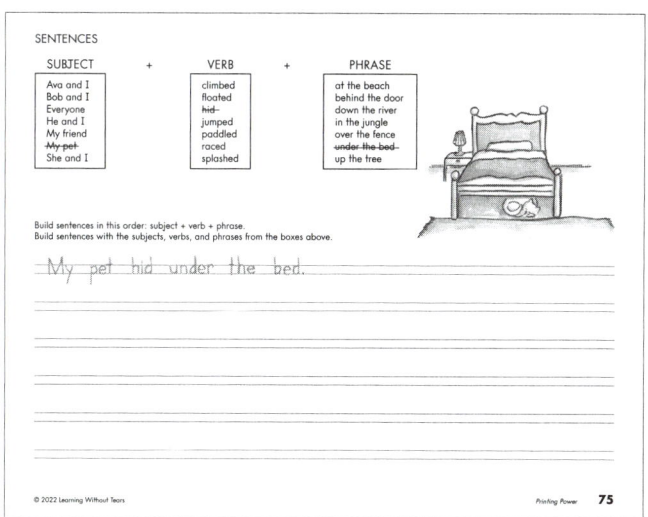

OBJECTIVE
To build sentences with correct syntax and grammar.

LESSON INTRODUCTION (Warm Up)
Take turns creating and saying sentences out loud using a subject, verb, and a phrase.

> Additional digital resources are available in the Interactive Digital Teaching Tool (IDTT).

LESSON PLAN

Handwriting

1. Direction Instruction (Demo)
Demonstrate on double lines using a subject + verb + phrase: **My pet hid under the bed.**
Remind children to start with a capital, put space between words, and end with a period.

2. Guided Practice
Children copy: **My pet hid under the bed.**
Observe as children build and write sentences on their own.
Remind children to cross out the words in the word bank.

3. Check Sentences
Monitor as children write their sentences for correct capitalization, word spacing, and ending punctuation.

Writing

Make your own sentence! Pick your subject and verb. Then add your topping (prepositional phrase). The subjects are a mix of singular and plural. Read them out loud and have the children tell you if the subjects are singular or plural. The verbs are past tense. Can they find the one irregular verb? The phrases are prepositional phrases. Can they tell you which word is the preposition or position word?

ENRICHMENT
Have children write explanatory paragraphs about an event in their lives. Each sentence must have a subject, verb, and phrase.

SUPPORT/ELL
Help children say the complete sentence. Model sentence for children who need extra help.

CROSS-CURRICULAR CONNECTIONS
Language Arts: Expand the activity with other subjects, verbs, and phrases. Have children make up silly phrases.

Elevators & Buildings

Printing Power – p. 76

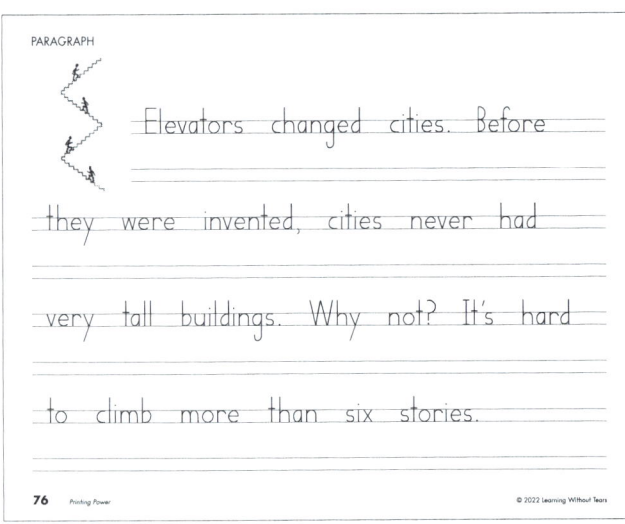

OBJECTIVES
To build writing fluency; to build paragraph skills.

LESSON INTRODUCTION (Warm Up)
Children take turns sharing elevator or tall building stories.

> Additional digital resources are available in the Interactive Digital Teaching Tool (IDTT).

LESSON PLAN

Handwriting

1. Direction Instruction (Demo)
Demonstrate on double lines: **Elevators changed cities.**
Remind children to start with an indent and a capital, put space between words, and end with a period.

2. Guided Practice
Children copy: **Elevators changed cities.**
Observe as children complete the paragraph on their own.

3. Check Paragraph
Monitor as children start with an indent and a capital, put space between words, and end with punctuation.

Writing
This is an example of informational writing. Children will come up with their own sentence by drawing on past experiences. For children with limited experiences of a topic use videos and books to help them connect.

ENRICHMENT
Have children research a skyscraper in the United States and write a paragraph about it (i.e., Willis Tower, Empire State Building, or John Hancock Center).

SUPPORT/ELL
Help children answer the question. Either have children copy or dictate what they tell you.

CROSS-CURRICULAR CONNECTIONS
Math: Consider an elevator math problem. Examples include: "Dan started on the fifth floor and went up 11 stories. What floor is he on?"

p. 77

Elevators & Buildings

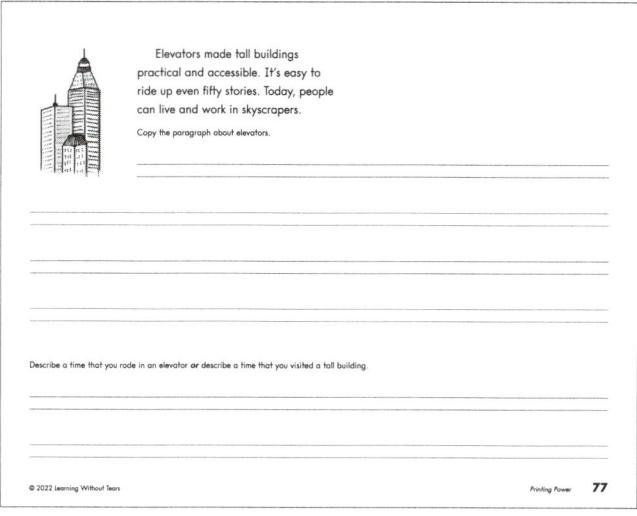

OBJECTIVES
To build writing fluency; to build paragraph skills.

LESSON INTRODUCTION (Warm Up)
Have children take turns sharing stories about elevators or tall buildings.

> Additional digital resources are available in the Interactive Digital Teaching Tool (IDTT).

LESSON PLAN

Handwriting

1. Direction Instruction (Demo)

Demonstrate on double lines: **Elevators made tall buildings practical and accessible.** Remind children to start with an indent and a capital, put space between words, and end with a period. Ask children to answer the question on their own.

2. Guided Practice

Children copy: **Elevators made tall buildings practical and accessible.** Observe as children copy and complete the paragraph and answer the question on their own.

3. Check Paragraph

Monitor as children start with an indent and a capital, put space between words, and end with punctuation.

Writing

This activity requires children to copy writing that is not placed on lines. Children often have to copy information. Throughout the handwriting student edition children have copied with examples on lines to guide them. In this example, they have to translate copying from print onto double lines.

ENRICHMENT
Discuss the tallest building the children have been in and have them write a paragraph describing their experience.

SUPPORT/ELL
Have children complete one sentence and review for errors before moving to the next sentence.

CROSS-CURRICULAR CONNECTIONS
Social Studies: Discuss and research the tallest skyscraper in New York City, the Freedom Tower.

Capitalization

Printing Power – p. 78

CAPITALS
Titles: Mr., Miss, Ms., Mrs., Dr.
Book titles: First, last, and important words

CAPITALIZE: Finish the sentences about yourself.

- Schools — My school is _____.
- Titles, names — My teacher is _____.
- Book titles — I read _____.
- Cities, towns — I live in _____.
- Rivers, lakes, and oceans — The closest water is _____.
- First word of a quote — My friend said, " _____ "

OBJECTIVE
To capitalize proper nouns correctly.

LESSON INTRODUCTION (Warm Up)
Children point out signs and labels in books that use capitals.

> Additional digital resources are available in the Interactive Digital Teaching Tool (IDTT).

LESSON PLAN

Handwriting

1. Direction Instruction (Demo)

Discuss titles: Mr., Miss, Ms., Mrs., Dr., and book titles. Talk about first, last, and important words and how capitals are used.
Demonstrate on a single line: **My school is_____.**

2. Guided Practice

Children copy: **My school is_____.**
Observe as children complete the sentences using the capital rule for each on their own.

3. Check Words

Monitor as children write their words for correct size, placement, and closeness.

Writing

Take this lesson to a keyboard! Show children how to get ALL CAPS by pressing the Caps Lock key with your left pinky. To get just one capital, press either the left or right Shift key. Pinky fingers make capitals in keyboarding.

ENRICHMENT

Expand the activity by having children capitalize other words such as US states and/or other countries.

SUPPORT/ELL

Dictate or have children copy words as needed.

CROSS-CURRICULAR CONNECTIONS

Language Arts: Write "about me" paragraphs. Pass out paragraphs and have children introduce their match.

Alliteration

p. 79

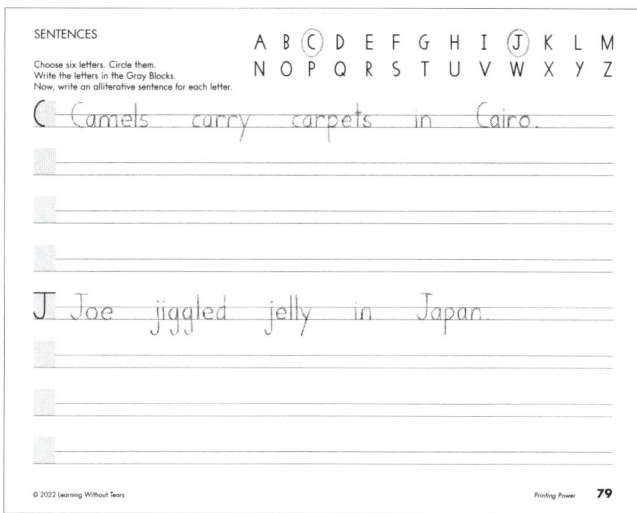

OBJECTIVE
To write sentences that feature alliteration (repeating the same beginning sound).

LESSON INTRODUCTION (Warm Up)
Have children stand up and take turns saying different alliterative sentences.

> Additional digital resources are available in the Interactive Digital Teaching Tool (IDTT).

LESSON PLAN

Handwriting

1. Direction Instruction (Demo)

Listen for the repeated sound in each sentence.
Demonstrate on double lines: **Camels carry carpets in Cairo.**
Say: **Choose six capitals. Circle them on the page. Write the capitals in the Gray Blocks. Now, write an alliterative sentence for each capital.**

2. Guided Practice

Observe as children copy the first sentence and create alliterative sentences on their own.

3. Check Sentences

Monitor to see if children write their sentences with correct capitalization, word spacing, and ending punctuation.

Writing

Alliteration is the repetition of an initial sound at the beginning of each word in a group of words. This is an engaging writing activity that is fun to learn and use in the classroom. It is often used in poetry to create unity.

ENRICHMENT
Have children write an alliterative sentence using the letter from their first name.

SUPPORT/ELL
If children struggle, allow them to copy the two example sentences and write additional sentences for them to copy.

CROSS-CURRICULAR CONNECTIONS
Social Studies: Using a map, have children find more areas around the world to write alliterative sentences.

Sentences & Numbers

Printing Power – p. 80

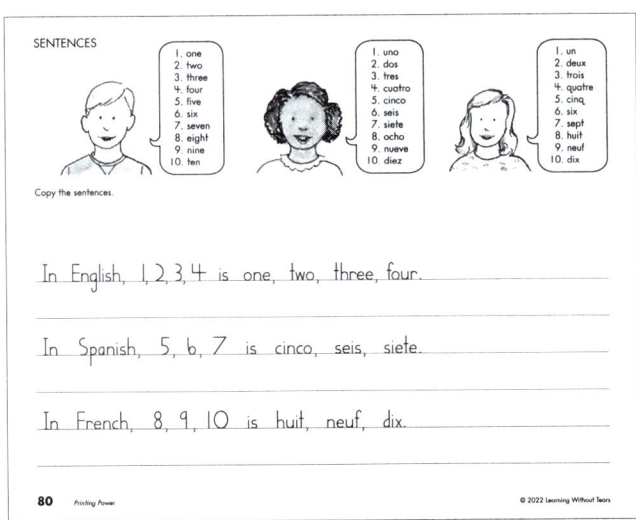

OBJECTIVE
To build writing fluency by writing sentences correctly.

LESSON INTRODUCTION (Warm Up)
Children stand and repeat counting to 3 in English, Spanish, and French.

> Additional digital resources are available in the Interactive Digital Teaching Tool (IDTT).

LESSON PLAN

Handwriting

1. Direction Instruction (Demo)
Say the words one, two, and three in Spanish and French.
Demonstrate on a single line: **In English, 1, 2, 3, 4 is one, two, three, four.**
Remind children to start with a capital, put space between words, and end with a period.

2. Guided Practice
Children copy: **In English, 1, 2, 3, 4 is one, two, three, four.**
Observe as children copy the other sentences on their own.

3. Check Sentences
Monitor as children write their sentences for correct capitalization, word spacing, and ending punctuation.

Writing

This "counting" page faces the first page of the number section. Children around the world count in their native tongues. How many languages are in your classroom? This is also a good page for commas after introductory phrases and serial commas. The number section has more math related sentences for your children.

ENRICHMENT
Have children count out loud up to 10 in Spanish and French. Copy the words on line paper.

SUPPORT/ELL
Repeat one, two, and three in Spanish and French slowly for children before they copy.

CROSS-CURRICULAR CONNECTIONS
Social Studies: Using a globe, identify some of the countries where Spanish and French are primarily spoken.

NUMBERS

Let's talk about numbers. If you're new to Handwriting Without Tears®, you are in for a surprise. You can joyfully and efficiently promote your students to write numbers correctly! That means numbers that start at the top, use the right strokes, and face correctly.

Review numbers at the beginning of the year, along with capitals. What about reversals? Not a problem! Our materials and strategies work to prevent letter and number reversal problems. When we use these strategies for second graders, reversals are never a problem.

And guess what? A smiley face in the top left corner of the Slate Chalkboard or Gray Block does the trick. The smiley face orients children. When the face is right side up, the number is right side up.

In this section, children will:

- Build correct habits for number formation
- Get extra practice in math skills

Teaching Numbers

Teaching numbers is satisfying. Lessons are visual, auditory, tactile, kinesthetic, and never boring The Slate Chalkboard, Gray Blocks, stories, and songs make learning appealing and effective. Expect excellence!

 The smiley face shows the top left corner. The smiley face helps children orient numbers. The frame gives them a practical frame of reference.

Numbers on the Slate Chalkboard

1, 2, 3, 4, 5, 6, and 7 start at the ☺ in the Starting Corner. When they start there, they are never reversed. Number 8 is a Center Starter and begins like capital S. Number 9 is so special—it has its own corner.

Numbers on the Gray Blocks

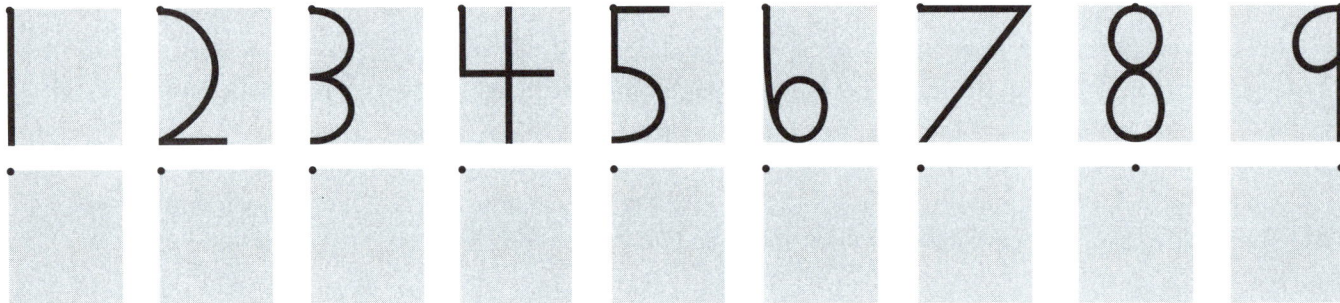

The Gray Blocks represent the inside of the Slate Chalkboard. With Gray Blocks, we transition to pencil and paper. By second grade, children are well on their way with number formations. Use Gray Blocks if you have students that struggle with number reversals.

Number Stories & More

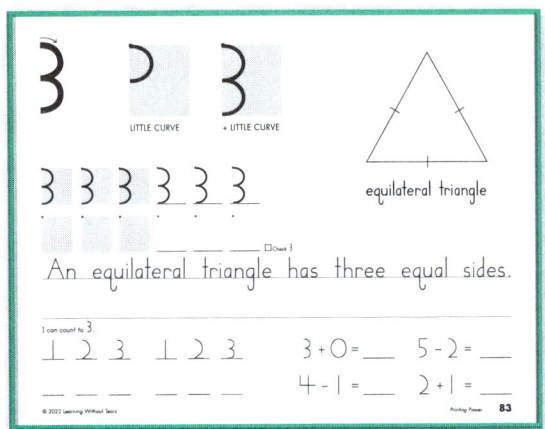

Here's how the student edition pages help you teach:

- Numbers large enough for finger tracing
- Things to count and color
- Number words to read
- Numbers to copy on Gray Blocks
- Numbers to copy on a base line

Number Stories

Fun stories help children remember numbers. Beyond our simple verbal cues, we made up stories that are fun to share and help make these numbers memorable.

1 starts in the Starting Corner.
1 makes a Big Line down.
1 stops in the corner.

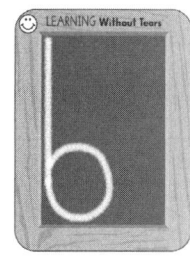

6 starts in the Starting Corner.
6 is a baby bear.
6 goes down to curl up in the corner.
6 is hibernating.

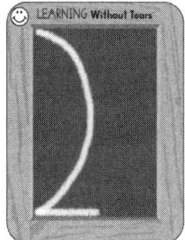

2 starts in the Starting Corner.
2 makes a Big Curve.
2 stops in the corner.
2 walks away on the bottom.

7 starts in the Starting Corner.
7 makes a Little Line across the top.
7 says, "I better slide down."

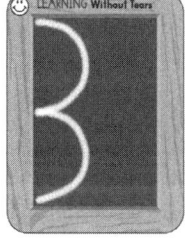

3 starts in the Starting Corner.
3 makes a Little Curve to the middle.
3 makes another Little Curve to the bottom corner.

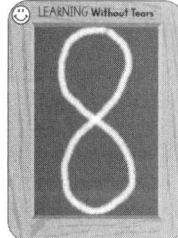

8 is different.
8 doesn't like corners.
8 starts at the top center.
8 begins with S and then goes home.

4 starts in the Starting Corner.
4 makes a Little Line down to the middle.
4 walks across the dark night.
4 jumps to the top and says, "I did it." (Big Line down)

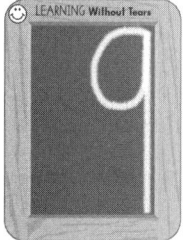

9 is so special.
9 has its own corner.
9 makes a Little Curve and goes up to the corner.
9 makes a Big Line down.

5 starts in the Starting Corner.
5 makes a Little Line down to the middle. It starts to rain.
5 makes a Little Curve around.
5 puts a Little Line on top to stop the rain.

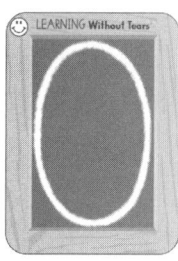

10 uses two places.
1 comes first.
0 is next.
0 starts at the top center.
10 is finished.

About Reversals

Understanding and Preventing Reversals

Do you wonder why children reverse numbers? It's simply because they're transitioning into symbols. They're applying what they know about the real world to symbols. In the real world, position doesn't change identity. A boy is a boy no matter which way he faces. But symbols are different. Position matters. Unlike a boy, letter **b** is not **b** if it faces a different way (**d**), and number **6** is not **6** when it's turned like this: **9**. Welcome to the world of symbols and reversals.

In the past, teachers and families thought of reversals as inevitable and something children had to outgrow. But reversals are not inevitable. They go away when you orient children spatially and teach directionality with the Slate Chalkboard, Gray Blocks, and Number Stories. Children especially enjoy the Wet-Dry-Try activity and you will enjoy the results. That multisensory activity carries over to the Gray Block in *My Printing Book*. Gray Blocks work the same way the Slate Chalkboard does to orient children spatially and help them place numbers correctly.

Correcting Reversals

Even with your good teaching, and even if children write numbers correctly in *My Printing Book*, reversals may still occur on math worksheets. Children are thinking about the answer, not how to write the number. They may just revert back to old ways. You may be tempted to ignore those reversals. Or you may be tempted to correct them all. We suggest a happier, more efficient strategy that works.

1. Check math papers for reversals.

2. Mark only one number reversal per paper. Always mark the lowest number that is reversed. Ignore all other reversals.

3. Help the child with that one number. Re-teach the number with the Slate Chalkboard or Gray Blocks.

Because you always help with the lowest number, that number (perhaps **2**) takes priority, and gets all the teaching it needs. Gradually and systematically, children stop reversing **2**, then **3**, and so on. Gradually, all reversals will be eliminated.

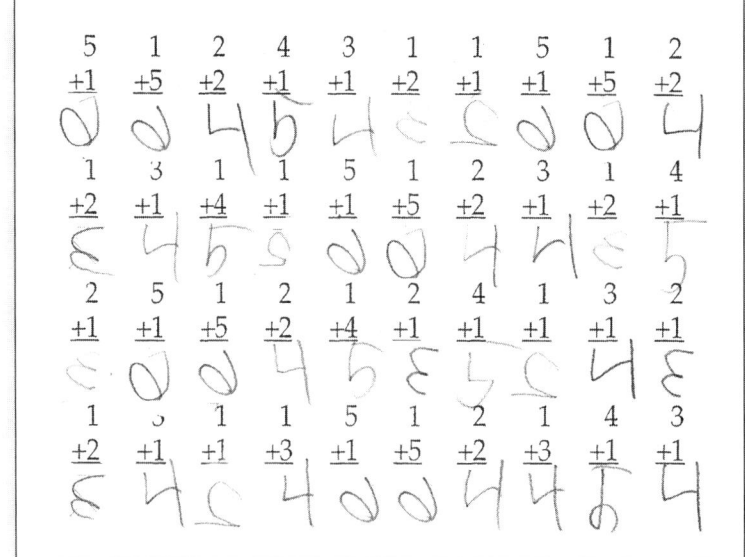

p. 81

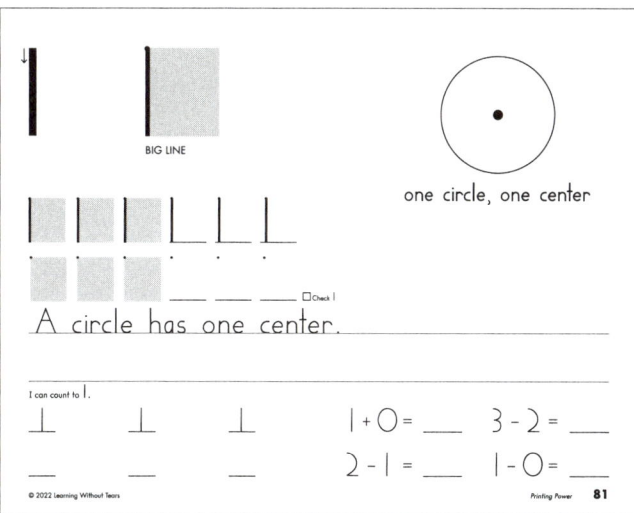

OBJECTIVE
To write number **1** and the word **one** with correct formation.

LESSON INTRODUCTION (Warm Up)
Wet-Dry-Try on the Slate Chalkboard (p. 156)

Additional digital resources are available in the Interactive Digital Teaching Tool (IDTT).

LESSON PLAN

1. Direction Instruction (Demo)

Demonstrate **1** on the Slate Chalkboard, Gray Block, or whiteboard.
Say the words for each step.

 Big Line down

Demonstrate on a single line: **A circle has one center.**

A circle has one center.

2. Guided Practice

Children copy: **1** and **A circle has one center.**
Monitor as children write the number to complete the math problems on their own.

3. Check Number

Help children ✓ their number for correct start and steps.

ENRICHMENT
Explain to children how "one" sounds like "won." and that these are homophones. Ask children to write two sentences using these homophones.

SUPPORT/ELL
Use Number Story **1** to reinforce correct formation (p. 131).

CROSS-CURRICULAR CONNECTIONS
Math: Practice word problems. Write real-life word problems and have children work together to solve.

2

Printing Power – p. 82

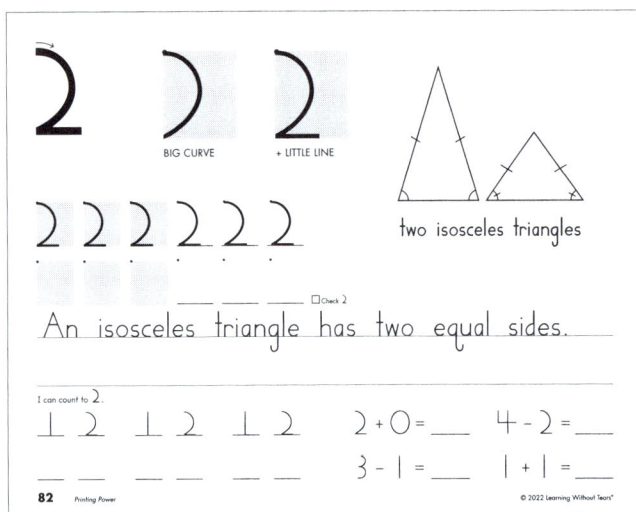

OBJECTIVE
To write number 2 and the word **two** with correct formation.

LESSON INTRODUCTION (Warm Up)
Door Tracing (p. 155)

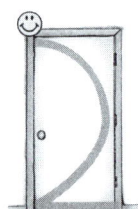

Additional digital resources are available in the Interactive Digital Teaching Tool (IDTT).

LESSON PLAN

1. Direction Instruction (Demo)

Demonstrate 2 on the Slate Chalkboard, Gray Block, or whiteboard. Say the words for each step.

Big Curve to the bottom
Little Line across

Demonstrate on a single line: **An isosceles triangle has two equal sides.**

An isosceles triangle has...

2. Guided Practice

Children copy: 2 and **An isosceles triangle has two equal sides.**
Monitor as children write the number to complete the math problems on their own.

3. Check Number

Help children  their number for correct start and steps.

ENRICHMENT
Use the student edition to read/count out loud by 2s. Start on page 2 and read the left-hand page numbers to 10 or more. Write the even numbers on single lined paper.

SUPPORT/ELL
Use Number Story 2 to reinforce correct formation (p. 131).

CROSS-CURRICULAR CONNECTIONS
Math: Practice understanding place value. Give children a two-digit number and have them mentally find 10 more or 10 less.

p. 83

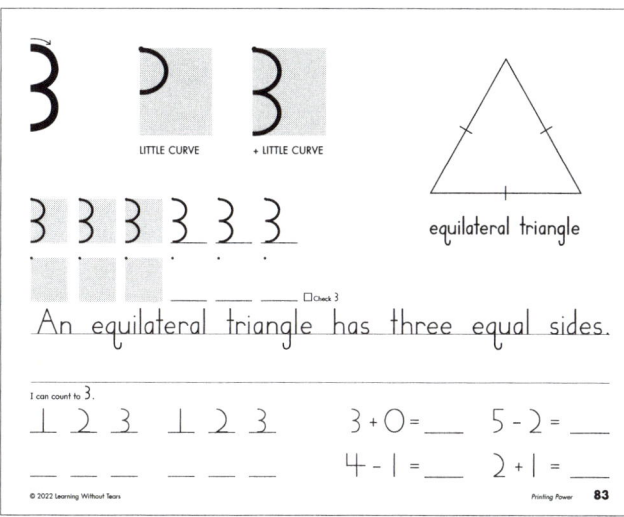

OBJECTIVE
To write number **3** and the word **three** with correct formation.

LESSON INTRODUCTION (Warm Up)
SONG: "My Teacher Writes" from *Rock, Rap, Tap & Learn* music album

Additional digital resources are available in the Interactive Digital Teaching Tool (IDTT).

LESSON PLAN

1. Direction Instruction (Demo)

Demonstrate **3** on the Slate Chalkboard, Gray Block, or whiteboard.
Say the words for each step.

Little Curve to the middle
Little Curve to the bottom

Demonstrate on a single line: **An equilateral triangle has three equal sides.**

An equilateral triangle has...

2. Guided Practice

Children copy: **3** and **An equilateral triangle has three equal sides.**
Monitor as children write the number to complete the math problems on their own.

3. Check Number

Help children  their number for correct start and steps.

ENRICHMENT
As a class, compare three-digit numbers using greater than, less than, and equal signs.

SUPPORT/ELL
Use Number Story **3** to reinforce correct formation (p. 131).

CROSS-CURRICULAR CONNECTIONS
Math: Have children draw triangles and label the angles: **1, 2,** and **3.** Review the terms "angle" and "tri."

4

Printing Power – p. 84

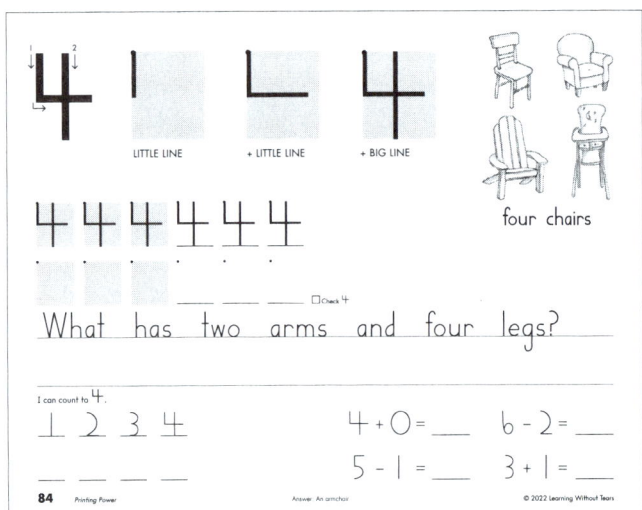

OBJECTIVE

To write number **4** and the word **four** with correct formation.

LESSON INTRODUCTION (Warm Up)

SONG: "Number Song" from *Rock, Rap, Tap & Learn* music album

Additional digital resources are available in the Interactive Digital Teaching Tool (IDTT).

LESSON PLAN

1. Direction Instruction (Demo)

Demonstrate **4** on the Slate Chalkboard, Gray Block, or whiteboard. Say the words for each step.

Little Line down
Little Line across the middle
Big Line down the center

Demonstrate on a single line: **What has two arms and four legs?**

What has two...

2. Guided Practice

Children copy: **4** and **What has two arms and four legs?**
Monitor as children write the number to complete the math problems on their own.

3. Check Number

Help children 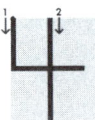 their number for correct start and steps.

ENRICHMENT

Have children draw different shapes that have four sides such as squares and rectangles. Have children draw a picture with these shapes.

SUPPORT/ELL

Use Number Story **4** to reinforce correct formation (p. 131).

CROSS-CURRICULAR CONNECTIONS

Math: Discuss how shapes with **4** sides are similar and different. Examples include: square, rectangle, trapezoid and rhombus.

p. 85

OBJECTIVE
To write number **5** and the word **five** with correct formation.

LESSON INTRODUCTION (Warm Up)
Wet-Dry-Try on the Slate Chalkboard (p. 156)

Additional digital resources are available in the Interactive Digital Teaching Tool (IDTT).

LESSON PLAN

1. Direction Instruction (Demo)

Demonstrate **5** on the Slate Chalkboard, Gray Block, or whiteboard. Say the words for each step.

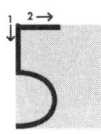 Little Line down to the middle
Little Curve to the bottom
Little Line across the top

Demonstrate on a single line: **I count by fives: five, ten, fifteen.**

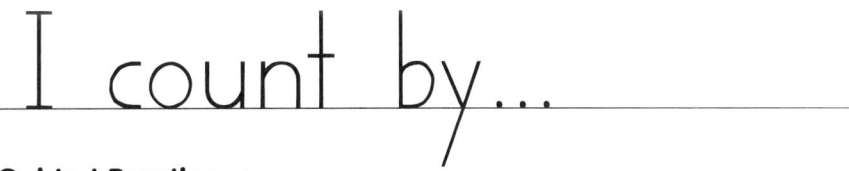

2. Guided Practice

Children copy: **5** and **I count by fives: five, ten, fifteen.**
Monitor as children write the number to complete the math problems on their own.

3. Check Number

Help children ✓ their number for correct start and steps.

ENRICHMENT
Have children trace fingers and hands and count by **5**s to see how many fingers are in the class.

SUPPORT/ELL
Use Number Story **5** to reinforce correct formation (p. 131).

CROSS-CURRICULAR CONNECTIONS
Language Arts: As a class, write a 5-line poem called a cinquain. Research online and decide what you want your focus to be.

6

Printing Power – p. 86

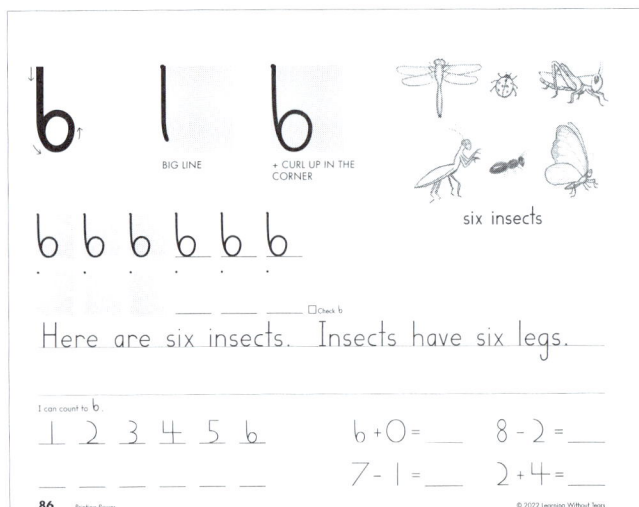

OBJECTIVE
To write number **6** and the word **six** with correct formation.

LESSON INTRODUCTION (Warm Up)
Digital Letter and Number Formations (p. 164)

Additional digital resources are available in the Interactive Digital Teaching Tool (IDTT).

LESSON PLAN

1. Direction Instruction (Demo)

Demonstrate **6** on the Slate Chalkboard, Gray Block, or whiteboard. Say the words for each step.

Big Line down
Turn and curl up

Demonstrate on a single line: **Here are six insects. Insects have six legs.**

2. Guided Practice

Children copy: **6** and **Here are six insects. Insects have six legs.**
Monitor as children write the number to complete the math problems on their own.

3. Check Number

Help children ✓ their number for correct start and steps.

ENRICHMENT
Have children write a number sentence using the number words five and six.

SUPPORT/ELL
Use Number Story **6** to reinforce correct formation (p. 131).

CROSS-CURRICULAR CONNECTIONS
Math: Have children practice telling time. Explain when the minute hand is on the **6**, you are half-way through the hour.

p. 87

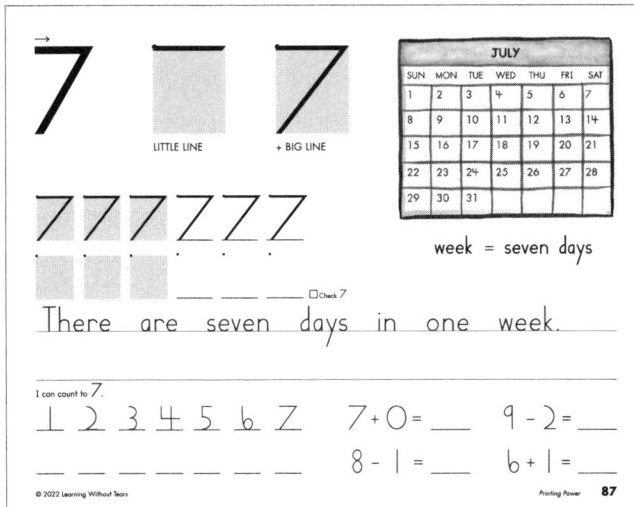

OBJECTIVE
To write number **7** and the word **seven** with correct formation.

LESSON INTRODUCTION (Warm Up)
Door Tracing (p. 155)

Additional digital resources are available in the Interactive Digital Teaching Tool (IDTT).

LESSON PLAN

1. Direction Instruction (Demo)

Demonstrate **7** on the Slate Chalkboard, Gray Block, or whiteboard. Say the words for each step.

Little Line across the top
Big Line slides down

Demonstrate on a single line: **There are seven days in one week.**

There are seven...

2. Guided Practice

Children copy: **7** and **There are seven days in one week.**
Monitor as children write the number to complete the math problems on their own.

3. Check Number

Help children  their number for correct start and steps.

ENRICHMENT
Add numbers to a blank calendar. Show children how there are **7** days in one week. Count the number of weeks.

SUPPORT/ELL
Use Number Story **7** to reinforce correct formation (p. 131).

CROSS-CURRICULAR CONNECTIONS
Language Arts: Discuss the days of the week. Compare what activities children do on weekends compared to activities during the school week.

8

Printing Power – p. 88

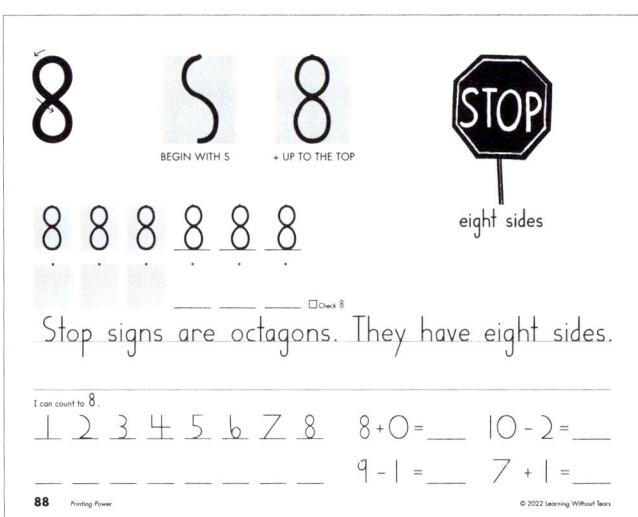

OBJECTIVE

To write number **8** and the word **eight** with correct formation.

LESSON INTRODUCTION (Warm Up)

Digital Letter and Number Formations (p. 164)

Additional digital resources are available in the Interactive Digital Teaching Tool (IDTT).

LESSON PLAN

1. Direction Instruction (Demo)

Demonstrate **8** on the Slate Chalkboard, Gray Block, or whiteboard. Say the words for each step.

 Begin with S
Up to the top

Demonstrate on a single line: **Stop signs are octagons. They have eight sides.**

2. Guided Practice

Children copy: **8** and **Stop signs are octagons. They have eight sides.**
Monitor as children write the number to complete the math problems on their own.

3. Check Number

Help children ✓ their number for correct start and steps.

ENRICHMENT

Have children draw shapes with **four**, **six**, and **eight** sides. Have children write the name of each shape.

SUPPORT/ELL

Use Number Story **8** to reinforce correct formation (p. 131).

CROSS-CURRICULAR CONNECTIONS

Math: Have children make an octagon from a square by folding a piece of paper and counting off the four corners.

p. 89

9

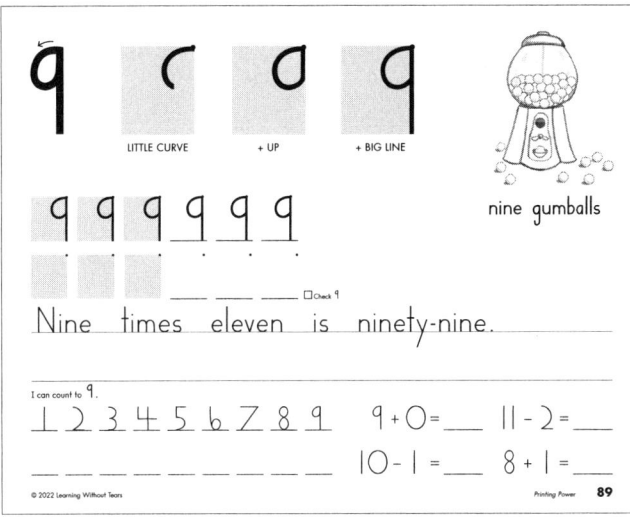

OBJECTIVE
To write number 9 and the word **nine** with correct formation.

LESSON INTRODUCTION (Warm Up)
Air Writing (p. 162)

Additional digital resources are available in the Interactive Digital Teaching Tool (IDTT).

LESSON PLAN

1. Direction Instruction (Demo)

Demonstrate 9 on the Slate Chalkboard, Gray Block, or whiteboard. Say the words for each step.

Little Curve up
Big Line down

Demonstrate on a single line: **Nine times eleven is ninety-nine.**

Nine times eleven...

2. Guided Practice

Children copy: 9 and **Nine times eleven is ninety-nine.**
Monitor as children write the number to complete the math problems on their own.

3. Check Number

Help children  their number for correct start and steps.

ENRICHMENT
Lowercase a and 9 start the same way. Demonstrate and ask children to show you how they can make an a change into 9.

SUPPORT/ELL
Use Number Story 9 to reinforce correct formation (p. 131).

CROSS-CURRICULAR CONNECTIONS
Social Studies: Discuss the importance of 911 and when it should be used.

10

Printing Power – p. 90

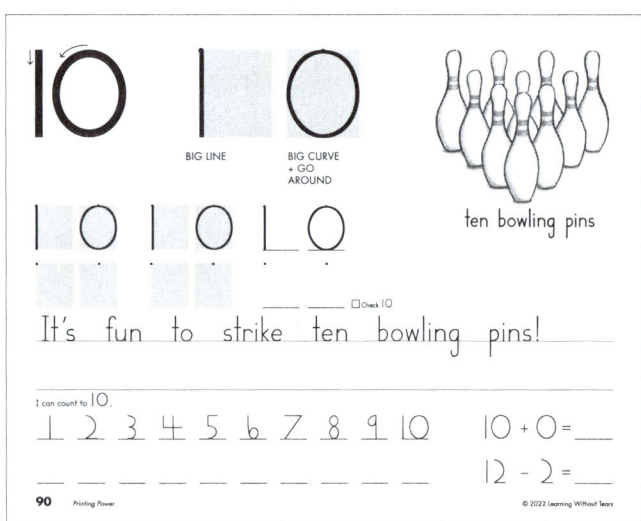

OBJECTIVE
To write number **10** and the word **ten** with correct formation.

LESSON INTRODUCTION (Warm Up)
Laser Letters (p. 163)

Additional digital resources are available in the Interactive Digital Teaching Tool (IDTT).

LESSON PLAN

1. Direction Instruction (Demo)

Demonstrate **10** on the Slate Chalkboard, Gray Block, or whiteboard. Say the words for each step.

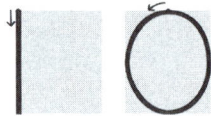

Big Line down
Big Curve go around

Demonstrate on a single line: **It's fun to strike ten bowling pins!**

It's fun to...

2. Guided Practice

Children copy: **10** and **It's fun to strike ten bowling pins!**
Monitor as children write the number to complete the math problems on their own.

3. Check Number

Help children ✓ their number for correct start and steps.

ENRICHMENT
Have children write in ten's up to **100**.

SUPPORT/ELL
Use Number Story **10** to reinforce correct formation (p. 131).

CROSS-CURRICULAR CONNECTIONS
Math: Practice mental math using **10**. Have children add or subtract **10** from a given number up to **100**.

Math Problems

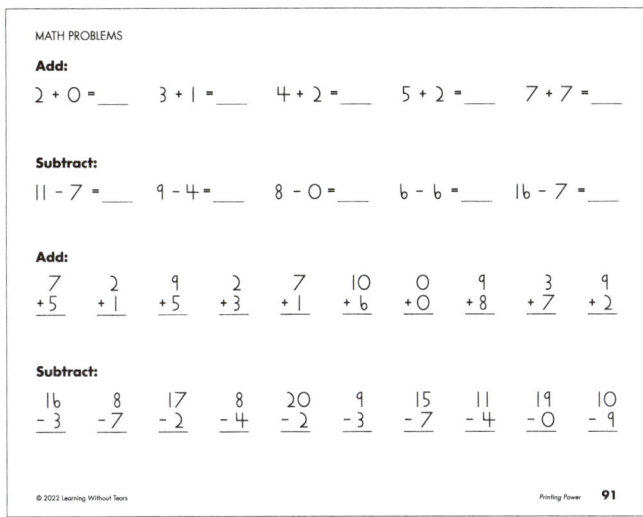

OBJECTIVE
To use numerals to write solutions for addition and subtraction problems.

LESSON INTRODUCTION (Warm Up)
Discuss addition and subtraction problems and how math problems can be written in different ways.

> Additional digital resources are available in the Interactive Digital Teaching Tool (IDTT).

LESSON PLAN

1. Direction Instruction (Demo)
Compare the two ways to write addition and subtraction problems. Demonstrate both.

Add: 2 + 0 = ___   **Subtract:** 11 − 7 = ___   **Add:** 7 + 5   **Subtract:** 16 − 3

2. Guided Practice
Monitor as children complete the addition and subtraction problems.

3. Check Numbers
Check to see if children solve the problems and write the answers correctly.

ENRICHMENT
Create other worksheets for children to solve math problems.

SUPPORT/ELL
If there is any difficulty with solving the math problems, give children counters to help them.

CROSS-CURRICULAR CONNECTIONS
Math: As a class, use **10** small plastic cups to make pyramids. Compare base and height when using different cups for the base.

1 & 2 Digit Numbers

Printing Power – p. 92

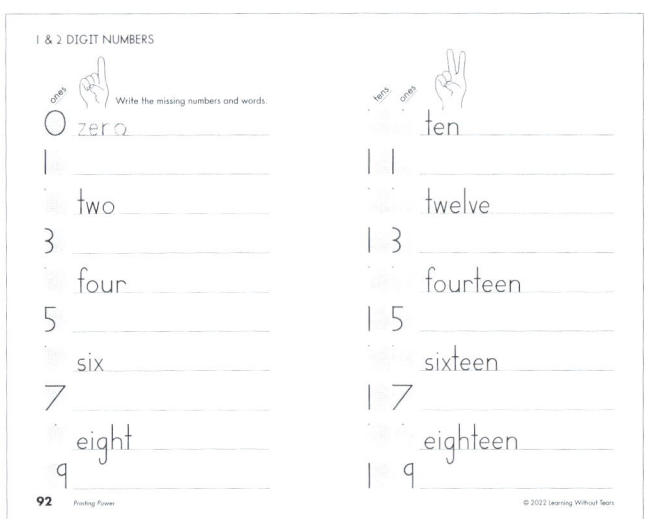

OBJECTIVES
To write one- and two-digit numerals and number words.

LESSON INTRODUCTION (Warm Up)
Laser Numbers (p. 163)

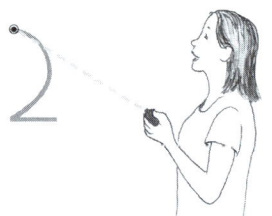

Additional digital resources are available in the Interactive Digital Teaching Tool (IDTT).

LESSON PLAN

1. Direction Instruction (Demo)

Demonstrate **0** and **1** on the Slate Chalkboard, Gray Block, or whiteboard. Demonstrate **zero** and **one** on double lines.

2. Guided Practice

Children copy: **0** and **1** and **zero** and **one**.
Observe as children complete the page on their own.

3. Check Numbers and Words

Monitor as children write their numbers for correct start and steps, and check their words for correct size, placement, and closeness.

ENRICHMENT
The "preteen" number words eleven and twelve don't follow the ending of "teen" in numbers 13–19. Have children write a sentence using one of these number words.

SUPPORT/ELL
In order to reinforce the numbers, have children count concrete objects in the classroom.

CROSS-CURRICULAR CONNECTIONS
Math: Have children practice counting backwards from **20–0**.

p. 93

2 & 3 Digit Numbers

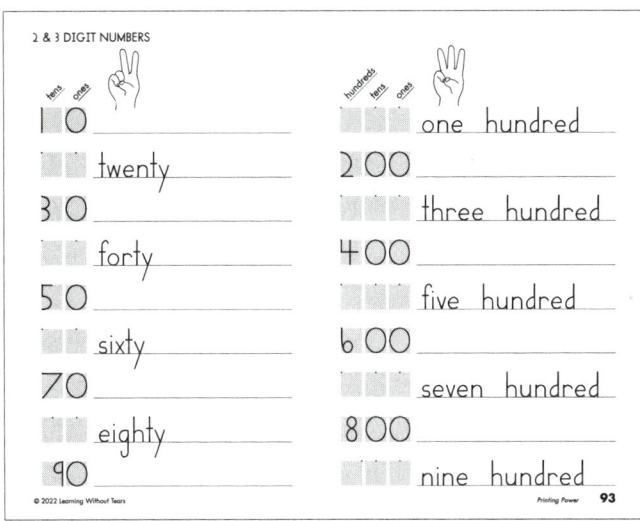

OBJECTIVES
To write two- and three-digit numerals and number words.

LESSON INTRODUCTION (Warm Up)
Digital Letter and Number Formations (p. 164)

Additional digital resources are available in the Interactive Digital Teaching Tool (IDTT).

LESSON PLAN

1. Direction Instruction (Demo)
Demonstrate **10** and **20** on the Slate Chalkboard, Gray Block, or whiteboard. Demonstrate **ten** and **twenty** on double lines.

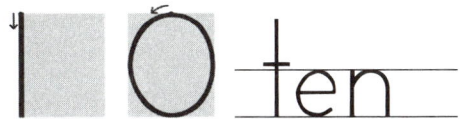 

2. Guided Practice
Children copy: **10** and **20** and **ten** and **twenty**.
Observe as children complete the page on their own.

3. Check Numbers and Words
Monitor as children write their numbers for correct start and steps, and check their words for correct size, placement, and closeness.

ENRICHMENT
Teach children to hyphenate between the tens and the ones when writing out numbers as words. Examples: **21**, twenty-one; **22**, twenty-two; etc.

SUPPORT/ELL
Help children say the irregular numbers: twenty, thirty and fifty. Then say the numbers sixty, seventy, eighty, and ninety to follow the pattern of adding **ty** or **y**.

CROSS-CURRICULAR CONNECTIONS
Math: As a class, add and subtract within **1,000**. Skip count by **10**s. Talk about how **10** bundles of **10** equals **100**.

Final Check

Printing Power – p. 94

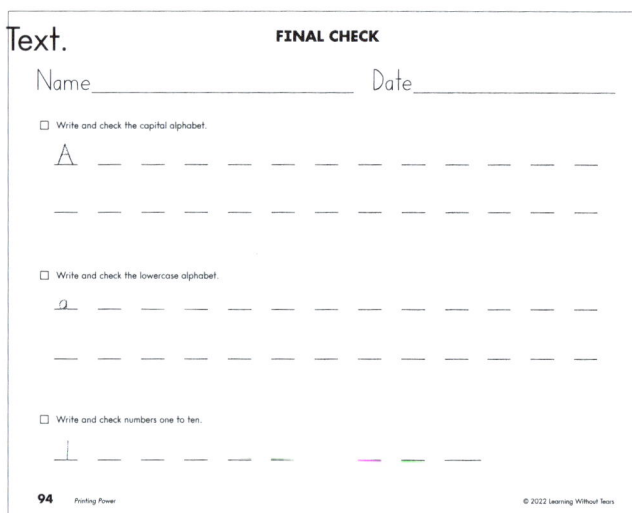

OBJECTIVE
To check letter and number skills.

LESSON INTRODUCTION (Warm Up)
SONG: "Where Do You Start Your Letters?" from *Rock, Rap, Tap & Learn* music album

FINAL CHECK

1. Administer the Final Check
Tell children to write the capitals, lowercase letters, and numbers in alphabetical and numerical order.

2. Review the Final Check
Review children's capitals, lowercase letters, and numbers.

3. Remediation
Help as needed with missing skills.

Memory: Teach any missing or unrecognizable letters or numbers. Use an Alphabet Desk Strip. Provide multisensory teaching strategies.

Orientation: Correct any reversals. Use Wet-Dry-Try on the Slate for capitals and numbers. Teach lowercase letters in groups. Don't forget about using the Mystery Letter Games!

Size: Use double lines to help children write a grade-appropriate size. Avoid poorly designed worksheets without lines.

Placement: For problems with placing small, tall, or descending lowercase letters, use the Hand Activity, the "Descending Letter Song", and double line paper. For problems with capitals and numbers use the gray block paper.

Note: **Start and sequence** errors can only be observed one-on-one. To remediate errors, use Gray Block Paper for capitals and numbers, the Wet-Dry-Try activity, Mystery Letter Games, and teach letters in similar groups with similar formations (for example: Frog Jump Capitals, Magic C Letters, and Diver Letters).

See pp. 185–191 for additional remediation activities.

MULTISENSORY ACTIVITIES

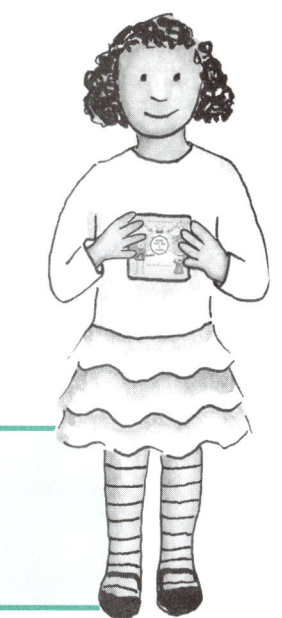

You know the importance of self-directed play and multisensory, active learning. Research is on your side. It supports multisensory teaching to address children's diverse learning styles: visual, tactile, auditory, and kinesthetic.

Activities with hands-on materials address different senses to teach correct formation, spacing, and sequencing. We help children develop their writing skills through explicit, multisensory, play-based instruction.

Each letter lesson begins with a multisensory introduction. There are many fun activities that rotate to add variety and appeal.

Multisensory activities can be hands-on. For example Wet-Dry-Try on the slate. There may also be a digital version of the activity on the Interactive Digital Teaching Tool and Digital Student App.

In this section, children will:

- Move, touch, feel, and manipulate real objects as they learn the habits and skills essential for writing

- Learn songs that make learning fun and memorable

- Engage with technology in a developmentally appropriate manner

- Develop social-emotional skills

Multisensory Cues

This guide has cues throughout the book to indicate that there is a correlating multisensory activity you can do with children in that section. Multisensory activities address children's different senses and bring your teaching to life.

Readiness

Stomp Your Feet   Pencil Grip   Music   Shake Hands With Me

CAPITALS

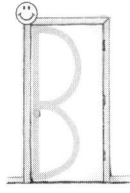 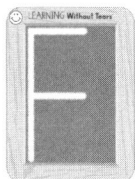

Capitals on the Door   Slate

CAPITALS and Lowercase Letters

Music   Letter Stories   Air Writing   Laser Writing

  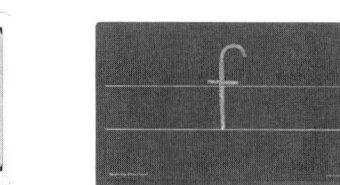 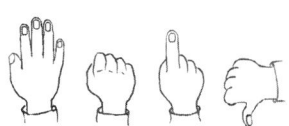

Digital Letter and Number Formations   Wet-Dry-Try App   Blackboard with Double Lines   Hand Activity

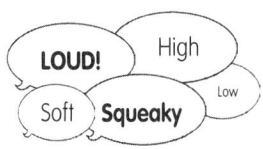  

Voices   "Sentence Song"   Syllables

Songs for Readiness

Music makes learning memorable and joyful. Start by playing the music in the background during free play. This builds familiarity. Then, when you sing during activities, children happily remember and are ready to participate.

Materials
- *Rock, Rap, Tap & Learn* music album

Activity

Choose a song and an activity to go with it.

"Hey, Hey Big Line"
This song teaches positions, (front, back, up, down, Etc.). While singing and dancing. Use the wood pieces and give each child a big line before the beginning of the song.

"Big Line March"
This song builds attention and responsiveness.
Children follow along to learn high/low, up/down, loud/soft. Etc.

"Tapping to the ABC's"
This song teaches the alphabet while having children tap along.
Give each child two wood pieces to tap.

"Diagonals"
This song teaches the diagonal movement. Children can stand up and use their bodies to move to the song.

Shake Hands With Me

Use shaking hands to teach another important skill: directionality. Children can learn to tell left from right easily with this activity. How does it work? We teach only the right hand and associate it with shaking hands. When children learn just the right hand, they're never confused. They know the right, and what's left is left.

Materials
- Lotion
- Rubber stamp
- Scent
- Cup of water

Activity

1. Greeting—Shake hands with each child. Smile and make eye contact.

2. Say, **Hello. This is your right hand. I'm going to do something to your right hand.**
   - Lotion—Put a dab on the right thumb. **Rub your fingers together.**
   - Rubber Stamp—Stamp the right hand. **Look at your right hand now.**
   - Scent—Dab a scent on the right hand to smell.
   - Water—Dip child's right fingertips in a cup. Have them shake fingers.

3. Direct students to raise their right hands and say with you, **This is my right hand. I shake hands with my right hand.**

Top to Bottom

English is a top-to-bottom, left-to-right language. Teaching a top-to-bottom habit is the secret to handwriting success. Children who start letters at the top develop speed and neatness. Those who start from the bottom generally struggle with handwriting.

Often, we judge a young child's writing only by how the letters look. Do not be misled by the appearance of children's letters and numbers. Children's fluency and, ultimately, their neatness depends on their habits for letter and number formation. This is particularly true when writing demands increase. Try this experiment:

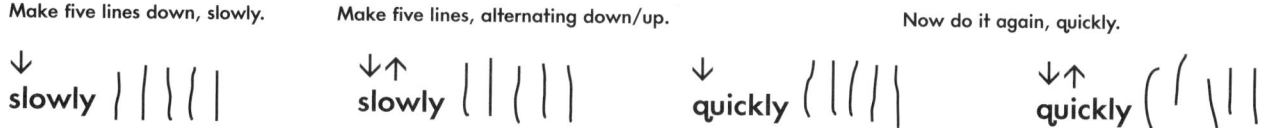

Notice that when you make lines slowly, it doesn't really matter where you start. But, when you add speed, it does matter where you start. Children who start at the top can be fast and neat! Tell families about this. Send children home singing this song to remind families to help children start at the top.

Where Do You Start Your Letters?
Tune: "If You're Happy and You Know It"

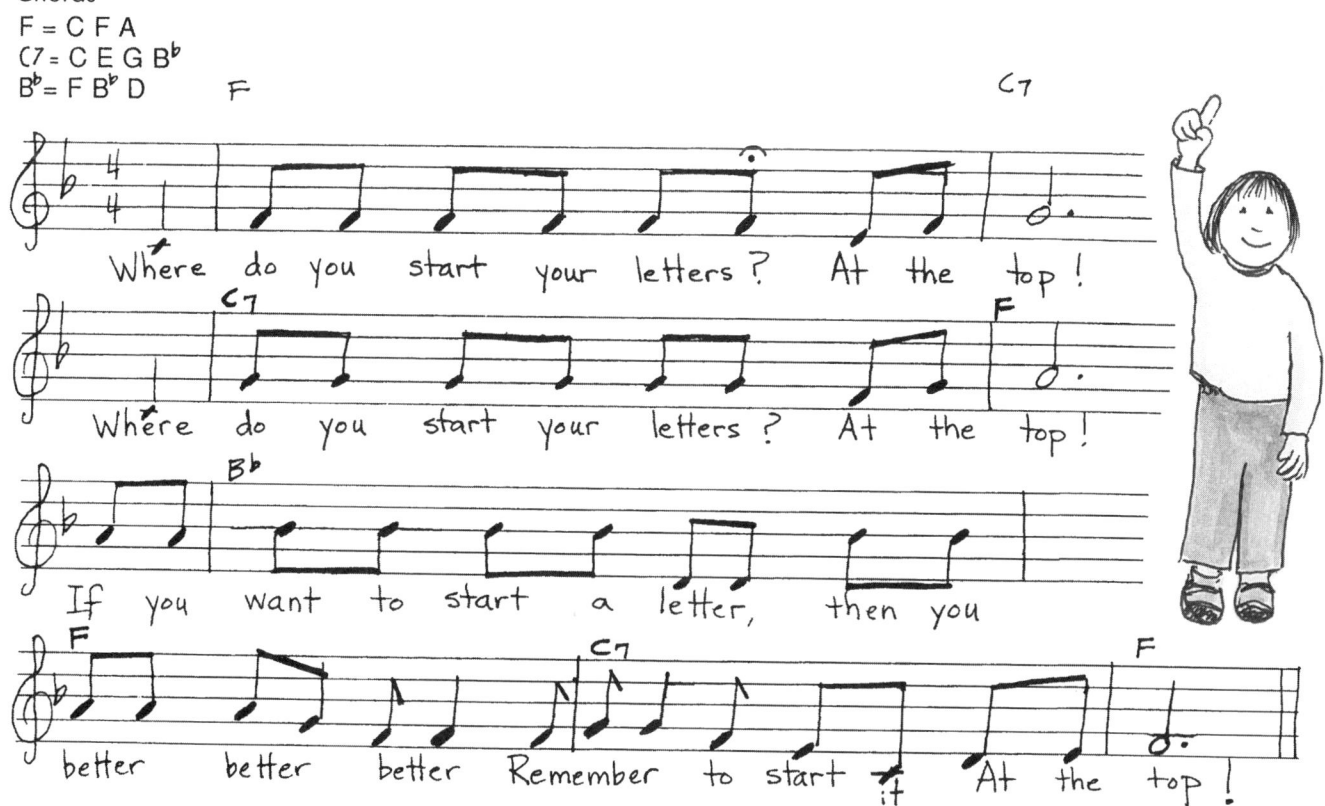

Where Do You Start Your Letters?

Children never forget where to start their letters with this fun song. Not only are they moving and having fun, they are learning prepositions, too!

Materials
- "Where Do You Start Your Letters?" from *Rock, Rap, Tap & Learn* music album

Activity

1. Play "Where Do You Start Your Letters?" in the background as children play so they will become familiar with the lyrics. They'll know the tune from "If You're Happy and You Know It."

2. Sing the song with children. Make a questioning gesture with hands for "Where?" and point high for "At the top!"

3. End by writing a letter on the board.

Capitals on the Door

Doors can do more than open and close. They can also help you teach lessons and end reversals. Just put a smiley face in the top left corner, and the door is ready to help. The smiley face brings a child's eye to the top and to the Starting Corner.

Materials
- Bright yellow smiley face mounted on top left corner of door
- Small laser pointer

Note: In place of a laser pointer, you may also use a flashlight or other small pointer.

Activity

1. Air Write a laser letter on the door for all to see. What letter will it be? Choose a familiar Starting Corner letter, perhaps **B, D, E, F, H, K, L, P, R, V, X,** or **Z** (hide laser beam when jumping to start another stroke).
2. Have children hold their pencils correctly in the air. Everyone checks pencil grips.
3. Children pretend to write on the door by following the laser beam.
4. Children name the letter after you finish writing.

Note: This activity also works well with numbers.

© 2022 Learning Without Tears

Wet-Dry-Try for Capitals

This is a favorite activity. You write a chalk letter and teach each step. Children wet the letter, dry it, and then try it with chalk. The Little Sponge Cubes and Little Chalk Bits reinforce correct grip. Repetition reinforces correct letter formation. Place Little Chalk Bits and Little Sponge Cubes in small cups so children can reach them. This is the physical version. The digital version is available on the Interactive Digital Teaching Tool and Digital Student App.

Materials
- Slate Chalkboard (1 per child)
- Little Chalk Bits (1")
- Little Sponge Cubes (1/2")
- Little cups of water
- Paper towel pieces
- ☺ Capital Formation Chart

Activity

1. **Prepare Slate Chalkboards**
   Write letter with chalk as a model to trace.

2. **Teacher's Part**
   Demonstrate letter on your own Slate Chalkboard. Say the words for each step.

3. **Child's Part - Use the Wet-Dry-Try method**
   (Child says the words for each step)
   Wet: Child uses a Little Sponge Cube to trace the letter.
   Dry: Child uses a Little Piece of paper towel to dry the letter.
   Try: Child uses a Little Chalk Bit to write the letter.

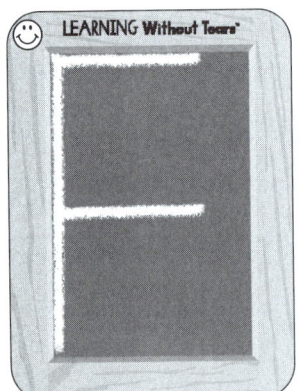  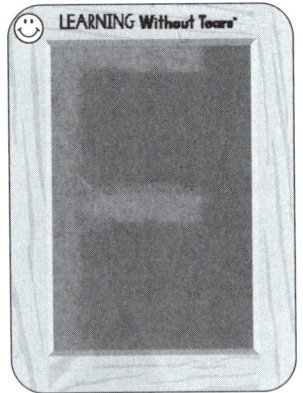 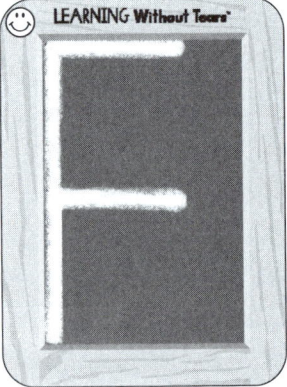

Start in the Starting Corner,
Big Line down, Frog Jump to ☺,
Little Line across the top,
Little Line across the middle

WET:
Wet **F** with sponge,
Wet **F** with wet finger,
Say the words

DRY:
Dry **F** with towel,
Dry **F** with gentle blow,
Say the words

TRY:
Try **F** with chalk,
Say the words

Digital Version

 Interactive Digital Teaching Tool: Share via your interactive whiteboard or smartboard

 Digital Student App: Integrated in lessons and on "My Tools" for additional practice

Mystery Letters on the Slate Chalkboard

You can play Mystery Letters with children as a fun way to develop good habits. Mystery Letter activities teach correct letter formation. The secret is to make the first stroke correctly before telling children the name of the letter they're going to make. This ensures they start the letter correctly.

Materials
- Slate Chalkboard (1 per child)
- Little Chalk Bits (1")
- Paper towel pieces
- Gray Block Paper

Activity

1. Gather the Slate Chalkboards, Little Chalk Bits, and paper towels for erasing.
2. Say the directions for a capital letter, leaving the last part a mystery (see directions below). Have children practice Wet-Dry-Try after completing the letter.

Note: Play the Mystery Letter games to reinforce correct habits for Starting Corner and Center Starting Capitals. You can play these games on Gray Block Paper.

Starting Corner Capitals

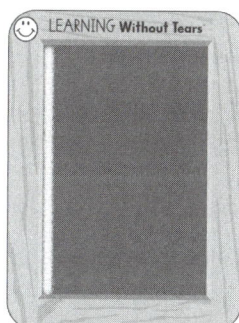

For **F, E, D, P, B, R, N, M,**
Start in the Starting Corner,
Big Line down,
Frog Jump to the Starting Corner,
Now make ____

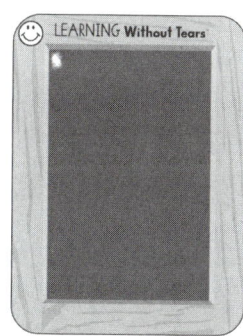

For **H, K, L,**
Start in the Starting Corner,
Big Line down,
Now make ____

For **U, V, W, X, Y, Z**
Start in the Starting Corner,
Now make ____

Center Starting Capitals

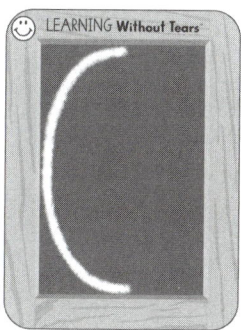

For **C, O, Q, G**
Start at the top center,
Make a Magic C,
Now make ____

For **S, A, I, T, J,**
Start at the top center,
Now make ____

Songs for Capitals

Music makes learning memorable and joyful. Start by playing the album in the background during free play. This builds familiarity. Then, when you sing during activities, children happily remember and are ready to participate.

Materials
- *Rock, Rap, Tap & Learn* music album

Activity

Choose a song and an activity to go with it.

"Frog Jump Letters"
Children stand up and finger trace the Frog Jump Capitals (p. 46) in the air. Let children jump around between the letter exercises.

"Give It A Middle"
This song helps children learn the middle position in letter formation as they finger trace or watch as you model letters on the board.

"Give It A Top"
Children learn about letters that have a top and can follow you as you model these letters on the board or in the air.

Songs for Lowercase

We also use music for lowercase letters. We even have a song to help children remember to leaves spaces when they write sentences. Try them all. Children will soon let you know their favorite.

Materials
- *Rock, Rap, Tap & Learn* music album

Activity
Choose a song and an activity to go with it.

"Sentence Song"
Children learn to start with a capital, write a word, and leave a space. Sung with the "Yankee Doodle" tune, sentences are such fun.

"CAPITALS & lowercase"
This song teaches capital/lowercase letters: **C c**, **O o**, **S s**, **V v**, and **W w**.

"Magic C Rap"
Magic c starts **a**, **d**, and **g**. This song teaches letters with the Magic c.

"Descending Letters"
Singing about **g**, **j**, **y**, **p**, and **q** is fun: **g** and **j** go down and turn, **y** goes sliding down, **p** goes straight down, and **q** goes down with a U-turn.

Letter Stories

Fun stories help children remember letters that are a bit tricky. Beyond our simple verbal cues, we made up some stories that are fun to share and help make these letters memorable. Many of these stories have a Live Teaching Video located in the Resource section of the Interactive Digital Teaching Tool.

b **Honeybee**
Say, "Let's make letter **h**. Now let's make another **h**. I have a surprise. This is an **h** for a honeybee." Turn **h** into **b**.

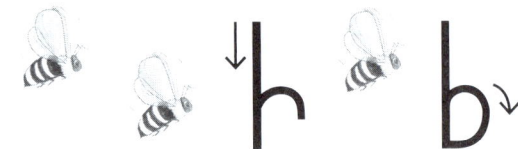

e **Run the Bases**
Place the pencil on the dot. Say, "Batter up to bat. Here comes the pitch. Hit the ball, wait, then run the bases: first, second, third, stop! It's not a home run."

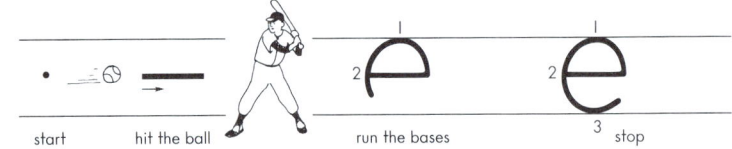

f **Fire Hose Squirts**
Say, "**f** is like water squirting out of a fire hose. It goes up and then falls down."

g **If George Falls**
Say, "Inside **g** lives a little man named George (draw a little face in **g**). He says, 'Ohhhh, if I fall, will you catch me?' Sure, I will catch you (turn the **g** to catch George) if you fall."

k **Karate K**
Say, "The Big Line is Mr. Kaye, your karate teacher. He wants you to show him your kick.

K: Put your chalk in the corner. That's you. Now kick Mr. Kaye. Hiiii-ya. That's the karate **K**.

k: Put the pencil on the line. That's you. Now kick Mr. Kaye. Hiiii-ya. That's the karate **k**."

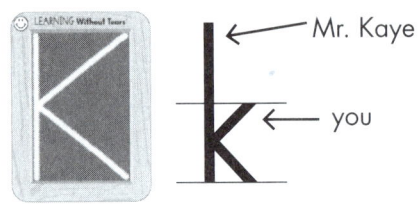

Letter Stories

m

Stinky m

Say, "If **m** has a big gap, people will throw trash in the gap. Don't make a big gap. Make the gap so little, there is only room for an upside down chocolate kiss."

q

U-Turn

Say, "The letter **q** is followed by **u**.
Think of quiet, quit, quibble, quaint, etc.
At the bottom of **q**, stop and make a U-turn."

s

Stop, Drop & Roll with S

Start **s** with a little **c**. Go over and say hello to the smiley face. Say, "What do you do if your clothes catch on fire? You stop, drop, and roll!"

 Say hello to the smiley face.

 Stop, drop, and roll.

Tt

T Is Tall, t Is Tall But…

Say, "Look at me. I can make capital **T**.
Look at me. I can make lowercase **t**.
Capital **T** is tall.
Lowercase **t** is tall, but it's crossed lower.
Capital **T** and lowercase **t** are both tall."

z

Z Chase

Say, "Left hand says, 'I'm going to chase you.' Right hand picks up the pencil and runs across the page.

Left hand says, 'I'm kidding! Come back.'
Right hand slides back down toward the left hand.

Left hand says, 'Ha! I'm going to chase you.'
Right hand runs back across."

(This story is for right-handers with z reversal problems, but can be adapted for lefties.)

 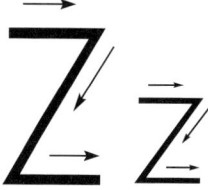

Air Writing

Air Writing is a kinesthetic strategy with visual and auditory components. Picking up and holding pencils adds a tactile component. This strategy allows you to watch the entire class and ensures that all students form their letters correctly.

Materials
- "Air Writing" from *Rock, Rap, Tap & Learn* music album (optional)
- Brightly colored ball

Activity

1. Sing "Air Writing" to prepare the class for participation.
2. Choose a letter. Use a brightly colored ball to trace the letter in the air in front of your class.
3. Have students hold a pencil correctly in the air. Everyone checks pencil grips.
4. Retrace the letter again with your students.

Note: If you are facing your students, make the letter backwards in relation to you so that the letter will be correct from your students' perspective. This activity also works well with numbers.

Laser Letters

Children are always amazed by this activity. You can easily catch their attention when you use a small laser. By using a laser, you provide a nice visual to follow while tracing letters in the air.

Materials
- Small laser pointer
- Chalk or markers
- Large board or easel

Note: In place of a laser pointer, you may also use a flashlight or other small pointer.

Activity

1. Students hold pencils ready to point to laser dot.

2. Teacher points to start of letter and slowly writes a laser letter saying its step-by-step directions.

3. Students follow the laser with their pencils, saying the directions with the teacher.

Note: This activity also works well with numbers.

Digital Formation Tools: Letter & Number

Introducing simple technology into your daily classroom experiences can make learning letters and numbers engaging and fun. This process also exposes young children to the world of technology at an early age.

How to locate:
- Go to +Live Insights, pli.lwtears.com
- Interactive Digital Teaching Tool: These formations are integrated in your letter and number lessons for you to share via your Interactive Whiteboard for in-class learning. They are also located on the Digital Formation Tools for additional practice outside of lessons.
- Student Digital App: Students can access the Letter & Number Formations on "My Tools" for additional practice.

Materials
- Computer or interactive whiteboard (IWB)

Activity

1. Go to the Interactive Digital Teaching Tool. Select Digital Formation Tools. Select Letter & Number Formations.

2. Select a letter or number. Prepare to demonstrate.

3. Children point their pointer fingers at the screen.

4. As children trace the letter, say the parts of the letter.
   We are going to trace F in the air.
   Big line down. Frog Jump, Little line across the top. Little line across the bottom.
   We made an F.

5. Children can take turns coming to the whiteboard to trace and write the letter or number.

A+ Worksheet Maker

The A+ Worksheet Maker includes customizable worksheets. These customizable worksheets can be used for extra practice on double lines. Worksheets include spelling, vocabulary, sentence writing, and more. You can use these worksheets in different subject areas throughout the classroom day.

How to locate:
- Go to +Live Insights, pli.lwtears.com
- Interactive Digital Teaching Tool: Select the A+ Worksheet Maker to create customizable worksheets that can be used for additional practice using the HWT font and double lines outside of handwriting lessons. Worksheets include spelling, vocabulary, sentence writing and more. You can use these worksheets in different subject areas throughout the classroom day.

Activity

1. Select the Interactive Digital Teaching Tool. The A+ Worksheet Maker has its own tab.

2. Select your grade and size of double lines.

3. Choose a worksheet.

4. Customize the worksheet and print.

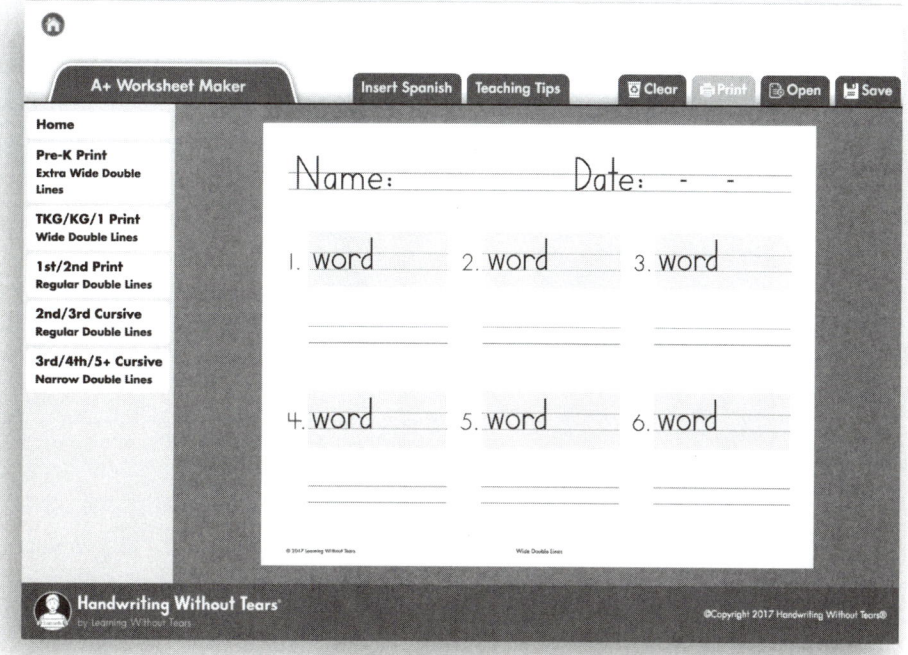

A+ Worksheet Maker

Wet-Dry-Try App

Children love using a tablet and participating in the Wet-Dry-Try App. They will listen to the personal handwriting coach to practice forming letters accurately in a fun way. There are three star levels with Level 1 having full letter formation guidance with audio and permanent visual cues. Level 2 has only flashed visual cues. Level 3 has no visual cues.

Materials
- Tablet with Wet-Dry-Try App installed

Activity

1. Confirm that the app is on each tablet in the classroom.

2. Children will begin by opening the Wet-Dry-Try App.

3. Children will put in their passcode. (This can be found in the teacher's account on Wet-Dry-Try +Live Insights.)

4. You can have children start in a particular section (i.e., capitals, lowercase, or numbers) or you can have them select or specific letter or number to work on.

Wet

Dry

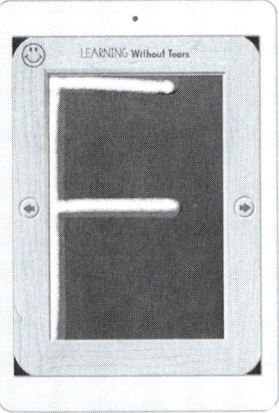
Try

Hand Activity

Children move their hands to show capitals and small, tall and descending lowercase letters. Share the digital animation of this activity located on the resource section of the Interactive Digital Teaching Tool.
Note: Avoid using the Hand Activity if there are children in your class who use sign language.

Activity
Capital & Lowercase Activity
1. Make left hand flat. Say **Capital C**.
2. Make right hand into a fist. Say **Lowercase c**.
3. Continue with **O o**, **S s**, **V v**, **W w**.

Small Lowercase Letters
14 lowercase letters are small: **c**, **o**, **s**, **v**, **w**, and **a**, **u**, **i**, **e**, **r**, **n**, **m**, **x**, **z**.

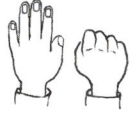  

tall small
C   c   o   s   v   w

Tall Lowercase Letters
7 lowercase letters are just as tall as a capital. Lowercase **t** is as tall as capital, but it's a lowercase letter.

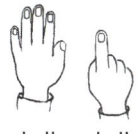      

tall tall
T   t   d   l   k   h   b   f

Descending Lowercase Letters
5 lowercase letters are descending letters. They go below the line.

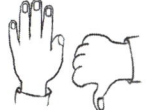  

tall descending
G   g   j   y   p   q

Digital Version

 Interactive Digital Teaching Tool: Share via your interactive whiteboard or smartboard

 Digital Student App: Integrated in lessons and on "My Tools" for additional practice

Wet-Dry-Try for Lowercase Letters

Wet-Dry-Try is an innovative teaching strategy. We use a slate chalkboard for capitals and numbers. For lowercase letters and words we use the Blackboard with Double Lines. This is the physical version. The digital version is available on the Interactive Digital Teaching Tool and Digital Student App. The latest research on brain development supports this activity. This research calls for fewer elements (just two lines), modeling, sensory engagement, and immediate feedback (Sousa 2011).

Materials
- Blackboard with Double Lines* (1 per child)
- Little Chalk Bits (1")
- Little Sponge Cubes (1/2")
- Little cups of water
- Paper towel pieces

Activity

1. **Prepare Blackboards**
   Write letter with chalk as a model to trace.

2. **Teacher's Part – Write f with Chalk**
   Use chalk to write a letter on double lines.
   Say the step-by-step directions.

3. **Child's Part – Wet-Dry-Try**
   As the child does each part, say the step-by-step directions to guide the child. The child is encouraged to join in, saying the words.
   Wet: The child uses a Little Sponge Cube to trace the letter.
   Dry: The child uses a little piece of paper towel to trace the letter.
   Try: The child uses a Little Chalk Bit to write the letter.

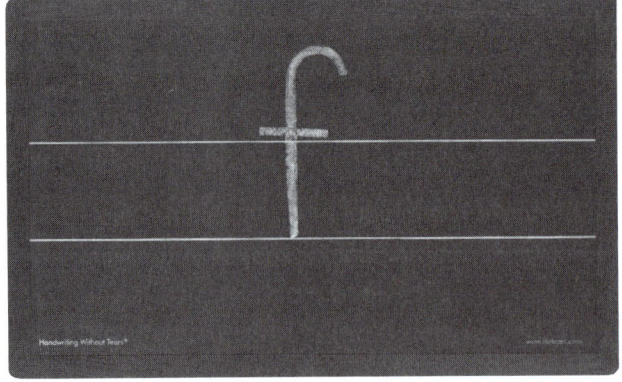 

*If you don't have a Blackboard with Double Lines, consider using our Double Line Writer on your whiteboard. This product is available at LWTears.com

Digital Version

 Interactive Digital Teaching Tool: Share via your interactive whiteboard or smartboard

 Digital Student App: Integrated in lessons and on "My Tools" for additional practice

Voices

Children should learn to write letters in the correct sequence. If you demonstrate with different voices, your students will quickly learn and memorize all the steps. This activity is filled with the repetition children need, but it is so much fun that the repetition is never boring.

Materials
- Large board, prepared with double lines
- Magic C Bunny puppet (optional)

Activity

1. Help children find the step-by-step words in their student edition.
   Read the words together as children point.
   Demonstrate the letter, saying the steps with the children.

2. Let the Magic C Bunny whisper a request for a different voice.
   Slowly demonstrate the letter again using a new voice.
   Children join in by saying the steps and modeling your voice. Repeat.

3. Write the letter. Children put their pencils on the dot. They use their voices together to say the steps as they write.

4. Repeat the activity with different voices: high, low, loud, soft, slow, fast.

Sentence Song

Why do some children runwordstogether? Speech doesn't use spaces between words. Children may naturally write like they talk, without spaces. Bad worksheets can also force children to squeeze words together. By teaching with "Sentence Song" and generous spaces, you boost sentence skills.

Materials
- "Sentence Song" from *Rock, Rap, Tap & Learn* music album

Activity

1. Teach sentence skills as you write on double lines: "We can write."

2. Teach each sentence part as you write:
   W = I start the sentence with a capital letter.
   We = I write a word and leave a space. (Be generous!)
   We can = I write a word and leave a space.
   We can write. = I write the last word. This is the end. I make a period.

3. Play "Sentence Song." Play it again and sing along while you point to the capitalization, spacing, and punctuation with your students.

Syllables

A small word part with one vowel sound is called a syllable. Children move their bodies using different motions for each syllable. Breaking (segmenting) words into syllables helps with reading and spelling.

Activity

1. Say the word for the children: for example, hippopotamus.

2. Have children stand up and complete the syllable activity together while saying the word. For each syllable, move hands to a different part of the body starting at head and moving to shoulders, waist, knees, and feet.

3. Repeat for other words.

hip - po - pot - a - mus

RESOURCES

School-to-Home Connections p. 174

Remediation Tips pp. 175–181

Strategies for English Language Learners pp. 182–184

Strategies for Children with Special Needs pp. 185–187

Handwriting Standards for Written Production pp. 188–189

References p. 190

Index pp. 191–195

School-to-Home Connections

Research consistently shows that a strong school-to-home connection helps children build self-esteem, curiosity, and motivation to learn new things. Home and school are the two most important places for young children. When teachers and families work together, everyone wins. Here are 10 ways to make a strong school-to-home connection:

1. Reinforce learning at home. We developed 😊 A Click Away and Home Links so you can share important handwriting information along the way. The icon above is featured throughout this teacher's guide. It will remind you when it's time to send something home.

2. Find opportunities to communicate during planned school events like family-teacher meetings, conferences, and school visits. Take a few extra steps to communicate through letters, email, and even podcasts. Download our "Second Grade Welcome Letter" from 😊 A Click Away resources at **idtt.LWTears.com/ext/TGPP/2022**.

3. Share important assessment information about your students' progress. Consider using our Screener of Handwriting Proficiency to monitor progress throughout the year at **myLWTears.com**.

4. Share this curriculum with families. Let them play with some of our hands-on products. Tell them about our website, **LWTears.com**, so that they can explore the many resources available.

5. Share music with families. Send children home singing songs from our *Rock, Rap, Tap & Learn* music album. If there is a fun song that families sing at home, ask them to share it with you.

6. Model language and thinking skills out loud. Children benefit from hearing adults talk and solving problems. Send home letter charts so families can use the same language you use in school when talking about letters.

7. Encourage families to read to children as much as possible and to look for letters in the books. Reading is fun and helps build comprehension and language skills. Hunting for letters builds alphabet knowledge.

8. Share the *Printing Power* student edition with families. Send it home when children have completed it. Encourage families to review it with their children and share it with other family members.

9. Help families prepare children to write. Encourage them to learn proper grip and encourage their children to hold a pencil correctly. Teach families how to help children write their names (see next page). These educational articles, along with others, are available for download on 😊 A Click Away resources at **idtt.LWTears.com/ext/TGPP/2022**.

10. Encourage families to help their children to recognize letters and notice letters all around them. Point out signs, logos, and letters wherever you go.

Remediation Tips

HANDWRITING ASSESSMENTS

Handwriting Without Tears® and Get Set for School® have three types of assessments. You can find more information about each assessment at **LWTears.com**. You will also find information about webinars and workshops related to each assessment.

Pre-K Assessments: 1:1 assessments
1. **Readiness & Writing**
2. **Language & Literacy**
3. **Numbers & Math**

Use the Readiness & Writing Assessment to check pre-writing skills: fill-in coloring, grip and hand preference, copying shapes, drawing a person, naming 10 capitals and numbers, and writing name in capitals. To check naming/recognizing all of capitals and lowercase letters, see the Language & Literacy Assessment. For shape and number naming use the Numbers & Math Assessment. See **LWTears.com** for more information.

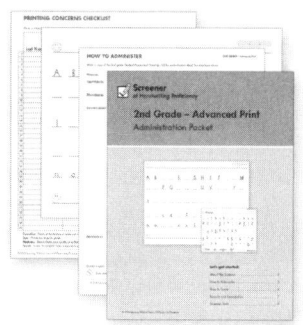

Screener of Handwriting Proficiency
(Printing: Grades K–3+)

Administer the class screener to check handwriting progress three times during the year. Use online scoring for these printing skills: letter/number memory, orientation, placement, and sentence writing. The results show progress for each child and the class. Use the results to plan class instruction and quickly identify children who need further evaluation with The Print Tool.

The Print Tool: 1:1 evaluation
(Printing: Grades K–3+)

The Print Tool is a complete evaluation that includes student and school information, a review of school papers, and careful observation of a child's physical approach and fine motor skills. Administered individually, The Print Tool evaluates capitals, numbers, lowercase letters, and seven specific handwriting components: memory, orientation, placement, size, start, sequence, and word spacing.

When scored, the Evaluate form shows exactly which letters/numbers and components are causing difficulty. Based on this information, remediation is targeted and specific. Children get precisely the materials and strategies they need to remediate their specific difficulties.

Remediation Tips

PHYSICAL APPROACH

Handedness
Switching hands does not allow one hand to become the skilled hand. Observe the child eating, cutting, tapping, etc. The child will usually begin with the skilled hand first. Work with families to promote the use of the dominant, skilled hand.

Pencil Grip
Teaching grip is essential as children begin formal handwriting instruction, but sometimes children will come to you with awkward grips. Start by using golf-size pencils. They are the perfect pencil size for young children and help promote an appropriate grip. We also suggest this strategy:

> **Remediate in 3 stages:**
> 1. Pick-Up – Make circles in the air with a correct grip. Drop and do it again. Repeat five times a day for a couple of weeks.
> 2. Scribble & Wiggle with Pencil Pick-Ups – Complete pencil pick-ups daily at home and at school using a correct grip. Access Pencil-Pickups on ☺ A Click Away.
> 3. Write – Have children write their names with a correct grip. Once they consistently write their name with a correct grip, give them permission to use it for all of their writing.

Adaptive Devices
Experiment with adaptive devices and use them only if they make it easier for the child to hold a pencil. With young children, physical devices should not be used as a substitute for physical demonstration.

Rubber Band Trick
If the pencil is pointing straight up in the air, it will be difficult to write. Loop two rubber bands or ponytail holders together. One goes around the child's writing hand, the other around the pencil.

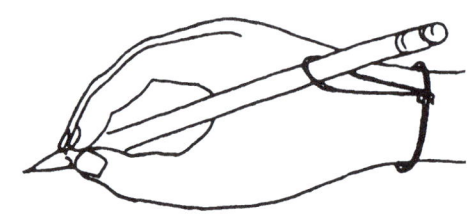

Remediation Tips

 Reward Good Grip
Try using the reward activity to motivate a good grip.

Pencil Pressure
Too Hard: Try a mechanical pencil or placing paper over a mouse pad to provide feedback.
Too Soft: Have children pencil in small shapes until they are black. Use pencils with softer lead.

Name the Helper Hand
A helper hand that twirls hair or props up a forehead will not support the paper. Try naming the helping hand, children find it funny. For example, John's helping hand is called Jacob. You talk to "Jacob" about how it's his job to hold the paper. You are not reprimanding the child, but just the name of their helping hand.

 The Eraser Challenge
Some children spend a lot of time erasing. We suggest giving children a pencil without an eraser and telling them to cross out the mistake. They are less likely to stop and do this. You can also try the Eraser Challenge. This activity is designed for children to be accountable. The goal is that all the erasers are left at the end of the day.

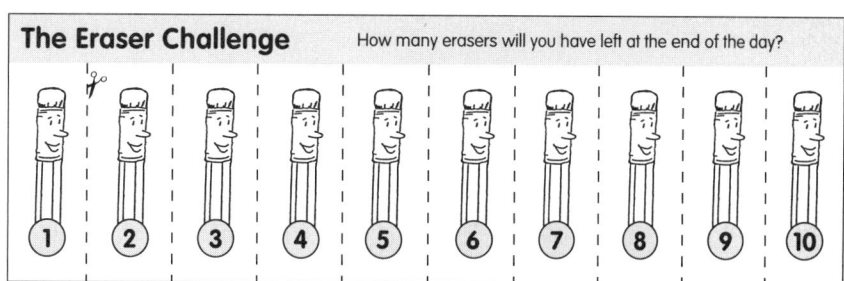

Remediation Tips

CAPITALS

Memory
Memory is being able to picture the letter in your mind. Use consistent language to help children picture the capitals: for example: B has a Big Line and two Little Curves, D has a Big Line and a Big Curve, etc. Active demonstration is the first step. We also suggest these activities:

 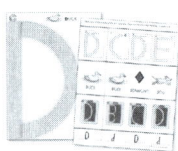   

"CAPITALS & Lowercase" | Capital Letter Cards for Wood Pieces | Mat for Wood Pieces | Wet-Dry-Try Slate | Digital Letter and Number Formations

Orientation
There are several capitals that can be reversed. Use the smiley face to orient children to starting their capitals at the top. Most capitals start in the top left corner. We also suggest these activities:

   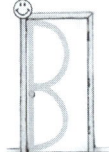 

Mat for Wood Pieces | Gray Block Paper | Wet-Dry-Try Slate | Capitals on the Door | Digital Letter and Number Formations

Placement & Size
All capitals are tall. They sit on the base line. Having children make tally marks and playing tic-tac-toe will help them learn to stop on a line, which is essential for placement. We also suggest these activities:

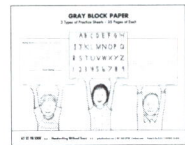  

Gray Block Paper | Digital Letter and Number Formations | A+ Worksheet Maker

Start & Sequence
All capitals will start at the top. Most will start in the top left corner. Some start in the center. Remediate in the three groups: Frog Jump Capitals, Starting Corner Capitals and Center Starting Capitals to help children use correct start and sequence. We also suggest these activities:

"Where Do You Start Your Letters?"
"Frog Jump Letters"
"Sliding Down to the End of the Alphabet" | Wet-Dry-Try Slate | Gray Block Paper | Frog Jump Mystery Letter | A+ Worksheet Maker

Remediation Tips

LOWERCASE

Memory
Quick and automatic recall of letters is important. Memory is essential for independent handwriting. Always spend time comparing capital letters to their lowercase partners so children can quickly and automatically write the correct letter. Demonstration and direct instruction are essential. We also suggest these activities:

"Frog Jump Capitals"

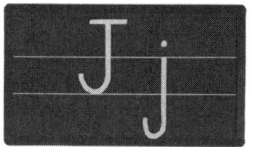
Blackboard with Double Lines

Wet-Dry-Try App

Digital Letter and Number Formations

Orientation
Facing letters in the correct direction is important for reading and spelling. Orientation errors are distracting because children stop and think about which way the letters go. The most common lowercase reversals are the **b** and **d**. Use the Honey Bee Story (p. 160) to fix. We also suggest these activities:

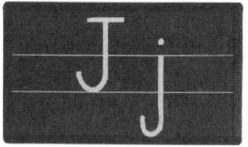
Blackboard with Double Lines

Wet-Dry-Try App

 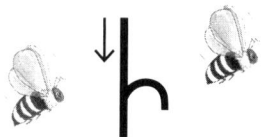
Honey Bee Story

Placement & Size
Placing letters on a line makes writing easier to read. Children need to be able to control their size so their writing isn't too big for their grade. Using the appropriate size double lines is the best way to help children place and write their letters a correct size. Our student editions also promote line generalization, as children will need to write on different lines for success in the classroom. We also suggest these activities:

"Capitals & Lowercase"
"Descending Letters"
"Vowels"

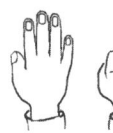 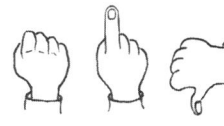 
Hand Activity

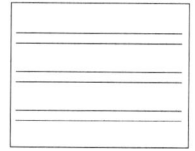
Double Line Paper

A+ Worksheet Maker

Start and Sequence
Correct start and sequence are essential for quick and automatic printing skills. The ability to write letters correctly is acquired through direct teaching and correct practice. We also suggest these activities:

"Where Do You Start Your Letters?"
"Magic c Rap"

Teach in groups:
Magic c
Diver Letters

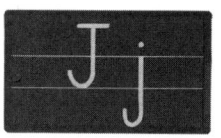
Blackboard with Double Lines

Mystery Letters

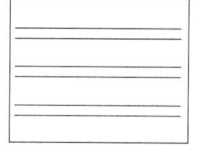
Double Line Paper

A+ Worksheet Maker

Remediation Tips

NUMBERS

Memory
Quick recall of numbers will allow children to focus on math. Active demonstration is the first step. We also suggest these activities:

"My Teacher Writes" Wet-Dry-Try Slate Wet-Dry-Try App Digital Letter and Number Formations

Orientation
There are several numbers that can be reversed. Use the smiley face to orient children to start their numbers at the top. Most capitals start in the top left corner. We also suggest these activities:

 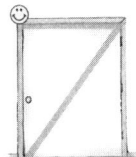 

Wet-Dry-Try Slate Door Tracing Gray Block Paper

Placement & Size
Numbers are the same size as capitals. Having children make tally marks and playing tic-tac-toe will help them learn to stop on a line, which is essential for placement. We also suggest these activities:

Gray Block Paper Digital Letter and Number Formations

Start & Sequence
All numbers will start at the top: numbers 1–7 will start in the top left corner, number 8 starts in the center, number 9 has its own corner. Remediate numbers in chronological order, starting with number 1. We also suggest these activities:

  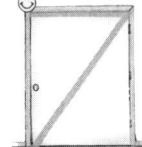  

"Number Song" "10 Fingers" Wet-Dry-Try Slate Wet-Dry-Try App Door Tracing Gray Block Paper Digital Letter and Number Formations

Remediation Tips

SPACING

Having appropriate spacing after words is essential for reading the content. We recommend playing the "Sentence Song" prior to teaching sentence skills to help children remember to leave a space. Direct instruction along with leaving plenty of room after each word is also key for children to understand and see what a space is. We also suggest these activities:

"Sentence Song"

Touching Fingers

Teach your students to put letters in a word close to each other. Have them put their index fingers up and bring them close together, without touching. Say, "In a word, the letters are close, but don't touch." Draw fingers for them on their paper as a reminder.

Sick Sentence Clinic

Write a sentence with the letters too far apart. Circle each word in the sentence. Now, copy the sentence over, putting the letters closer. For example:

I a m b i g.   I am   big.

Now, write a sentence with the letters too close. Children underline each word in the sentence. Now, copy the sentence over with spaces between the words.

Icanrun.   I can   run.

The Nothing Bottle

If students run their words together: Say that you will give them what they need to create spaces. Have them hold out their hands to catch it. Take a huge empty bottle (or any container) and make a big show of pouring into their hands. Ask, "What did you get?" Nothing! Tell them to put nothing after every word they write.

© 2022 Learning Without Tears — Printing Power Teacher's Guide: **Resources** — 181

Strategies for English Language Learners

Our program and research-based teaching strategies help diverse learners master handwriting. We developed them to meet the needs of all learners, including English language learners (ELLs). Our strategies provide simple best practices you can seamlessly integrate into a classroom setting, benefiting all children. Use the following strategies to help your ELL children succeed in your classroom:

Prior Knowledge Activation

Research tells us that children learn more effectively when they already know something about a content area and when concepts in that area mean something to them and to their particular background or culture. When you link new information to a student's prior knowledge, you activate the child's interest and curiosity and infuse instruction with a sense of purpose. Prior knowledge has a large influence on student performance (Dochy, Segers, & Buehl, 1999). English language learners need opportunities to practice previously learned knowledge and what they are presently learning. Hill and Bjork (2008) acknowledge the importance of practice to prevent ELLs from learning incorrectly.

We use child-friendly, consistent language with clear, direct instruction that uses simple verbal cues paired with fun stories for children to make connections and activate prior knowledge. When teaching particular groups of letters, you may ask children what they already know about the letter group like shape, size, and starting position.

Conducive Learning Environment

Research indicates that the prevention of failure among English language learners involves two critical elements: the creation of educational environments that are conducive to their academic success and the use of instructional strategies known to be effective with these students (Ortiz, 1997; Ortiz & Wilkinson, 1991).

To maximize a child's ability to master handwriting, prepare your classroom or teaching space so children can see and hear what you are modeling. You should also ensure that children have the proper materials, including the correct size chairs and desks. Children's feet should be flat on the floor with their arms resting comfortably at the desk. While instructing, you should have children arrange their desks in rows or in a V shape. During guided instruction, you should be strategic in grouping ELLs, rotating them to allow interaction with a variety of English speaking peers.

Strategies for English Language Learners

Cooperative Learning Strategies

According to research, cooperative learning is particularly beneficial for any child learning a second language. Cooperative learning activities promote peer interaction, which helps language development and concept and content learning. It is important to assign ELLs to different teams so they can benefit from English language role models. ELLs learn to express themselves with greater confidence when working in small teams and pick up vocabulary by observing how their peers learn and solve problems.

"Having students work together cooperatively is a powerful way for them to learn and has positive effects on the classroom climate" (David Johnson and Roger Johnson, 2001). Skill grouping reduces anxiety among ELLs, thus, making it an effective format for teaching skills that are difficult to comprehend (MacIntyre and Gardner, 1994). Our program and multisensory activities offer many opportunities for children to be move around and work together in diverse groups to reinforce letter formation.

Multisensory Instruction

Numerous individuals report the importance of using visual, auditory, and tactile aids to make content more understandable to ELLs (Carey, 2007; Herrell & Jordan, 2008; Samway & Taylor, 2008). Our multisensory instruction and interactive activities include strategies to address the diverse learning styles of all children. We have methods to meet the needs of auditory, visual, tactile, and kinesthetic learners. For auditory learners, we use consistent, child-friendly language that helps children learn and remember easily. To meet the needs of visual learners, we provide step-by-step illustrations of letter formation and give clear visual direction. Our clean, uncluttered, and black and white pages also support a visually simple format to support the learning style of visual learners. Our student editions have step-by-step models that are big enough for finger tracing to meet the needs of tactile letters, and we use music and movement to engage kinesthetic learners. Additional strategies include using dough to form letters and playing visual memory games.

Thematic Instruction

Research reports that themes help children understand new concepts. They provide mental organizing schemes for students to approach new ideas (Caine & Caine, 1997; Kovalik, 1994). Our teaching order helps children learn handwriting skills in the easiest, most efficient way. Specifically, we teach letter formation in groups that have similar strokes. These thematic groups allow children to repeat important vocabulary words that are common to letter groups and promote good writing habits.

Repeated Lesson/Concept/Vocabulary

Recent research (Rydland & Aukrust, 2005) states the importance of second language learners' use of repetition for conversational participation and language learning. Research also indicates that word repetition is a favorable condition in vocabulary learning (Nation, 2001). We use consistent, child-friendly terminology for teaching letter formation and specifically repeat the same vocabulary through the lessons and grade levels. We do not make assumptions about what a child knows, and our direct instruction only uses words that children are familiar with and uses as few words as possible. As children practice writing letters and words, have them repeat the letter formation steps as they form letters and words.

Strategies for English Language Learners

Ensure that they use the same vocabulary. You can also have children create flash cards with the letters on one side and vocabulary/pictures on the other side (review the cards repeatedly). Alternate the side of the card that is used as the prompt and have children work in pairs to quiz one another.

Immediate Feedback

Research shows that "immediate feedback motivates students to make necessary adjustments, encourages cooperation with and support of others, increases student response, and promotes activity and harmony within the group" (Weissglass 1996). Research also shows that learning improves with consistent feedback (Linnenbrink & Pintrich, 2002; Pintrich & Schunk, 2002; Heath & Glen, 2005). In addition, when children work cooperatively, you should strive to provide immediate feedback.

We provide ample opportunities to assess skill mastery within the student editions, enabling you to quickly determine if you need to re-teach or give specific support. We also provide additional resources online for additional skill assessment.

Think-Aloud Modeling/Metacognition (Show and Tell)

According to research, modeling thought processes helps students become more aware of their own thinking (Simons 1995; Resnick and Klopfer 1989, Paris and Winograd 1990). As you model letter formation, we provide simple step-by-step instructions to help children learn the correct steps for forming letters. After you model thinking aloud, children can work in pairs and model to one another.

Differentiated Instruction

Research indicates that a student's learning profile includes learning style (i.e., visual, auditory, tactile, or kinesthetic), grouping preferences (i.e., individual, small group, or large group), and environmental preferences (i.e., lots of space or a quiet area to work). You may differentiate instruction based on any one of these factors or any combination of factors (Tomlinson, 1999). Research also indicates that although some of the techniques may remain the same, it is necessary that you differentiate instruction for ELLs to accommodate the different levels of language development (Genesee, Lindholm-Leary, Saunders, & Christian, 2006).

We provide many opportunities to differentiate instruction for diverse learners. By recognizing a child's prior knowledge, readiness, language, learning styles, and interests, you are able to meet the needs of all learners. You can group children according to different learning styles or you can also group them by level of mastery (i.e., advanced children may be grouped with and can support struggling children).

Strategies for Children with Special Needs

Handwriting Without Tears® can be used easily and effectively for children with disabilities. Here are some suggestions:

Fine Motor Activities
To help children with fine motor delays, use the first 10–15 minutes of a session doing fine motor work. If children are delayed in their fine motor skills, they will likely need extra help with handwriting. Spend the last 10 minutes of a session forming letters.

Autism Spectrum Disorder (ASD)
Often, concentration and compliance are challenging for children with autism, so they may struggle with handwriting, fine motor skills, or perceptual delays. Children on the autism spectrum who are high functioning, such those with Asperger's Syndrome, tend to relate well to tangible, hands-on materials. Children who do not respond well to verbal cues (language) usually do well with the Handwriting Without Tears program. You can demonstrate many of the teaching techniques with few or no verbal cues as the child attends visually to the task. Teacher demonstration and child imitation are the keys to successful handwriting. Keep these tips in mind when teaching children with ASD:

- Use as many multisensory experiences as possible
- Use the Magic C Bunny to incorporate socialization and interaction
- Be very consistent with the child
- Be careful when using abstract teaching strategies; children with ASD tend to take things literally.

Down Syndrome
Use several multisensory activities and repetitions. If the child has a classroom assistant (IEP aide), allow extra time for the child to practice handwriting. Because the child may be easily distracted, you may want to schedule extra time for breaks. Here are some tips for working with children who have low muscle tone (hypotonia) due to Down Syndrome:

- If the child struggles with writing because of low muscle tone, have them write in all capital letters
- Assess the child's comfortable size of writing
- Use a modified pencil grasp
- Adapt seating in the classroom and at home
- Work on extra fine motor activities to strengthen the hands.

Strategies for Children with Special Needs

Poor Vision

If a child has poor vision, modify teaching materials appropriately. Here are some ideas to increase the visibility of teaching materials:

- Use brightly colored paints with a bright contrasting mat (black and white works well)
- Enlarge all student edition pages
- Use a larger slate for capitals and numbers (11" x 17")
- Use a window guide to grade the size of handwriting
- Double lines can work well for children with poor vision
- Enlarge or thicken lines with a marker until the child is comfortable with the chosen size
- Provide a texture on the lines to help the child locate the line position.

Cerebral Palsy

To help a child with cerebral palsy, begin by establishing good positioning. If the child is in a wheelchair, try using a lap tray during writing time for support and stability of the arms and shoulders. If the child only has use of one extremity, clamp down paper and other materials using a clipboard clamp screwed into the lap tray. Once good writing position has been established, try these tips for writing success:

- If the child has problems with muscle tone, try an adapted pencil grip for more control of the pencil.
- Children with cerebral palsy may do better initially writing in capitals, which are developmentally easier to read and write.
- If the child has perceptual or visual problems, it may help to enlarge the worksheets and darken the print.

Dyslexia

Dyslexic children typically struggle with organization and using language effectively. Often, they struggle with writing because letter formation is not automatic. The teaching techniques help the child develop good habits: starting at the top with letter formation; learning a left-to-right flow in the sequence of reading and writing; and learning consistent, child-friendly terminology when learning letter formation. Help a child with dyslexia in the following ways:

- Use the Slate and Gray Blocks to correct letter and number reversals.
- Introduce Wood Pieces to teach correct formation of all capital letters.
- Use the double lines to teach consistency in placement of letters on the lines.
- Teach letters in groups of similar strokes, as taught in the student editions.
- Provide many opportunities for review and mastery lessons.

Strategies for Children with Special Needs

Dysgraphia
Children with dysgraphia have trouble producing written language due to poor motor planning. They may struggle with organizational skills and movements that need to be in an automatic and specific order, such as the formation of letters for writing. This can cause handwriting to be illegible or contain irregular and inconsistent letter formations. Children with dysgraphia can be scattered in their writing habits. For example, their writing is sometimes a mixture of lowercase and capital letters. You can help organize these children in the following ways:

- Teach the shapes (parts and pieces) of the letters using the Wood Pieces Set and the Mat for Wood Pieces, which has a smiley face in the top left corner.

- Use the Slate Chalkboard and Gray Block Paper to correct capital letter and number reversals. The smiley face will become a consistent reminder of the starting corner and will orient the child to the left side of the Slate Chalkboard.

- Provide visual models for the child to follow. Refer the child to the pictures in the student editions that give additional visual cues for letter formation.

- Provide many practice sessions to develop patterns for letter formation.

- Teach the letters in the recommended groups of similar strokes to help develop consistent patterns of letter formation.

Handwriting Standards for Written Production

Handwriting instruction must adhere to developmental principles to ensure success for all children. Yet, educational guidelines often are limited to one standard in the English Language Arts standards—"produces legible handwriting." When students fail to meet this standard, teachers have no means for examining which skills are lacking. To review standards visit our website: **LWTears.com/freeresources**.

Handwriting is an essential skill for both children and adults (Feder and Majnemer 2007). Even in the age of technology, handwriting remains the primary tool of communication and knowledge assessment for students in the classroom. The demands for handwriting are great, whether in the classroom or beyond. A 1992 study (McHale and Cermak) found that 85 percent of all fine motor time in second-, fourth- and sixth-grade classrooms was spent on paper and pencil activities. A more recent study (Marr, Cermak, Cohn and Henderson 2003) noted that kindergarten children are now spending 42 percent of their fine motor time on paper and pencil activities. The addition of handwritten components to many state standardized assessments and of a handwritten essay to the College Board SAT further emphasize the importance of handwriting. Furthermore, good handwriting is important long after graduation. In Script and Scribble, Florey writes in reference to handwritten job applications, "Like it or not, even in our machine-driven world, people still judge you by your handwriting" (2009).

Research literature extensively documents the consequences of poor handwriting on early literacy and academic performance. Children who experience difficulty mastering this skill [handwriting] may avoid writing and decide they cannot write, leading to arrested writing development (Graham, Harris and Fink 2000). Handwriting is critical to the production of creative and well-written text (Graham and Harris 2005) affecting both fluency and the quality of the composition. Handwriting instruction must adhere to developmental principles to ensure success for all children. According to the National Association for the Education of Young Children, newborn to eight-year-old children learn best from methods that are consistent with developmentally appropriate practice (1998). However, due to a general lack of professional development in the area of handwriting, educators are not always aware of the specific objectives to be addressed at various age and grade levels.

Seeing the need for a more specific analysis of skills, a team of occupational therapists and educators developed a set of handwriting standards. We hope it serves as an example to educators and curriculum decision-makers and brings increased attention to this crucial, yet often overlooked, area of education.

Physical Skills
1.1 Physical Approaches & Skill Development
Students will develop necessary physical skills for handwriting. Each student will:
- A. Use a correct and efficient pencil grip for writing
- B. Stabilize paper with non-writing hand while writing
- C. Position writing paper appropriately
- D. Maintain sitting posture for writing

Printing Skills
2.2 Letter Skills
Students will demonstrate skills in printing letters and numbers from memory. Each student will:
- A. Demonstrate correct formation of letters and numbers
    1. Start capital letters at the top
    2. Start numbers at the top

Handwriting Standards for Written Production

      3. Start lowercase letters (except d and e) at the top
      4. Follow standard formation sequence for letters and numbers
   B. Orient letters and numbers correctly (without reversals)
   C. Place letters and numbers on a base line (within 1/16" above or below)
   D. Write letters, numbers, and symbols in a grade-appropriate size
   E. Follow the writing guidelines of various styles of paper (double and single lines)

2.3 Word Skills

Students write letters together to form words. Each student will:
   A. Write names
      1. Begin with a capital
      2. Form each letter in a name, moving left to right
      3. Write courtesy titles correctly (Mr., Mrs., Ms., Miss., Dr.)
      4. Leave clearly defined space between title, first name, and last name
   B. Write two- to ten-letter words
      1. Form each letter in the word, moving left to right
      2. Use appropriate spacing (i.e., letters close together, NOT touching or overlapping)
      3. Capitalize proper nouns
      4. Place apostrophe correctly in possessives and contractions
      5. End abbreviations with a period

2.4 Sentence Skills

Students write words to express thoughts, forming sentences. Each student will:
   A. Write sentences with two to eight words
   B. Write from left to right, returning to left margin of subsequent lines as needed
   C. Use sentence writing conventions:
      1. Begin with a capital letter
      2. Leave a clearly defined space between words
      3. Use ending punctuation (period, question mark, or exclamation point)
   D. Use comma and quotation marks to indicate speech

2.5 Writing Conventions

Students will combine sentences to express ideas or opinions, using formatting conventions that are extensions of handwriting skills. Each student will:
   A. Write paragraphs using proper conventions
      1. Write three- to five-sentence paragraphs
      2. Indent the first line of each paragraph
   B. Write titles of written works, capitalizing the first, last, and important words
   C. Follow standard format for friendly letters
      1. Write date, beginning at left margin or center of line
      2. Write greeting, beginning at left margin
      3. Write body, using paragraph skills
      4. Write closing, matching starting point of date
      5. Place name, matching starting point of date and closing

References

Boyd, Judi, W. Steven Barnett, Elena Bordova, Deborah J. Leong, and Deanna Gomby. 2005. "Promoting Children's Social and Emotional Development Through Preschool Education." New Brunswick, NJ: National Institute for Early Education Research.

Dennis, Julie L., and Yvonne Swinth. 2001. "Pencil Grasp and Children's Handwriting Legibility During Different-Length Writing Tasks." *American Journal of Occupational Therapy* 55 (2): 175–183.

Dolch, Edward William. 1948. *Problems in Reading*. Champaign, IL: The Garrard Press.

Feder, Katya P., and Annette Majnemer. 2007. "Handwriting Development, Competency, and Intervention." *Developmental Medicine & Child Neurology* 49: 312–317.

Florey, Kitty Burns. 2009. *Script and Scribble: The Rise and Fall of Handwriting*. New York: Melville House.

Florida International University. 2012. "Good Handwriting and Good Grades: FIU Researcher Finds New Link." *FIU News*, January 18. http://news.fiu.edu/2012/01/good-handwriting-and-good-grades-fiu-researcher-finds-new-link/34934.

Gesell, Arnold. 1940. *The First Five Years of Life: A Guide to the Study of the Preschool Child*. New York: Harper and Brothers.

Graham, Steve, and Karen R. Harris. 2005. "Improving the Writing Performance of Young Struggling Writers: Theoretical and Programmatic Research from the Center on Accelerating Student Learning." *Journal of Special Education* 39 (10): 19–33.

Graham, Steve, Karen R. Harris, and Barbara Fink. 2000. "Is handwriting causally related to learning to write? Treatment of handwriting problems in beginning writers." *Journal of Educational Psychology* 92: 620–633.

Knapton, Emily. 2011. "Exploring the Levels of Emergent Literacy." *Indiana Reading Journal* 43 (2): 16–18.

Lust, Carol A., and Denise K. Donica. 2011. "Effectiveness of a Handwriting Readiness Program in Head Start: A Two-Group Controlled Trial." *American Journal of Occupational Therapy* 65 (5): 560–568.

Marr, Deborah, Sharon A. Cermack, Ellen S. Cohn, and Anne Henderson. 2003. "Fine Motor Activities in Head Start and Kindergarten Classrooms." *American Journal of Occupational Therapy* 57 (5): 550–557.

McHale, Kathleen, and Sharon Cermak. 1992. "Fine Motor Activities in Elementary School: Preliminary Findings and Provisional Implications for Children with Fine Motor Problems." *American Journal of Occupational Therapy* 46, 10: 898–903.

National Association for the Education of Young Children & International Reading Association. 1998. "Learning to Read and Write: Developmentally Appropriate Practices for Young Children." *Young Children* 53 (4): 30–46. http://www.naeyc.org/files/naeyc/file/positions/PSREAD98.pdf.

National Governors Association Center for Best Practices and Council of Chief State School Officers. 2010. *Common Core State Standards*. Washington, D.C.: National Governors Association Center for Best Practices, Council of Chief State School Officers. www.corestandards.org.

Sousa, David. 2011. *How the Brain Learns*, 4th ed. Thousand Oaks, CA: Corwin Press.

Strickland, Dorothy S., and Judith A. Schickedanz. 2009. *Learning About Print in Preschool*, 2nd ed. International Reading Association: Newark, DE.

Tompkins, Gail E. 2010. *Literacy for the 21st Century: A Balanced Approach*, 5th ed. Boston, MA: Pearson.

Full list of references available on **LWTears.com**.

Index

A
A, 60
a, 60
abbreviations, 112, 124
active teaching, 4
Activity Design, 8
adaptive devices, 186
addition, 119, 142–143
Air Writing, 155, 162
alliteration, 125
alphabet desk strips, 11
alphabet knowledge, 20
Alphabet Wall Cards, 11
American Sign Language, 99
antonyms, 109
A+ Worksheet Maker, 72, 165
assessments, 14, 185
auditory skills, 130
autism spectrum disorder, 195

B
B, 81
b, 81
Blackboard with Double Lines, 10
body (letter), 113
body parts, 74
buildings, 122–123

C
C, 58
c, 58
calendars, 112, 119, 139
capitalization rules, 64, 87, 100–101, 106–107, 124
capitals, 5, 41–50, 124
    Capitals on the Door, 155
    Center Starting Capitals (C, O, Q, G, S, A, I, T, J), 44, 49, 157
    Frog Jump Capitals (F, E, D, P, R, N, M), 44, 46–47, 158
    multisensory activities and, 155–159, 167
    remediation tips, 188
    review, 91, 146
    Starting Corner Capitals (H, K, L, U, V, W, X, Y, Z), 44, 48, 155, 157
    teaching guidelines for, 26
Center Starting Capitals. *See capitals*
cerebral palsy, 196
child development, 6, 20–21
A Click Away, 5, 15, 184
closeness. *See spacing*
closings, 112
coloring, 20
comics, 100
compound words, 102
computer keyboard, 118, 124
continents, 106
contraction, 108
cooperative learning strategies, 193
copying, 21, 23
counting, 126, 134, 137
Cross-Curricular Connections, 7, 9
    Language Arts, 46–50, 58–64, 66, 68–70, 74, 77–79, 82–83, 85–86, 90–91, 94–95, 97, 102, 108–109, 111–112, 114–118, 120–121, 123, 137, 139
    Math, 51, 80, 88–89, 119, 122, 133–136, 138, 140, 142–145
    Resources, 45
    Science, 65, 67, 72, 76, 87, 103–105, 110
    Social Studies, 71, 73, 75, 81, 84, 96, 98–101, 106–107, 113, 125–126, 141
cross strokes, 36
curves. *See Wood Pieces Set*

D
D, 61
d, 61
dates, 112–113
demonstration, 9, 21
descending letters, 7, 55, 68, 159, 167
developmental order, 6, 42, 44, 176–177
diagonals, 88, 151
differentiated instruction, 5, 9, 15, 194
Digital Products Portal, 12, 15, 184–185
Digital Teaching Tools, 12–13
digraphs, 114
direct instruction, 21
directionality, 7, 132
Diver Letters. *See lowercase letters*
Door Tracing, 155
dots, 66
Double Line Notebook Paper, 11
double lines, 7, 10, 55
Down Syndrome, 195
Draw and Write Notebook, 11
drawings, 20, 96
dysgraphia, 197
dyslexia, 196

Index

E
E, 67
e, 67
English language learners (ELL), 15, 192–194
Eraser Challenge, 187

F
F, 84
f, 84
feedback, 194
Final Group. *See lowercase letters*
fine motor skills, 20, 36, 39, 195
fingerspelling, 99
finger tracing, 130
FLIP Crayons®, 39
foreign languages, 126
Frog Jump Capitals. *See capitals*

G
G, 62
g, 62
geography, 106–107
geometry, 89
golf-size pencils, 11
Gray Blocks, 7, 43, 130, 132
Greek & Latin, 86
greetings, 113, 152
grip, 18, 34, 37–39, 186–187
guided practice, 21

H
H, 80
h, 80
the Hand Activity, 167
handedness/hand skills, 88, 152, 161, 186
Handwriting All Year, 25
handwriting fluency, 93
handwriting process, 18
handwriting standards, 198–199
helper hand, 187
Home Links, 15, 59, 62, 81, 89, 186
homophones, 98, 133

I
I, 66
i, 66
IDTT, 13. *See Interactive Digital Teaching Tool*

imaginary play, 10
imitation, 20–21, 39
indenting for paragraphs, 75, 87, 96, 101, 117–118, 122–123
independent writing, 11, 21
inflection, 64
informational writing, 97, 110–111, 122
Infrequently Used Letters. *See lowercase letters*
instructional design, 21
Interactive Digital Teaching Tool, 13. *See IDTT*

J
J, 73
j, 73

K
K, 71
k, 71

L
L, 70
l, 70
labels, 104–105, 116
laser letters, 155, 163
learning environment, 192
left-handed, 6, 36, 88, 161, 179
legibility, 19
letter charts, 184
letters
    capitals–teaching order, 42, 44
    directionality, 7, 132
    formation, 18, 158, 164. *See also individual letters*
    learn & check, 44, 57
    lesson design, 9
    lowercase–teaching order, 42, 56
    orientation, 6, 18–19, 44, 56
    positioning, 153–154, 158
    reversals, 18, 42, 44, 161
    singing, 47, 50
    size, 68, 90
    skills, 198–199
    stories, 160–161
Letter Stories, 160–161
letter writing, 112–113
line generalization, 7, 55
lines, 123
    double lines, 7, 10, 55
    single lines, 43, 48, 55
    triple lines, 43, 55

Index

lines for poems, 105, 108, 115
lists, 107
lowercase letters, 5, 44, 53–91
    Diver Letters (p, r, n, m, h, b), 28, 56, 76–82
    Final Group (f, q, x, z), 29, 56, 84–89
    Magic c Letters (a, d, g), 27, 56, 60–63, 159
    multisensory activities and, 159–161, 167–168
    positioning, 56
    remediation tips, 189
    review, 90, 146
    Same as Capitals and t (c, o, s, v, w, t), 27, 44, 56, 58–59
    teaching guidelines for, 27–29
    Transition Group (u, i, e, l, k, y, j), 28, 56, 65–73

M

M, 79
m, 79
Magic c. *See lowercase letters*
Magic C Bunny, 10, 169
Magic C Capitals, 44
Mat for Wood Pieces, 188
Mat Man®, 20
metacognition, 194
modeling, 194
models, 6, 11
months, 112
movement, 10, 35, 103, 171
multisensory activities, 5, 10, 149–171
    Air Writing, 162
    capitals and, 155–158, 167
    digital letter and number formations, 164
    Hand Activity, 167
    icons for, 150
    laser letters, 163
    lowercase letters and, 159–161, 167–168
    movement with syllables, 171
    music and singing, 151, 153–154, 158–159, 170
    shaking hands, 152
    voices activity, 169
    Wet-Dry-Try, 156, 166, 168
    worksheet maker, 165
multisensory instruction, 193
music and singing, 10, 38, 45, 151, 153–154, 158–159, 170, 191
Mystery Letters, 47, 157
"My Teacher Writes," 135

N

N, 78
n, 78
name with capitals, 45, 106–107, 124
neatness, 19
nouns, 120. *See also proper nouns*
    irregular, 74, 120
    plural, 74, 120
    regular, 120
    singular, 74
numbers, 5, 129–146
    irregular numbers, 145
    numerals, 133–147
    one-digit, 133–141, 144
    place value, 134
    practice, 51
    preteen and teen, 144
    remediation tips, 190
    reversals, 130, 132
    review, 146
    in sentences, 126
    stories, 130–131
    teaching guidelines for, 26–27, 130
    teaching math, 29
    three-digit, 135, 145
    two-digit, 134, 144–145
    Wet-Dry-Try, 132
    writing/formation, 18, 51, 130, 164

O

O, 58
o, 58
oceans, 106
online resources, 5, 10, 12, 15, 184–185
onsets and rimes, 54

P

P, 76
p, 76
paper placement, 23, 34, 36
paragraphs, 75, 87, 96, 99, 101, 115, 117, 122–123
parental involvement, 184. *See also Home Links*
pencil grip, 11, 18, 34, 37–39, 186–187
    quadropod, 37
    tripod, 37
Pencil Pick-Ups, 45, 186
pencil pressure, 187

Index

physical skills, 198
plurals, 74, 120
poems, 108, 115
posture, 23, 34
prefixes, 86, 109
prepositional phrases, 121
prepositions, 154
pre-strokes, 23
pre-writing, 20
printing
    scope and sequence, 22–23
    skills, 22–23, 42, 198–199
    speed and legibility, 19
Printing Power student edition, 11, 43, 57
The Print Tool®, 185
prior knowledge activation, 192
professional development, 15
proper nouns, 87, 106–107, 124
punctuation, 64, 100–101
    apostrophe, 75, 108
    comma, 107, 126
    exclamation point, 64
    period, 64
    question mark, 64
    quotation marks, 100–101

Q
Q, 85
q, 85
question & answer, 110–111
quotations, 100–101
QWERTY layout, 118

R
R, 77
r, 77
readiness, 5, 20, 23, 33–39, 151
remediation tips, 15, 146, 185–191
repetition, 193–194
resources, 5, 183–199
reversals, 7, 18, 130, 132, 161
rhymes/rhyming, 69, 82, 115
rimes, 54
Rock, Rap, Tap & Learn album, 10, 151, 154, 158–159
rubber band trick, 186

S
S, 58
s, 58
Same as Capitals and t. *See lowercase letters*
School-to-Home Connections, 184
Screener of Handwriting Proficiency, 14, 185
sea words, 104–105
self-portrait writing, 97
sentences
    building, 121
    practice, 54, 94–95, 126
    "Sentence Song," 159, 170, 191
    skills, 199
    spacing, 94–95
shaking hands, 20, 152
shapes, 133–136, 140
signature, 113
sign language, 99
Silly Spelling, 63
Simply Smart Student Materials, 4, 10–11
singing. *See music and singing*
singulars and plurals, 74, 120
size, 68, 90
Slate Chalkboard, 20, 130, 132, 156–157
smiley face, 129, 155
social skills, 20, 152
songs. *See music and singing*
spacing, 7, 19, 64, 75, 94–95, 191
spatial organization, 7, 43
special needs children, 195–197
speech bubbles, 100
speed, 19
stages of learning, 20–21
standards for handwriting, 198–199
Start and Sequence, 19, 146
Starting Corner Capitals. *See capitals*
student edition design, 6–7, 43, 54
student materials, 10–11
subject, 121
subtraction, 119, 142–143
suffixes, 54
syllables, 103, 110, 171
symbols, 132
synonyms, 109

Index

T
T, 59
t, 59
teacher support, 4, 14–15
teaching guidelines, 14, 25–31
teaching order
    capitals. *See letters*
    lowercase. *See letters*
technology, 12–13, 164, 166
thank you letter, 113
thematic instruction, 193
title for poem, 108, 115
topic, for paragraph, 87, 99, 115, 122
tracing, 20, 137. *See also Door Tracing; finger tracing*
triangles, 134–135
trigraphs, 114

U
U, 65
u, 65
uppercase. *See capitals*

V
V, 58
v, 58
verbs
    action, 120
    irregular, 120–121
    regular, 120
vision problems, 196
visual cues, 11
visual skills, 162–163
vocabulary, 98, 104–105, 116, 193–194
voices activity, 169
vowels, 27, 50, 69, 78, 98, 114

W
W, 58
w, 58
Wet-Dry-Try, 20, 132, 156, 166, 168. *See also Slate Chalkboard*
Wood Pieces Set, 20
word banks, 104–105, 116
word roots, 86

words
    compound words, 102
    learn & check, 57
    practice, 54
    singulars and plurals, 74, 120
    skills, 199
Word Search, 83
writing
    big and little curves, 131
    big and little lines, 131
    capital letters. *See capitals*
    developmental order, 6, 42, 44
    lowercase. *See lowercase letters*
    numbers. *See numbers*
    process, 18
    readiness, 20, 23, 33–39, 151
    teaching guidelines for, 30–31
writing activities, 93–126
writing conventions, 199

X
X, 88
x, 88

Y
Y, 72
y, 72

Z
Z, 89
z, 89